Evidence
for
Faith 101

Bruce BICKEL
&
Stan JANTZ

HARVEST HOUSE PUBLISHERS

EUGENE, OREGON

Cover by Left Coast Design, Portland, Oregon

Cover illustration © Krieg Barrie Illustration

Bruce Bickel: Published in association with the literary agency of Mark Sweeney & Associates, 28540 Altessa Way, Ste. 201, Bonita Springs, FL 34135

Stan Jantz: Published in association with the literary agency of Mark Sweeney & Associates, 28540 Altessa Way, Ste. 201, Bonita Springs, FL 34135

CHRISTIANITY 101 is a registered trademark of Bruce Bickel and Stan Jantz. Harvest House Publishers, Inc., is the exclusive licensee of the federally registered trademark CHRISTIANITY 101.

EVIDENCE FOR FAITH 101
Copyright © 2008 by Bruce Bickel and Stan Jantz
Published by Harvest House Publishers
Eugene, Oregon 97402
www.harvesthousepublishers.com

Library of Congress Cataloging-in-Publication Data

Bickel, Bruce, 1952-
    Evidence for faith 101 / Bruce Bickel and Stan Jantz.
        p. cm.—(Christianity 101)
    Includes bibliographical references (p.) and index.
    ISBN-13: 978-0-7369-2295-1 (pbk.)
    ISBN-10: 0-7369-2295-4
    1. Apologetics. I. Jantz, Stan, 1952- II. Title.
BT1103.B52 2008
239—dc22

                                                                        2008020754

Bruce and Stan are part of a faith-based online community called ConversantLife.com. At this website, people engage their faith in entertainment, creative arts, science and technology, global concerns, and other culturally relevant topics. While you're reading this book, or after you have finished reading, go to www.conversantlife.com/101 and use these icons to read and download additional Christianity 101 material from Bruce and Stan:

 Resources: Download study guide materials for personal devotions or a small-group Bible study.

 Videos: Click on this icon for interviews and video clips on various topics.

 Blogs: Read through blogs and articles and comment on them.

 Podcasts: Stream ConversantLife.com podcasts and audio clips.

conversant **life** .com

engage your faith

Contents

Introduction

*A*pproximately 6.7 billion people share our planet, and about one-third of them follow the Christian faith. If that's the case, why isn't the world a better place? After all, Christianity is a religion based on Jesus Christ. If all these Christians acted the way Jesus acted, we would see a lot more love and goodwill and a lot less feuding and fighting. But the world is full of feuding and fighting and evil and suffering. So either many of those people who call themselves Christians aren't doing what they're supposed to do, or Christianity isn't really all that it's cracked up to be. Or maybe Jesus wasn't who He said He was—the Son of God.

And what about God? Almost everybody believes in God, including Muslims (over a billion people) and Jews. But do they believe in the same God as the Christians? And what about the Hindus (750 million people), who believe in lots of gods? Who's to say they aren't on to something? How can any one religion have a corner on God?

Given all of these variations, what's wrong with finding your own path to God? We can't see Him, and He's not talking, so we just have to have faith, because we can't actually prove whether or not...

God exists

God made the world

Jesus is the Savior of the world

the Bible is true and trustworthy

Christianity makes sense

God cares about evil and suffering

heaven and hell really do exist

your life makes a difference

Can We Know These Things?

A lot of people—including many Christians—believe these statements are true, but they don't think it is possible to actually *know* they are true. They think that faith in God is a personal, subjective thing and cannot be known in the same way you know, for example, that the sun will come up tomorrow, or that you have a cousin in Baltimore. So they believe in God because it's the right thing to do, or because it helps them deal with life, or because that's what they were taught. But they don't believe anyone can actually *know* that God exists.

Then there are those people who flat out deny that God exists, precisely because no one can prove He does. They believe that ultimate reality includes only what you can experience with the five senses. The bottom line is that only nature is real. Anything above nature—otherwise known as the *supernatural*—is not real.

We happen to disagree with these two conclusions: that God cannot be known and that God doesn't exist because He cannot be known. We believe you can know God, and you can know that God exists. We believe in a reality that goes beyond what we can touch, taste, smell, hear, or see. You may not be able to prove this reality in a science experiment, but neither do you have to accept it without any evidence.

Belief in God is more than a leap in the dark. He may be full of mystery and wonder, but we can know Him just as surely as we can know the sun will come up tomorrow. Yes, faith is involved in knowing God, but it is a faith based on evidence.

What You'll Find Inside

The purpose of this book is to help you think through many of the important questions that many people are asking about God, Jesus, the Bible, the origin of the universe, the Trinity, Christianity, suffering and evil, heaven and hell, and other hot-button topics. We don't take offense when someone inquires about these, and neither should you. When you take questions and objections about God personally, you have a tendency to get defensive, and that rarely leads to a productive dialogue.

The Bible never asks you to get defensive about your faith. What it does say is this:

> *And if someone asks about your Christian hope, always be ready to explain it. But do this in a gentle and respectful way* (1 Peter 3:15-16).

These verses are at the heart of a field of study known as Christian apologetics. Too often people have used apologetics in order to *defend* the Christian faith. But apologetics is more about *explaining* the truth about God than it is about defending God. Christian apologetics is most useful when it points to a correct point of view, rather than trying to disprove someone else's view.

The ideas and points of view presented in this book are introductory. They aren't meant to be a comprehensive treatment of the various issues and questions that are coming up more and more in our culture. Our goal is to get you thinking and to point you in the right direction so that you will be motivated to learn more about the Christian faith. After all, if God and Christianity can be known, then we always have more to learn.

This Book Is for You If...

Between the two of us, we have more than a few decades of Christian experience, and we have done a lot of reading and research over the years in the field of Christian apologetics. We have personally responded to thousands of questions asked by people just like you who want answers to the deep and sometimes troubling issues of their faith. Furthermore, we have explained the truth about God to hundreds of people who don't believe God can be known or that He exists. That's why we are excited to enter into this informal relationship with you through this book. We think it will be helpful to you, especially if you fall into any of the following categories:

- You are a new Christian and have a whole bunch of questions about God and the Christian life.

- You have been a Christian for a while, but you still aren't comfortable when people ask you to explain your faith and what you believe. Your lack of confidence may even be keeping you from growing as a Christian.

- You have done a lot of reading and study about God and the Christian life, but the answers that satisfy you don't seem to have any effect on the people around you who don't have a relationship with God. They are fine with you being a Christian, but they don't want anything to do Christianity.

- Some of your friends and acquaintances have a problem with Christianity because they think it's intolerant. They think the notion that Jesus is the only way to God is narrow-minded.

- You believe in God, but you can't accept the idea that God would send anyone to hell. You are convinced that everyone who believes in God, regardless of who or what that is, will make it to heaven.

- You don't believe in God at all, but you are curious to see what a book like this has to say. You have some Christian friends, and you aren't opposed to learning more about what they believe.

How to Use This Book

Although this book follows a logical sequence, you don't have to begin reading at the beginning and then continue straight through until you finish. If you want to go first to a chapter that you're just itching to read, that's fine. Each chapter pretty much stands on its own. However, if you're reading this book as part of a group, you may want to go from start to finish. Small group studies just seem to work better that way.

Whether you are going through *Evidence for Faith 101* on your own or as part of a small group, we hope you take time at the end of each chapter to work on the *Questions for Reflection and Discussion*.

These are designed to get you thinking about the material and interacting with it.

Speaking of interaction, we have made a high priority of helping you interact with the material in this book. If you go to www .conversantlife.com/101, you will be guided to some online digital resources, including videos, audio files, additional study questions, and a study guide. In addition, you will be able to ask questions and get answers from real people.

We think these features, designed to enhance your experience with this and all of the Christianity 101 books, are unique. Where else can you find a resource where you have an opportunity to interact with the authors and other trustworthy people anytime you want!

So enjoy *Evidence for Faith 101*. We hope it gives you lots to think about and even more to believe in.

Part I
Faith and Apologetics

Introduction to Part I

*W*hen you talk about faith and evidence, what you're really talking about is *apologetics*. So before we get into the nitty-gritty details of what it means to have faith, and how important it is to have evidence for faith, let's have a discussion about apologetics, the area of study that brings these two important elements together.

What exactly is apologetics, and how does it relate to faith? On the surface, it sounds like making excuses for what you believe. But that can't be right. If you're a Christian, you don't want to go around telling people, "Excuse me, but I'm a Christian, and I want to apologize for that." (Actually, we Christians may sometimes need to apologize for doing or saying certain things, but that's not what *apologetics* means.)

The word *apologetics* comes from the Latin word *apologia* (defense). So at its most basic level, when you engage in apologetics, you are giving a defense, or an explanation, for the things you believe. In the introduction, we saw the verse in the Bible that speaks to this most clearly. It's in Peter's first letter to suffering Christians in the first century:

> *And if someone asks about your Christian hope, always be ready to explain it* (1 Peter 3:15).

Engaging in apologetics isn't about getting defensive about what we believe. That happens all too often and it gets us nowhere.

More correctly, apologetics is the process of providing reasonable explanations—or evidence—for the truth claims of the Christian faith.

Answers for Difficult Questions

Let's face it. Christianity has some pretty outrageous truth claims. Here are a few for starters:

- There is an all-powerful, all-knowing, perfect being called God, whom no one has ever seen.
- God created the universe and everything in it out of nothing.
- God had a Son named Jesus, who is the same as God in substance but is a different person. Oh, and by the way, Jesus isn't just God; He's also human.
- Jesus died a physical death but was raised from the dead and returned to heaven, where He is preparing a place for those who put their trust in Him.
- Jesus is coming back to earth someday.
- God has communicated this information to us through a book known as the Bible, which contains important information a Christian needs for living a godly life.

Now, if you're a Christian, you have probably accepted these truth claims and more. But do you really believe they have reasonable explanations? Or have you just taken a leap of faith? Maybe you did some investigation, and you came to the conclusion that these truth claims are really true. What prompted you to believe? Was it evidence, like you might have in a court case? Or were other factors involved? What part did faith play in your belief? Now put yourself in the place of a non-Christian (or simply think back to the time when you were not yet a Christian). Does this stuff seem reasonable or rational? Or does it sound more like a fairy tale?

The field of apologetics attempts to provide answers for tough questions like these, and in doing so, it can help the Christian and non-Christian alike.

The Benefits of Apologetics for the Christian

For the Christian, being able to explain the truth claims of the Christian faith serves a very important purpose: It gives you a much greater appreciation for God, Jesus, the Bible, and everything else that is part of your faith. When you know the reasons for what and why you believe, you gain confidence and assurance.

Over the years of writing the Christianity 101 books, we have received many e-mails and letters from Christians who aren't sure they are saved, and that has them worried. Honestly, every Christian has been in this position at one time or another. The reason we feel this way isn't that God has somehow abandoned us. To the contrary, it's that we don't know enough about God. The more we know Him, the more we will feel His presence, His love, and His care for us because our feelings for God will be based on our knowledge of God.

> Apologetics gets at the heart *through* the head. The head is important precisely because it is a gate to the heart. We can love only what we know.
>
> —*Peter Kreeft*

The Benefits of Apologetics for the Non-Christian

Many Christians believe that their faith is being attacked by non-Christians, especially in this postmodern age of moral relativism when there doesn't seem to be much room for objective truth. Because Christianity claims to offer objective truth—that is, truth that is the same for all people regardless of the context—many non-Christians criticize it for being narrow-minded and judgmental of other beliefs. That's a legitimate issue, and it's something Christians need to address, but they shouldn't be afraid of such criticism and the questions that come out of it.

As we said earlier, Christians shouldn't get defensive. If someone is questioning God or Jesus or the Bible, they must be interested in having answers. When Christians know what they believe and are able to answer the questions and objections posed by those who don't yet accept the truth claims of the Christian faith as valid, they are using apologetics to open up productive conversations that can lead others to a saving faith in Christ. That's a pretty big benefit for the non-Christian.

In a Gentle and Respectful Way

Providing explanations isn't optional for the Christian. As the apostle Peter says, it's a responsibility. Christians always need to be ready to explain their hope. But when we offer our explanations, we aren't to do so with a condescending or judgmental attitude. As Peter advises, we should give our answers "in a gentle and respectful way" (1 Peter 3:16).

Apologetics isn't about winning arguments. It's all about presenting the truth in love. Yes, a battle is raging in the spiritual realm, and the marketplace of ideas is full of conflicts. But as Peter Kreeft writes, "the warfare is against unbelief, not unbelievers, just as insulin is against diabetes, not diabetics. The goal of apologetics is not victory, but truth."[1]

Let's keep these two foundational characteristics of apologetics in mind as we move forward through the next two chapters: We need to know what we believe, and we need to present the truth in love to those who are asking questions about our faith.

Chapter 1

Faith is to believe what you do not yet see;
the reward for faith is to see what you believe.

—*Augustine*

Faith is an amazing thing. Everybody has faith, and everybody talks about faith. "Keep the faith," "Don't lose faith," and "Have faith" are just some of the faith expressions we throw at each other, usually to offer encouragement. That's because faith offers hope. Faith tells us not to give up.

But faith isn't much more than an expression or a wishful feeling if it's not rooted in something or someone real. A child may have faith in Santa Claus, but it's not a real faith because Santa Claus isn't real. Besides being real, the object of our faith must be trustworthy. A Chicago Cubs fan can have all the faith in the world that this will be the year for his beloved team to win the World Series. But can the Cubs be trusted to deliver a championship?

In this chapter, we're going to look at what it means to have faith. More importantly, we're going to look at what it means to have faith in God, who is both real and completely trustworthy. Having faith in God doesn't mean you take a leap in the dark. To the contrary, it means you step into the light as you trust the living God with your present and future life.

A Case for Faith

*I*f you were to ask a random sampling of people—some Christians, some non-Christians—to give you a definition of faith, you would probably get a wide variety of answers. To give you an idea of what kind of responses you would receive, here are some definitions we've collected (along with the people who said them):

"Faith is believing something you know ain't true" (Mark Twain).

"Faith is not being sure of where you're going, but going anyway" (Frederick Buechner).

"Faith is belief without, or in spite of, reason" (George H. Smith).

"Faith is the strength by which a shattered world shall emerge into the light" (Helen Keller).

"Faith is the opening of all sides and at every level of one's life to the divine inflow" (Martin Luther King, Jr.).

"I think that faith is, in principle, in conflict with reason" (Sam Harris).

That's quite a collection of quotes, isn't it? And did you notice that we left out one very important definition? It's from the Bible:

> *Now faith is the substance of things hoped for, the evidence of things not seen* (Hebrews 11:1 NKJV).

Notice the contrast between the Bible's definition of faith and our sample definitions. Rather than describing faith as something nebulous or impractical, or a blind leap into the darkness, the Bible talks about faith as having substance and being the evidence of the things we can't see. And what are these things? Well, for starters, that God exists, that Jesus was raised from the dead, and that all who believe in Jesus will have eternal life.

More Than a Feeling

So what are we to conclude from this quick glance at the Bible's definition of faith? For one, faith is more than a feeling, more than a blind leap in the dark, and certainly very different from "believing something you know ain't true." Neither is faith subjective. In other words, faith is not a private thing, subject to your own interpretation. Faith has substance, and it includes evidence that is clear and available for everyone, regardless of their background or circumstances.

Everybody Has Faith

When people hear the word *faith,* they usually think of religion, and because Christianity is the most popular religion in the world, they usually think of *Christian* and *faith* together. We're going to talk about the Christian faith in a little while, but first we want to talk about faith in general.

The thing is, everybody has faith, and they have it every day. If you didn't have faith, you would never leave your home. But you do.

- You have faith that your car is going to start and get you to work or school or wherever you're going;
- you have faith in the other drivers on the road, that they won't slam into you;

- you have faith that your job or class will be there when you arrive; and
- you have faith that at a certain designated time in the future, which you can't see, you will receive a paycheck or a grade for your efforts.

Now is it possible that your car won't start, or that you could get into an accident, or that your job could be eliminated or your class cancelled? Yes, those things are possible, but they're not likely, so you move through your day on faith for two basic reasons:

- You've done all of this enough to know that your chances for success are pretty good; and
- You trust the manufacturer who built your car, you have confidence in the other drivers on the road, and you believe that your boss or your teacher will be where they are supposed to be.

In other words, your faith in these objects (your car, other drivers, your boss or teacher) rests in your knowledge of them and your experience with them, which add up to trust, confidence, and belief.

> Properly understood, from both a Christian and philosophical perspective, faith is compatible with knowledge.
>
> —David Hoerner

Faith and Belief

Now we're getting to the heart of what faith is all about. Faith isn't blind, irrational, or stupid. Every person exercises faith every day—many times each day. Faith doesn't take away from belief. Faith adds to belief in that it adds trust, and in doing so, faith gives you the confidence to act on or to commit to the things you believe. In fact, without faith, we would never act on our belief in a car, belief in people, or belief in God.

Does that mean that your faith in cars and their drivers is the same as your belief in God? No. The difference between everyday faith and the kind of faith described in Hebrews 11:1 has to do with the object of your faith.

A Different Kind of Faith

Christianity is a religion (just like Islam or Judaism). But it is also called a faith. You may have even told someone that you believe in the Christian faith. That's good! In this sense, faith includes a body of knowledge that Christians believe and affirm. It means that true Christians believe that God exists and that what He says in His word (the Bible) is true. That in itself is good, but it's not good enough. It's not enough just to believe in God (even the demons believe in God—see James 2:19). We need to put our trust in God and commit ourselves to Him. That's what having faith in God means.

This is what distinguishes the Christian faith from other kinds of faith. The object of the faith is completely reliable and completely trustworthy. We can't say that about other objects of faith, whether it's a person, an organization, a machine, or even a religion. As good as those objects are, they aren't 100 percent reliable. At some point, regardless of how much you think these things won't happen, your best friend may betray you, your job may not live up to your expectations, your car could stall on the freeway, and that religious leader you admire so much may have a secret sin that comes to light. Consequently, you would never want to completely stake your life on these objects, especially your life for eternity. It's just too risky. Only one object is worthy of that kind of faith, and that's God.

*T*alk about Mr. Dependable

We're going to talk more about God and His personality traits (sometimes called *attributes*) in chapter 3. But this is a great place to mention a few traits that show us just how reliable and trustworthy God is.

God is holy. He is righteous. No fault is found in Him. His moral character is without flaw. In the negative context, God has no evil in Him; from a positive perspective, He is completely pure.

> *Holy, holy, holy is the Lord Almighty; the whole earth is full of his glory* (Isaiah 6:3 NIV).

God doesn't change. He is *immutable*—the same yesterday, today, and forever. And He cannot be changed.

> *Whatever is good and perfect comes down to us from God our Father, who created all the lights in the heavens. He never changes or casts shifting shadows* (James 1:17).
>
> God is just. He is fair and impartial. He does not play favorites.
>
> *He is the Rock; his deeds are perfect. Everything he does is just and fair. He is a faithful God who does no wrong; how just and upright he is!* (Deuteronomy 32:4).

The Object of Faith

When we talk about God being the object of our faith, we don't mean to reduce Him to something you can put on your shelf or stick in a box and carry around with you. That kind of object is an idol. Rather, we are focusing on the whole person of God—His character traits and the way He interacts with His creation. For the Christian, this includes everything that God has revealed in the Bible about Himself and the world He created.

We have access to everything God has revealed in the Bible, but that doesn't mean we can know everything about Him. Even though God has revealed enough for us to know Him, we will never know or understand God completely.

> *"My thoughts are nothing like your thoughts," says the* LORD. *"And my ways are far beyond anything you could imagine. For just as the heavens are higher than the earth, so my ways are higher than your ways and my thoughts higher than your thoughts"* (Isaiah 55:8-9).

At the same time, God is knowable. He has given us enough information about Himself for us to trust Him completely as the object of our faith. That doesn't mean that knowing these things is easy. As we will see in chapter 5, the Bible gives us what we need in order to know God and live for Him, but the information about God and His dealings with humankind isn't laid out in some kind of easy-to-follow outline. The Bible contains great literature, and like all great literature, you have to read it carefully and study it diligently in order to get the most out of it.

Even then, some aspects of the Christian faith aren't easy to grasp. In order to help people understand the basis and the basics of the Christian faith—and to put the basic elements of the Christian faith into some kind of systematic order—thoughtful people throughout the history of the church have organized the teachings of the Bible (called *doctrines*) into a series of propositions (called *creeds*) or doctrinal statements of belief. Basically, a creed is a set of statements that Christians consider and accept as true.

$\mathcal{A}$ Creed Is a Measurement

The purpose of a creed is to act as a measurement or standard of correct belief. The historic creeds of Christianity—such as the Apostles' Creed and the Nicene Creed—were written in order to present in an organized fashion what God has revealed in the Bible about Himself and the world.

Though comprehensive and accurate, a set of propositions like those contained in the Nicene Creed is a little formal for people today. We like more informal doctrinal statements, such as the one formulated at Rock Harbor, where our friend Mike Erre is the teaching pastor. In a very simple yet accurate way, these five statements define what it means to have faith in God.[1]

- God is a Trinity who exists and is the self-existent Creator of all.

- Jesus is fully God and fully human; He died for our sins, rose from the dead to give us new life, and will return again.

- Human beings are created in the image of God. We have each rebelled against God's kingdom and are in need of the salvation that He alone can provide.

- God's salvation comes to us through trusting the life, death, and resurrection of Jesus and is given to us by grace alone. We can do nothing to earn God's favor.

- The Bible is inspired by God and is authoritative over everything on which it speaks.

Keep in mind that these propositions, though accurate in the way they describe God and what He has told us in the Bible about

Himself and the world He created, are not the ultimate objects of faith. They are more like a map that points us to God or a structure that shows us what God is like. Ultimately, the object of our faith is God Himself. God is not a proposition or an idea or set of beliefs. God is the living, personal Creator who loves you and wants a relationship with you. You can't have a relationship with a proposition or set of beliefs, but you can have a relationship with the living God, something that is essential to faith. It's not enough to know *about* God; we need to actually know Him.

That doesn't mean we can throw out the propositions. We need objectivity in our understanding of who God is and what He wants for us. Otherwise faith is reduced to a subjective feeling, where one person's opinion about God and Christianity is as good as another's, even if the opinions are very different. As Peter Kreeft writes, "without propositions, we cannot know or tell others what God we believe in and what we believe about God."[2]

The Author of Faith

God is not only the object of faith but also the author of faith in that He is the one who revealed the propositions we believe. God "authored" faith in two ways:

- through His written word, the Bible (more about the Bible in chapter 5)
- through the living Word, Jesus Christ (more about Jesus in chapter 6)

Here's how the writer of Hebrews summarizes these two ways God the author has spoken to us:

> *Long ago God spoke many times and in many ways to our ancestors through the prophets. And now in these final days, he has spoken to us through his Son* (Hebrews 1:1).

The Act of Faith

So far we have looked at God as both the object and also the author of our faith. We've briefly considered why God is worthy of our faith (and we will consider many more reasons in chapter 3). But another aspect of faith goes beyond merely believing that God exists. Faith certainly includes this kind of belief, but it isn't enough to connect us with God on a personal level. James writes about this rather sarcastically:

> *You say you have faith, for you believe that there is one God. Good for you! Even the demons believe this, and they tremble in terror* (James 2:19).

Faith at this level puts us in the same category of the demons, which is pretty lousy company. The point James is making is that believing *in* God is not enough. We need to actually *believe* God and put our trust in Him, that who He is and what He says in His word are not only true but also true for us.

ℱaith Is Not Ignorance

Yes, knowledge about God and all He created is absolutely critical to faith. In fact, we're going to spend several chapters in part 2 discussing what we can know about God, the world, the Bible, and Jesus. We'll see that all of them point to God as holy, unchanging, just, and much more. Without knowledge, faith is reduced to wishful thinking and empty hope, and at that level it doesn't help us at all. As Harold Lindsell writes, "No man can be saved without knowing something. Faith is not ignorance. It is not closing one's eyes to the facts. Faith is never afraid to look the truth squarely in the face."

Knowledge about God guides us to belief in God, and then we must act by faith by adding trust and commitment to our belief. Here's what we mean.

Faith and Trust

When the Bible talks about faith and belief, it means much more than mere confidence in knowledge of a fact. It goes beyond the kind of belief that is based on seeing the truth for ourselves. After Jesus was resurrected from the dead, He appeared to all of His disciples except for one, the disciple famously known as "doubting Thomas." Thomas was not with the disciples when Jesus first appeared to them in bodily form. Even though the other disciples told Thomas they had seen Him, Thomas refused to believe. He said, "I won't believe it unless I see the nail wounds in his hands, put my fingers into them, and place my hand into the wound in his side" (John 20:25). Thomas wanted absolute proof that Jesus was alive. He wanted to verify with evidence the fact that Jesus had risen from the dead. That wasn't a bad thing. Jesus didn't criticize Thomas for this. In fact, a week after Thomas expressed his desire for evidence, Jesus appeared to His disciples again, and this time Thomas was there. The first thing Jesus did was to offer Thomas the marks on his physical body—the nail holes in His hands and the wound in His side—as evidence for His bodily resurrection. He told Thomas, "Stop doubting and believe" (John 20:27 NIV).

Thomas believed, of course (who wouldn't after that dramatic episode), and he probably felt satisfied that his faith was based on empirical knowledge. But Jesus understood that faith must go beyond what we can personally know and experience with our senses. So He told Thomas the obvious: "Because you have seen me, you have believed." Then Jesus defined the aspect of faith that goes beyond the senses, including sight: "Blessed are those who have not seen and yet have believed" (John 20:29 NIV). This is the *trust* part of faith. This is what the writer of Hebrews means by "the evidence of things not seen" (Hebrews 11:1 NKJV). This is what Paul means when he writes, "For we live by believing and not by seeing" (2 Corinthians 5:7). This is the part of faith that moves from your mind to your heart.

Faith and Commitment

Knowledge and trust are both essential to faith, but there is one more aspect of faith that is critical. Having true faith means that you also commit yourself to God by conforming your will to God and His will. At this level, faith involves attitude and emotions and behavior. Your faith should be so strong that you voluntarily conform to God's principles, not because you are forced to, but because you have faith that God's values and God's will are best for you. This is where faith goes into action.

The Bible is very clear that our actions (or *works*) don't save us.

*God saved you by his grace when you believed. And you
can't take credit for this; it is a gift from God. Salvation is
not a reward for the good things we have done, so none of
us can boast about it* (Ephesians 2:8-9).

At the same time, unless we make a commitment to obey
God and to "do the good things he planned for us long ago"
(Ephesians 2:10), our faith is quite literally "dead and useless"
(James 2:17).

Committing Yourself to Fly

Flying in an airplane is a great way to see how trust and commitment
add to belief. Let's say that you have never flown in a plane before, but
you believe airplanes can fly because you've read about the principles of
aerodynamics, and you've seen airplanes fly with your own eyes. You could
actually say that you have faith in air travel because you trust the airplane
and the flight crew to fly you safely to your destination (again, because
you've read about it, you've seen it, and you've talked to people who have
flown in airplanes). Is your faith worth anything? Not until you put your
faith into action by actually committing yourself to fly.

Saving Faith

In the book of Acts, an entire chapter is devoted to an encounter
between the apostle Paul and King Agrippa, who ruled over much
of Palestine in the middle of the first century. Paul has been on
trial for two years (talk about a slow judicial system), accused by
the Jews of subversion against the Roman state (these are trumped-
up charges brought by those who want Paul eliminated). Paul
has already defended himself before Governor Felix and then his
replacement, Governor Festus (now you know where those colorful
names came from). Now, after two years, Paul ends up pleading
his case before Agrippa II, the son of Agrippa I, who had executed
James and imprisoned Peter 15 years earlier.

As the scene opens in Acts 26, Paul is in the royal court, giving
his *apologia* before the king. This is classic apologetics, delivered
with gentleness and respect. Paul tells his story and explains his

beliefs—in effect, he gives an explanation for the hope he has in Christ—beautifully summarizing the gospel (or *good news*) of Jesus Christ. In fact, Paul quotes Jesus, who spoke these words to Paul on the day of his conversion:

> *Yes, I am sending you to the Gentiles to open their eyes, so they may turn from darkness to light and from the power of Satan to God. Then they will receive forgiveness for their sins and be given a place among God's people, who are set apart by faith in me* (Acts 26:17-18).

This is what God does for people when He saves them: He opens their eyes so they may turn from darkness to light (Ephesians 5:8); He frees them from Satan's power (Hebrews 2:14); He forgives their sins (Acts 2:38); and He sets them apart by virtue of their faith in Him (1 Peter 2:9). This is saving faith.

And how does Agrippa respond? We know he has knowledge of God, and he believes the prophets (what we call the Old Testament). Yet Agrippa doesn't put his trust in Jesus for salvation. He isn't a Christian because he doesn't have saving faith, and he says so directly to Paul: "Do you think you can persuade me to become a Christian so quickly?" (Acts 26:28).

Faith Is a Decision

Many people are like King Agrippa (only without the *king* part). They believe in God, and they have knowledge about God through the stories of other people and the content of the Bible, but they haven't decided to completely trust in God to save them through the person and work of Jesus. Theologian Wayne Grudem puts it this way:

> In addition to knowledge of the facts of the gospel and approval of those facts, in order to be saved, I must decide to depend on Jesus to save me. In doing this I move from being an interested observer of the facts of salvation and the teachings of the Bible to being someone who enters into a new relationship with Jesus Christ as a living person. We may then define saving faith in the following way: *Saving faith*

is trust in Jesus Christ as a living person for forgiveness of sins and for eternal life with God.[3]

*W*hy Did God Choose Faith?

For many people, one of the frustrating things about the Christian faith—and Christians and non-Christians alike can struggle with this—is that it has enough evidence to show that it's a reasonable faith but not enough to demonstrate that it's absolutely true. Why didn't God leave us a "smoking gun" as irrefutable evidence to show that He exists and to demonstrate without question to the whole world that the Bible is true? In a word, the answer is that God didn't want saving faith to depend on us, but on Him. He didn't want saving faith to be just a condition of the mind. It must also be an attitude of the heart. As Grudem says, "When we come to Christ in faith, we essentially say, 'I give up! I will not depend on myself or my own good works any longer.'"[4]

Two Extremes to Avoid

We're going to talk a lot about balance in this book. As you seek evidence and reasonable explanations for your faith, you'll want to avoid two extremes:

Evidentialism. This view says that everything we know by faith can and should be understood or proved by reason. People who emphasize this view believe that the Christian faith should be anchored in evidence and historically verifiable facts. They argue that defending Christianity should rest primarily in the evidence for creation, the Bible, and Jesus (especially His resurrection).

Fideism. This term comes from the Latin word *fide*, meaning faith. The fideistic view holds that the only knowledge we can have is by faith. While evidentialism says that the best way to come to faith in God is *through* reason and evidence, fideism says that you should come to faith by believing in God *apart from* reason and evidence. Faith in God cannot be rooted in rational argument because faith is a matter of the heart, not the head.

A Balanced Approach

The Christian faith is a balanced faith. It is reasonable, and the evidence supports the truth claims of Christianity, so you don't have to check your brains at the door when you act in faith to trust and commit yourself to Jesus Christ. But neither do you need to have rational answers for every question in order for your faith to be valid. It's not either faith or reason. It's both faith and reason.

What's That Again?

1. Christian apologetics is the process of providing reasonable explanations for the truth claims of the Christian faith.

2. Faith is more than a feeling or a blind leap in the dark. Faith has substance, and it includes evidence for faith that is available for everyone.

3. Faith doesn't take away from belief. Faith adds to belief in the form of trust and commitment.

4. It's not enough to believe *in* God; we need to *believe* God by trusting Him and committing ourselves to Him.

5. The difference between the Christian faith and other kinds of faith is that the object of the Christian faith is completely reliable and trustworthy. The object of the Christian faith is, of course, God, including everything God has revealed about Himself in the Bible.

6. We have propositions (statements of belief) to help us understand the basis and the basics of the Christian faith. Although propositions help us define what it means to have faith in God, they are not the objects of our faith.

7. God is not only the object of faith but also the author of faith. God has "authored" faith through the Bible and through Jesus.

8. Knowledge about God guides us to believe in God, and then we must act in faith by adding trust and commitment to our belief.

9. Saving faith is trust in Jesus Christ as a living person for forgiveness of sins and for eternal life with God.

10. The Christian faith is a reasonable faith. We can find reasons and evidence to support the truth claims of Christianity, but we don't have to have rational answers to every question in order for our faith to be valid.

Dig Deeper

We consider three books to be indispensable for anyone who wants to get good at Christian apologetics:

Handbook of Christian Apologetics by Peter Kreeft is well organized, thorough, and written in a conversational manner.

The *Baker Encyclopedia of Christian Apologetics* by Norman Geisler is exactly what the title says: an encyclopedia. This is a great resource for anything even remotely related to Christian apologetics.

Systematic Theology by Wayne Grudem gives an excellent explanation of Christian doctrine. This is a book you will use throughout your life.

In the first of what will be a series of shameless self-promotions, we also want to recommend one of our books in the Christianity 101 series: *Knowing God 101* explains the basics of the Christian faith in a way that is correct, clear, and casual (our trademarks).

■ ■ ■

*Q*uestions for *R*eflection and *D*iscussion

1. Take a look at the truth claims listed in the introduction to part 1. Why do you believe these are true? Are there any on this list—or some that aren't listed—that trouble you?

2. What's the difference between defending your faith and getting defensive about your faith? What kind of signal do you send to someone when you get defensive? What kind of signal do you send when you present the truth in love?

3. Other than driving your car or flying in an airplane, give an example of something you do every day that requires faith. Why do you think some people who exercise faith in ordinary things have trouble exercising faith in God?

4. St. Augustine once said, "A god we understand completely is an idol." What does that mean to you? How can we know God without understanding Him completely? Why is it important that there are things about God we don't understand?

5. Read the five statements of belief written by Rock Harbor. If these are considered essential statements about the Christian faith (and they are), what makes them essential? Are there any other essential statements you think should be included in this list? Why is it important to avoid adding nonessential statements to a list like this?

6. What's the difference between knowing God and knowing about God? Has there ever been a time in your life when you knew about God but didn't really know Him?

7. What's the difference between believing in God and believing Him? Why doesn't mere belief in God lead to salvation? What do we mean when we say, "This is the part of faith that moves from your mind to your heart"?

8. Explain the elements of saving faith as found in Acts 26:17-18.

Moving On...

We hope you are beginning to see that the Christian faith is a matter of both the head and the heart. And we don't just exercise this balanced faith once when we come to faith in Christ. We need to live our lives in faith every day, trusting God for the things we can't see and believing that God will deliver on His promises. Part of that belief comes from a conviction of the heart, and part of it comes from a confirmation of the mind that the things we believe are really true. In chapter 2 we will consider a number of these confirmations and evidences for faith.

Chapter 2

And you will know the truth,
and the truth will set you free.

—*Jesus Christ*

In the opening chapter of their excellent book *20 Compelling Evidences That God Exists,* Ken Boa and Robert Bowman make this rather startling statement. "There's only one good reason to believe that God exists: *because it's true."*

Why is that such a startling statement? Because in our culture, with its pluralism of beliefs and competing world-views, having a belief simply because it's true is a bit of an anomaly. We happen to agree with Boa and Bowman, but it's not enough just to say Christianity is true. We have to have some very good reasons to believe that the Christian faith is true. That's not to say that you can't believe the truth claims of Christianity without evidence. But you're not going to get very far in your faith until your belief is supported by some very compelling evidence.

We're not going to lay out the evidence for your faith in this chapter (that comes in part 2). What we want to do is explain that evidence and reason have a place in your faith—a very important place.

A Place for Evidence

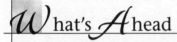

What's Ahead

- A Reasonable Faith
- A Brief History of Faith and Reason
- Evidence, Faith, Reason, and Truth
- Your Worldview Is Showing
- The Difference Between Knowing and Showing

*O*ver the years of writing books, we've done lots of radio interviews, mostly on Christian stations. Each interview has a host, usually a lively, inquisitive, opinionated person (necessary qualities for an engaging host). Recently we were all set to do an interview with a well-known radio host in the Southwest. After the obligatory "bumper" music, but before she introduced us to her listening audience, our host launched into an editorial about the nature of faith. As she was about to bring us into the conversation with, "Please welcome Bruce and Stan," she uttered this little phrase: "Faith goes beyond reason."

Mind you, our host was a Christian, and her remark wasn't meant to be derogatory. To the contrary, in her mind she was giving faith a compliment. But was her statement accurate? Was she trying to say that faith is deeper and more personal than mere reason? Or was she implying that faith and reason don't mix very well, like oil and water?

A Reasonable Faith

Regardless of the motive, it was clear that this particular radio host—a mature Christian by all accounts—didn't have a clear understanding of the role that reason plays in faith. In our experience, this is common. We have found that many Christians are unclear of the relationship between faith and reason. What we want to do in this chapter is to show the dynamic relationship between the two. Much more than a belief system based on subjective feelings and personal preference, Christianity is a reasonable faith.

---

*Q*uick Review: What Is the Christian Faith?

Let's review what we said about the Christian faith in chapter 1: Faith includes a body of knowledge that Christians believe and affirm. Furthermore, the object of faith is the whole person of God—His character traits and the way He interacts with His creation—as revealed by God in the Bible.

That doesn't mean that Christianity is purely rational or that faith in God requires that we absolutely prove that God exists. What it means is that we have good reasons for believing that the Christian faith is true. We like what J.P. Moreland says:

> Understood in this way, we see that faith is built on reason. We should have good reasons for thinking that Christianity is true before we dedicate ourselves completely to it. We should have solid evidence that our understanding of a biblical passage is correct before we go on to apply it.[1]

This understanding of faith stands in sharp contrast to the current perception of the Christian faith held by many non-Christians and, sadly, some Christians:

- The Christian faith is distinct from reason;
- becoming a Christian is a decision to believe something that has no basis in fact; and
- there is no evidence for faith.

Have you ever felt that way? Do you think that's the perception of the people you know at work or at school? Do your friends or maybe even your family members view your faith like this? Is that why you're reluctant to engage them in conversations about faith, especially when questions about God and the Bible come up?

If this is the case, don't feel bad. Many Christians share your feelings. However, just because you're in good company doesn't mean that you shouldn't make an effort to discover the true nature of faith. An understanding of faith separated from reason is not biblical. And it isn't the view that has characterized Christianity and the church—until recently.

A Brief History of Faith and Reason

Throughout the history of the church, faith and reason have been connected. Here are some highlights.

The apostle Paul. Nobody did more to establish the early church than Paul. As we pointed out in the last chapter, Paul was skilled in apologetics—that is, providing a reasonable explanation for his faith—whether he was offering a defense before governors and kings (Acts 24–26) or debating Greek philosophers in Athens (Acts 17). Throughout his letters to young churches and Christians, Paul consistently teaches that the Christian faith is something they can *know.* In his letter to the Roman church, Paul writes this about the ability of people to know the truth about God:

> *They know the truth about God because he has made it obvious to them. For ever since the world was created, people have seen the earth and sky. Through everything God made, they can clearly see his invisible qualities—his eternal power and divine nature. So they have no excuse for not knowing God* (Romans 1:19-20).

The early church fathers. After the last of the original apostles— those who saw Jesus with their own eyes—died at the end of the first century, leaders of the church known as the early church fathers continued to use apologetics to show that the Christian faith is true. In the second century, at a time when Christians were still being persecuted by the state, Justin Martyr argued that Christianity should be tolerated because it was a true philosophy like Platonism (a popular philosophy of the day). In fact, he argued that it was even better! Justin Martyr also used the Old Testament prophecies to prove that Jesus is the Messiah. In the third century, Origen offered a defense of the resurrection of Jesus and showed that the miracles of Jesus, while not natural, were credible.

Augustine. Widely considered to be one of the greatest theologians and apologists of all time, Augustine (354–430) taught that faith and reason work together to help people know God, although he is sometimes hard to follow. On the one hand, said Augustine, rather than trying to prove such truths as the existence of God and the resurrection of Christ, we need to accept what Scripture says about them because God is invisible and the resurrection occurred in the past and cannot be observed. On the other hand, Augustine believed that it was foolish to "believe in Christ without any proofs concerning Christ." Even though Augustine didn't think it was possible to come to faith through reason alone, he saw the two as interactive and interdependent.

The Middle Ages. Far from being a period of darkness, the Middle Ages was a time of intellectual development for the Christian faith. Many prominent apologists showed that Christianity is a reasonable faith. Anselm (1032–1109) developed several proofs to answer the questions of unbelievers, including the famous (and controversial) ontological argument for the existence of God (more about this in the next chapter). However, Anselm's primary goal in combining faith and reason was to help Christians gain a better appreciation for their faith as a reasonable faith. Anselm is famous for saying, "I believe in order to understand."

Thomas Aquinas (1225–1274) developed many of the traditional arguments used to this day to show God exists, including the cosmological and moral arguments and the argument from design. At the same time, Aquinas didn't believe that faith is just about reason. He taught that some truths about God are discoverable through reason and faith working together, while others are known only through faith.

The Reformation. The two giants of the Reformation presented two different views of faith and reason. Martin Luther (1483–1546) taught that reason has its limits in helping people trust in Christ for salvation. Not only did Luther believe that the only way to be justified in God's sight is by faith alone, but he also believed that reason plays no part in knowing the true God. Later in his life, Luther admitted that non-Christians can gain a general knowledge about God through evidence (he must have taken another look at Romans 1:19-20), but this knowledge alone is not enough to save them.

By contrast, John Calvin (1509–1564) taught that faith is always reasonable. However, he clarified that faith doesn't always *appear* to be reasonable to non-Christians because their reason has been corrupted by sin. This is what Paul means when he writes about "wicked people who suppress the truth by their wickedness" (Romans 1:18).

Colonial America. The Pilgrims (or Puritans) who came to America in the seventeenth century weren't stupid. They were highly educated, and they valued education. (Most of the great universities founded in the seventeenth and eighteenth centuries—Harvard, Princeton, and Yale are just three examples—were founded by Christians.) Christian scholars like Jonathan Edwards, who possessed a towering intellect to go along with a deep spirituality, demonstrated by their writings and teachings that faith and reason belong together.

When Reason Was Pushed to the Margins

J.P. Moreland says that three different European trends in the eighteenth and nineteenth centuries began to push reason to the margins as a factor in people coming to Christ in faith. First, philosophers such as David Hume (1711–1776) and Immanuel Kant (1724–1804) said that we cannot know God exists because we can't experience Him with the five senses. Second, German higher criticism of the Bible questioned its reliability as a historical document. Third, the publication of *On the Origin of Species* by Charles Darwin challenged the belief that God created the universe.

In America, Christians responded in two ways to these challenges to biblical authority. First, they withdrew from the arena of public intellectual debate and focused on the inner life, with an emphasis on the Holy Spirit. "To be sure," writes Moreland, "Christians must rely on the Holy Spirit in their intellectual pursuits, but this does not mean they should expend no mental sweat of their own in defending the faith."[2] The second response from Christians to these challenges was the rise of fundamentalism. The term came from an emphasis on the fundamentals of the Bible. Rather than engage the culture with the foundational truths of Scripture, the fundamentalists started their own Bible institutes and gathered in their own Bible conferences. The net result, according to Moreland, was the "marginalization of Christian ideas from the public arena."

Apologetics in the Twentieth Century and Beyond

Thankfully, a dramatic revival of sound apologetics and cultural engagement sprang to life in the second half of the twentieth century. A number of brilliant scholars with a heart for Christ reshaped the landscape. Chief among them was C.S. Lewis (1898–1963), an Oxford scholar who has influenced many Christian apologists and philosophers as well as tens of millions of Christians. Through such popular books as *The Problem of Pain, The Screwtape Letters, Miracles,* and *Mere Christianity,* Lewis showed that Christianity is based on reasonable evidence.

As the twenty-first century has unfolded, a new generation of Christian apologists is delivering the timeless message of truth in new contexts. Gifted communicators such as Lee Strobel *(A Case for Christ),* William Lane Craig *(Reasonable Faith),* and Timothy Keller *(The Reason for God)* are communicating the truth about God in ways that are relational and culturally relevant.

Evidence, Faith, Reason, and Truth

When we talk about evidence for faith, what we're really after are the reasons for our faith. In the last chapter, we dug into the details about faith. Now it's time to define what we mean by *evidence.* In order to do that, we also need to look at two related terms: *reason* and *truth.*

- *Evidence.* This is the data presented to prove the facts (especially in a court case). In a broader sense, evidence is anything that tends to prove or disprove something. From a positive perspective, evidence gives us grounds for belief. From a negative perspective, evidence gives us grounds to no longer believe something previously thought to be true.

- *Reason.* The act of reason is the mental process we engage in order to form a conclusion about something, whether that conclusion is taken as a fact, a judgment, or an inference.

- *Truth.* The best definition of truth we have found is this: Truth corresponds to reality. Or how about this: Truth conforms to the way things are. Truth is the objective of evidence and the object of reason. In other words, evidence is presented in order to reveal the truth about something, and we use reason in order to point us to the truth.

You Can Know the Truth

Jesus was big on truth. No surprise! He claimed to be truth (John 14:6) and said that truth was knowable. Not only that, but knowing the truth will set us free (John 8:32). Obviously, Jesus had something concrete in mind, namely Himself. As we will see in chapter 6, there is good reason to believe that Jesus was who He said He was—the true Son of God—and that He truly came to life after dying for the sins of humanity. But for our discussion now we need to be reminded that the truth of the Christian faith is rooted in reality and backed by evidence. Its truth is objective.

By contrast, today's culture places an emphasis on subjective (or relative) truth. Objectivity is passé unless you can tie it to empirical scientific data (and even then the data can be interpreted in different ways, depending on the situation). What counts is individual opinion and perspective (what's true for you may not be true for me). This is one of the main reasons why Christianity is under fire these days. The Christian faith, based in the person of Jesus, dares to suggest that you can know the truth. It's also why Christians are often accused of being intolerant. How dare we think that there is objective standard for truth! In our culture, tolerance is often valued more highly than truth.

When it comes to establishing the Christian faith—that is, everything God has revealed in the Bible about Himself and the world He created—evidence and reason are important, but they aren't the only way we can know truth. As we discovered in the last chapter, reducing faith to the level of empirical evidence—that which we can experience with the five senses—results in evidentialism.

So we don't want to go to that extreme. But neither do we want to throw out evidence and reason. That results in the other extreme of faith, which is fideism.

When it comes to reason and faith and the way they relate to truth, it isn't either/or. It's both/and. Both reason and faith help us get to the truth. Reason gets us there by enabling us to discover, understand, and prove certain things that correspond with reality. But faith is also necessary because you can't personally prove everything that is real in the world.

To illustrate this point, we're going to assume three things about you: You've never been to Nepal, you weren't alive during the Civil War, and you've never been bitten by a rattlesnake. That being the case, how do you know that Mt. Everest is a real place, that Abraham Lincoln was a real person, and that rattlesnake bites can be fatal? The reason you know these things is that you have exercised faith by believing what other people—such as parents, friends, teachers, and scientists—tell you about real places, people, and things. You can't personally prove these things, but you have good reason to believe that what other people have concluded about them is true.

A Balanced Approach

If our goal is truth—that is, everything that corresponds to reality—then we need to find a balance between evidence, reason, and faith as they relate to truth. In coming up with this balance, Peter Kreeft distinguishes between three categories of truth and how we arrive at them.[3]

1. *Truths of faith and not of reason.* These are truths revealed by God in the Scriptures that are not understandable, discoverable, or provable by evidence and reason. An example of something in this category of truth is the Trinity (one God in three persons).

2. *Truths of both faith and reason.* These are things revealed by God, but they are also understandable, discoverable, or provable by reason. An example of something in this category of truth is the existence of God.

3. *Truths of reason and not of faith.* These are truths that aren't

revealed by God but are known through evidence and reason. An example of something in this category is the existence of the universe.

Just because we arrive at truth in these different ways doesn't mean that one truth is better or more reliable than another. Truth is truth, whether it is understandable, discoverable, provable by science, or revealed by God in His word. However, this doesn't mean there won't be questions or objections to certain kinds of truth, especially the truths in categories 1 and 2. If someone questions the existence of God or the nature of the Trinity, we can't just smile, fold our arms, and say, "Hey, what can I tell you? God said it, I believe it, and that settles it for me." That kind of approach is irresponsible and unproductive.

According to Kreeft, our job as apologists is twofold. First, we need to prove the propositions about the Christian faith that fall in category 2. This is the *positive* task of Christian apologetics. For example, we can show that belief in an invisible God is logically coherent (more about this in chapter 3).

Second, we need to answer the objections to the propositions in category 1. This is the *negative* task of Christian apologetics. For example, we can't prove that God is one God in three persons, but we can answer the objections to this truth through sound reasoning (more about this in chapter 6).

Christianity is not a patent medicine. Christianity claims to give an account of facts—to tell you what the real universe is like. Its account of the universe may be true, or it may not, and once the question is really before you, then your natural inquisitiveness must make you want to know the answer. If Christianity is untrue, then no honest man will want to believe it, however helpful it might be: if it is true, every honest man will want to believe it, even if it gives him no help at all.[4]

—C.S. Lewis

A Reason to Believe

Taking a balanced approach to evidence, reason, and faith as a way of getting to the truth should give you a sense of security and comfort. On the one hand, you don't need to rely on reason alone to prove everything you believe about Christianity. On the other hand, you don't have to throw reason out the window. Christianity is a reasonable faith that corresponds to reality whether that reality can be backed by evidence or is simply revealed by God through His word.

Your Worldview Is Showing

One of the best ways to show that Christianity is reasonable is to compare it to other belief systems. Another way to describe a belief system is to call it a *worldview*. At its most basic level, a worldview is a framework through which or by which we make sense of the world. More simply, according to Norman Geisler, "a *worldview* is how one views or interprets reality."[5] Because your worldview is like a lens through which you view and come to conclusions about reality, it shapes the way you live your life.

Remember what we said about truth? Truth corresponds to reality, to the way things really are. So blending these two definitions together, we can say that your worldview helps you get to the truth. With that in mind, it would seem that choosing a worldview is a pretty important task in life. It would be a shame for anyone to adopt a certain worldview and live within that framework, only to discover that it isn't pointing to the truth. It's kind of like the joke about the guy who climbs to the top of the ladder of success, only to find out that it's leaning against the wrong building. Of course, getting to the truth about the world is a lot more important than climbing the corporate ladder. Your framework for life affects everything you do and pretty much everything you believe.

Searching for and choosing the right worldview should be at the top of everyone's to-do list. The trouble is, most people aren't proactive when it comes to investigating worldviews. Instead, they do one of two things. Either they inherit their worldview from their family through tradition, or they merely absorb the ideas and lifestyles of the culture around them, whether that involves tracking the media or following the crowd.

We're not saying that you can't adopt a true and cohesive worldview this way. But why take the chance? Why not do your own research? The stakes are just too high not to take charge of your own choice. Besides, even if you are confident that you are living within the framework of the best of all possible worldviews, doing some investigation into the other options out there will help you understand why your worldview is the best one and why it helps you answer questions about these things:

Origins—where we came from

Identity—who we are

Purpose—why we are here

Meaning—what life is all about

Destiny—where we are going

*Y*our Search Matters

How you go about your search is up to you. Reading a book like this (along with the books and resources we suggest along the way) is a great place to start. And don't limit yourself to reading books you agree with. You may also want to personally interview people who hold to worldviews that are different from yours. If you're a student, you are already being exposed to all of the worldviews out there, whether you hear about them from your teachers or your fellow students. Don't take what they say at face value. Do your own investigation. Be smart. After all, it's your life, not theirs.

One of the main benefits from putting so much effort into this search is that when you have arrived at a worldview that is reasonable, well thought-out, and consistent with reality, you will be able to live your own life as a reasonable, thoughtful person who makes decisions based on the ultimate realities of the universe. That may sound rather cosmic, but the benefits are extremely practical, the biggest one being that you are able to confidently answer life's big questions: where you came from, who you are, why you're here, what your life is all about, and where you are going when you die.

What Are the Options?

A lot of religions are out there (a religion is simply a set of beliefs) as well as a lot of ideas about the world. But all belief systems actually stem from three major worldviews. Let's take a look at them.

Naturalism. This worldview says that reality includes the natural world and nothing else. Naturalism begins with *scientism*, a belief that the only things we can truly know—physical objects, properties, events, and propositions—are things that can be proven scientifically. Obviously, this worldview leaves no room for the supernatural (*supernatural* simply means above nature), and therefore no room for God. Consequently, when you try to answer the questions about origins, identity, purpose, meaning, and destiny, you are left with these answers:

- There's no explanation for how the natural world came to exist; evidently it came out of nothing.
- After the "nothing," matter, energy, and forces just happened.
- Eventually, life forms developed.
- No planning or design was involved because no planner or designer exists. Everything has happened by random mutation and natural selection.
- Human beings aren't any better than other life forms, just more advanced.
- Humans have no purpose for life larger than what they can create.
- There's no life beyond this life; everything ends at death.

*D*oes Naturalism Correspond with Reality?

Naturalists believe their worldview provides answers for everything that is real in the universe. There's only one problem (and it's a big one). By definition, naturalism leaves out the supernatural. By implication, it says that supernatural beings and supernatural occurrences aren't real. However, if God, who is supernatural, exists, then naturalism falls short of reality.

Moral relativism. In this worldview, propositions about the nature of reality are not simply true or false. What we believe depends on the cultural, social, and linguistic contexts of the particular situation in question. In other words, truth is relative. What's true for one person may not be true for another. What's true in one location may not be true in another. And what's true today may not be true tomorrow.

Relativism doesn't necessarily rule out the existence of God, but it doesn't establish God as an objective reality. Because truth is relative, belief in God and the supernatural is relative. The relativistic framework doesn't include the objective, transcendent God who created humanity in His image and who exists apart from His creation. In this worldview, God is who or what we want Him to be.

Clearly, there are different forms of relativism, just as there are different forms of naturalism. But the bottom line is that both worldviews lead you to one bleak conclusion: There is no objective meaning or purpose to life. You are on this earth for a few years, you do the best you can, trying to make the world a better place (or not, if that isn't your cup of tea), and in the end you die.

That's not to say that people with a naturalist or relativist worldview can't be happy and productive. And don't think for a minute that these worldviews rule out faith. The naturalist can have faith, as long as it's faith in some kind of physical object, property, or event. And someone with a relativist worldview can have faith as well, as long as it's personally helpful or enriching. However, in both cases, if you're talking about a reasonable faith that leads you to the objective reality of God, then it's an entirely different matter. In fact, it's at the heart of our third worldview.

$\mathcal{D}$oes Relativism Correspond with Reality?

This is an interesting question because in this framework, reality is subjective. There's no such thing as objective truth. The problem is that in saying that all truth is relative, the relativist is making an objective statement (in philosophical terms, that means the argument about all truth being relative is self-refuting). The other problem is that when push comes to shove, two people with alternate views or perceptions of something that is real—let's say a car sitting in a parking lot—will ultimately agree that the car belongs to the person to whom it's registered rather than the person who wants to steal it.

Theism. This worldview includes an infinite, personal God who created the universe. God is both transcendent over the universe (that means He exists apart from it) and immanent in it (that means He is involved in it). Biblical theism answers the great questions about the universe and life with these propositions:

- God created the world out of nothing (Genesis 1:1).
- God created people in His image, which means all humans share some of His characteristics (Genesis 1:26-27).
- God lovingly created us in order to glorify and enjoy Him (1 Corinthians 10:31).
- We find meaning in life as we invest in His eternal values (Matthew 6:33).
- Each of us has an eternal destiny and can, by God's grace and an exercise of faith in Jesus Christ, choose to spend eternity in heaven (1 Peter 1:3-4).

For many people—in particular those who hold a naturalistic or relativistic worldview—these propositions sound like the wishful thinking of people who willfully set aside the harsh realities of our universe and instead believe in a fairy tale that promises eternal rewards and happiness. And all you have to do is believe in Jesus.

It's understandable that people would view theism and Christianity in this way. The story told in the Bible does sound pretty amazing, especially the many supernatural elements. However, when considering a worldview, the issue is not how good it sounds or how satisfying it is to the people who believe it. Only one issue counts, and only one question is worth asking: It is true? Does it correspond with the way things are?

In part 2 we're going to take an in-depth look at the way theism in general and the Christian faith in particular correspond to the real world, which includes more than science can measure. And we will discover a basis for objective truth. The truth claims of the Christian faith aren't made-up fairy tales. They are factual claims that you can investigate and find to be true because they are supported by evidence and reason.

The Difference Between Knowing and Showing

William Lane Craig, one of the world's most respected Christian apologists, makes a distinction between *knowing* that Christianity is true and *showing* that Christianity is true. His purpose in doing this is to encourage Christians on two counts. First, you can know your faith is true even if you don't know everything about your faith or have an answer to every question and every doubt. As we said in chapter 1, faith is more than belief. Faith adds trust and commitment to belief. Faith is a decision to trust in Jesus Christ. If it were simply a matter of mental understanding, even the demons would be saved. But faith is more than knowledge. The act of faith comes from the heart, and saving faith comes from God. Second, you're not alone when you attempt to use reason and evidence to show the truth of your faith. God has given you some extra help.

Knowing Christianity Is True

For the Christian, knowing Christianity is true comes through the "self-authenticating witness of God's Holy Spirit."[6] This kind of knowing is along the lines of confidence or assurance. That's because God sent the Holy Spirit to be Christ's presence in us. Jesus explains it this way:

> But when the Father sends the Advocate as my representative—that is, the Holy Spirit—he will teach you everything and will remind you of everything I have told you (John 14:26).

Years after the Holy Spirit had come upon the believers on the Day of Pentecost (Acts 2:1-4), the apostle Paul confirmed the Holy Spirit's role in a letter to the Roman church:

> So you have not received a spirit that makes you fearful slaves. Instead, you received God's Spirit when he adopted you as his own children. Now we call him, "Abba, Father." For his Spirit joins with our spirit to affirm that we are God's children (Romans 8:15-16).

Craig concludes that evidence and reason are necessary to support the faith of the believer, but they are not the basis of that faith.

The Holy Spirit also plays a role in the life of the unbeliever. The Bible is clear that people don't seek God on their own (Romans 3:10-11). The only way any of us open our hearts and minds to even consider God is through the Holy Spirit. Jesus explains it this way:

> *And when he [the Holy Spirit] comes, he will convict the world of its sin, and of God's righteousness, and of the coming judgment. The world's sin is that it refuses to believe in me* (John 16:8-9).

*T*he Holy Spirit Is the Key

How many people have you known who have all the evidence they need for the existence of God and yet still refuse to believe? It isn't because they lack evidence, but because they are resisting or ignoring the work of the Holy Spirit in their lives. Or because they have been hurt by a negative experience with the church or other Christians. Or because they have been misled by a false presentation of the Christian message. When you are in conversations about faith with unbelievers, be aware that there could be many reasons why they are closed to the truth about God. And pray that their hearts would be open to the Holy Spirit's influence.

Showing That Christianity Is True

> Effectiveness in apologetics is presenting cogent and persuasive arguments for the Gospel in the power of the Holy Spirit, leaving the results to God.
>
> —*William Lane Craig*

You may know your faith is true, but how do you show it to be true to someone who wants to know? Here the role of evidence and reason is very important. But the Holy Spirit doesn't take a backseat while you lay out persuasive arguments and evidence. It isn't either/or, as in either the evidence or the Holy Spirit. It's both/and. The Holy Spirit will act to use your arguments to convince unbelievers that Christianity is true.

This should give you great confidence as you explain your faith to people who ask. It isn't your job to convince or convict anyone. That's the Holy Spirit's job. Your task is to provide reasonable explanations for the truth claims of the Christian faith.

Some Final Thoughts on Faith and Evidence

As we come to the end of this section on faith and evidence, we want to give you two additional thoughts that will help you make

> Preach the gospel at all times. When necessary, use words.
>
> —*St. Francis of Assisi*

sense of all of this. First, faith and evidence will never contradict each other. How do we know this? Here's how: If the Christian faith is true, and if the evidence is true, there will never be a contradiction. Truth cannot contradict truth. Now, the evidence may be faulty, resulting in an incorrect conclusion and an apparent contradiction (for example, the evidence once showed that the earth was flat), but evidence leading to the truth will never contradict true faith.

Second, as you study the evidence (that's what you're doing by reading this book), keep in mind that your own life—the integrity you show and the love you demonstrate—will often speak more powerfully than the words you use. That's not to say that you shouldn't use words, but without a life characterized by the love of Christ to back them up, they will only be like "a noisy gong or a clanging symbol" (1 Corinthians 13:1).

What's That Again?

1. Christianity is a reasonable faith and not just a belief system based on subjective feelings and personal preference.

2. Throughout the history of the church, faith and reason have been connected:

   • In his letters to the early church, Paul wrote

about the ability of people to know the truth about God;

- the early church fathers used apologetics to show the Christian faith to be true;

- Augustine saw faith and reason as interactive and interdependent;

- Calvin taught that faith is always reasonable although it doesn't always appear that way;

- the Puritans taught that faith and reason belong together; and

- after a lapse in the nineteenth century, there was a revival of sound apologetics led by C.S. Lewis.

3. As the twenty-first century unfolds, a new generation of Christian apologists is communicating the truth about God in ways that are relational and culturally relevant.

4. When it comes to reason and faith, it's both/and, not either/or. Reason enables us to discover, understand, and prove certain things, but faith is necessary to know certain truths that we can't discover, understand, or prove for ourselves.

5. Peter Kreeft distinguishes between three categories of truth: truths of faith and not of reason, truths of both faith and reason, and truths of reason and not of faith.

6. The positive task of apologetics is to prove the propositions of the Christian faith that are known by both faith and reason. The negative task is to answer the negative objections of propositions known by faith alone.

7. The three main belief systems or worldviews are naturalism, relativism, and theism. It's important to arrive at a worldview that is reasonable, well thought-out, and consistent with reality.

8. When considering a worldview, the issue is not how good it sounds or how satisfying it is, but whether or not it is true.

9. There is a difference between *knowing* and *showing* that Christianity is true. For the Christian, knowing Christianity is true comes through the self-authenticating witness of the Holy Spirit. Evidence and reason help the Christian to show Christianity is true.

10. Faith and evidence leading to the truth will never contradict each other.

Dig Deeper

Three books get our seal of approval for providing a balanced approach to faith and reason:

The main purpose of *20 Compelling Evidences That God Exists* by Kenneth Boa and Robert Bowman is to help the reader discover why believing in God makes so much sense.

William Lane Craig's book *Reasonable Faith* is pretty dense but well worth the effort to study.

That's Just Your Interpretation by Paul Copan does a great job deciphering the various worldviews. Copan also answers several challenges to Christianity.

We wouldn't be doing our duty if we didn't recommend that you read *Mere Christianity* by C.S. Lewis. Aside from the Bible, this classic book has influenced more people with the reasonable claims of Christianity than any other.

■ ■ ■

Questions for Reflection and Discussion

1. If you had to guess, what do you think your family, friends, and coworkers would say about the Christian faith? Have

these perceptions ever kept you from engaging them in conversations about faith?

2. For nearly two thousand years, people believed that faith and reason belonged together. What happened to change this belief, especially in the nineteenth century? What happens in any era when Christians withdraw from the arena of public intellectual debate?

3. Review the definitions of evidence, reason, and truth. Why are all three necessary components of faith?

4. We provided an example for each of these categories of truth:

> truths of faith and not of reason
>
> truths of both faith and reason
>
> truths of reason and not of faith

Give one more example for each one.

5. How deliberate have you been about choosing your worldview? How did you arrive at it? How has your choice affected the way you live?

6. Which of the three worldviews is most common today? Which one has the most appeal for today's culture? Why do you think popular culture has disdain for the theistic worldview?

7. Summarize what it means to know that Christianity is true. What does it mean to show that Christianity is true? Is this optional for the Christian?

8. As best you can, explain how the self-authenticating witness of God's Holy Spirit helps you to know your faith in Christ is real and true. What can you do to increase the power of the Holy Spirit in your life? (See Galatians 5:16-26.)

Moving On...

Now that we've taken a good look at faith, evidence, reason, and the way they relate to one another, it's time to move to part 2, where we will consider various kinds of evidence for God, the Bible, and Jesus. These chapters contain a lot of information, so you may have to take your time. That's okay. The information is too important to gloss over or rush through. You will notice that just about all of the evidence—whether it's philosophical, natural, or historic—is connected so that no one piece of evidence has to stand on its own as irrefutable. Remember, God has given us enough information to know Him by faith but not so much that we can do it on our own.

$\mathcal{P}$art II
Faith, Evidence, and God

Introduction to Part II

*I*n the beginning God created the heavens and the earth." Those ten words are among the best known and most controversial in history. As you no doubt know, they are the first words of the Bible: Genesis 1:1. What's amazing about that short verse is that it describes three foundational claims about the universe and how it came to be:

> There is a God.
>
> God existed before the beginning, and
>
> God created the universe.

Even though nearly half the world—2.3 billion Christians, 1.2 billion Muslims, and 14 million Jews—professes to believe in one Creator God, a lot of people don't automatically buy into the claims of Genesis 1:1. These aren't evil, ignorant people who are making sacrifices to pagan gods like Baal, Ra, or Zanex (okay, we made that last one up). They probably aren't actual atheists, who deny the existence of any kind of God, or even agnostics, who don't think it's possible to know whether or not God exists. (A recent Pew Forum survey on the U.S. religious landscape says that just 4 percent of Americans say they are either atheist or agnostic.[1])

More than likely these skeptics and doubters include some of your coworkers, friends, and maybe even family members—intelligent, loving, honest people who have nothing against you for believing in God. They are probably fine with the notion of God as a higher power or a positive force that is part of the universe but doesn't get involved in our lives. But the idea of a personal God who has always existed and who interacts with the world He made is a bit of a stretch for lots of people.

Open-Minded, Insecure, or Hungry for More

In the next four chapters, we want to address the concerns and questions of three kinds of people. First are the open-minded skeptics. These people are skeptical of God's existence, but they aren't closed to the idea. The problem is that no one has ever offered a reasonable explanation for God's existence and His creation of the world, not to mention His involvement in it.

Then there are the insecure doubters. These people consider themselves believers, but they've never actually explored the evidence for God's existence. They accept Him by faith, but it's not a reasonable faith. Consequently, they have some doubts about God, but they are afraid to express their doubts to their Christian friends and family for fear that they will be criticized or ridiculed.

Then there are those who are hungry for more. These people think their faith is reasonable, and they know there is good evidence to believe in God. The problem is they don't know enough to answer the tough questions that people are asking about God these days. They would like to speak intelligently to the legitimate questions of open-minded skeptics and insecure doubters. Additionally, they would like to know there are good answers to the questions being asked by the hard-nosed atheists who seem to be coming out of the woodwork.

What About the Atheist?

For most of the twentieth century, the Christian worldview dominated Western culture. God was part of most people's personal belief system, and He was also accepted in the public square—government, schools, and the media. That's not the case anymore. The public square is no longer dominated by a Christian worldview, and those who believe in God are no longer calling the shots (or if they are, they are less vocal).

As the twenty-first century unfolds, a new voice is gaining a footing. This voice doesn't speak for God, but rather opposes Him.

Or more correctly, it opposes the idea that God exists. Whether you call the people who hold this position skeptics, atheists, or agnostics, their influence is being felt everywhere—in the schools, in the government, and most vocally in the media.

We actually think this is a positive trend because it has startled many Christians who were, quite frankly, a bit sloppy in their beliefs about God. When your view is the dominant view and few oppose you, the tendency is to get soft and let your guard down. But when someone challenges your beliefs about something, especially your beliefs about God, it tends to upset you. And when that happens, you can do one of two things. You can either hide like a wounded animal, or you can determine to get stronger by learning more about what you believe about God.

Our purpose is not to challenge or rebut the atheist directly. Some very capable people are doing just that, and we'll give you some resources at the end of chapter 3 in case you're interested in doing a deeper study. However, we want to assure you—whether you're an open-minded skeptic, an insecure doubter, or hungry for more—that you have nothing to fear from the new atheists (as they are sometimes called) like Richard Dawkins, Sam Harris, or Christopher Hitchens. They may be more articulate and more popular than the old atheists (think Madeline Murray O'Hair), and they may sound as if they consider Christians to be a lower form of life on the evolutionary chart, but the truth of the matter is that anyone who is trying really hard to deny God's existence and to keep any belief about God out of the public arena is probably dealing with his or her own doubts about the non-existence of God.

$\mathcal{D}$oubt Goes Both Ways

Nothing is wrong with having doubts about God, the Bible, and Jesus. We're going to deal with the nature of doubt in part 3. But don't think for a minute that believers are the only ones who deal with doubt. Unbelievers have doubts too—not about God, but about their unbelief.

A Cumulative Case for God

As we're going to show you in the next four chapters, an impressive amount of evidence is available for...

the existence of God

God's hand in creation

the reliability of the Bible

the reality of Jesus

However, despite the preponderance of the evidence we're going to present, we want to be very clear that no single piece of evidence—no smoking gun, if you will—tips the scales in favor of God. But the cumulative effect of the evidence in the next few chapters is so compelling that it is reasonable to believe that God exists, that God created the universe, that the Bible offers a trustworthy account of reality, and that Jesus truly existed and was the person He claimed to be.

In chapter 3, we will look at three traditional philosophical arguments for the existence of God: the cosmological argument, the moral argument, and the ontological argument. In chapter 4 we will consider the evidence from the natural world, as expressed in the argument from design (sometimes called the teleological argument). In chapter 5 we will examine evidence for the Bible (the written word of God) as a reliable historic and prophetic document. And in chapter 6 we will look at the evidence for Jesus (the living Word of God), who was raised from the dead.

Chapter 3

From the first glimmerings of philosophy among the ancient Greeks through the dawn of the third millennium after Christ, the world's greatest thinkers from Plato to Plantinga have wrestled with the question of God. Is there a personal, transcendent being who created the universe and is the source of moral goodness? I think there is and there are good reasons to think so.

—*William Lane Craig*

The famous philosopher Bertrand Russell was once asked how he would explain his unbelief if he were to die and find out that God really does exist. "Not enough evidence, God," Russell allegedly replied. "Not enough evidence." Russell had every right to his opinion, and a lot of people today share his view. But is it the correct response? Has God failed to leave us enough evidence for His existence?

We don't think God has failed in any respect. He has been generous in leaving us plenty of evidence for His existence, and that evidence is built into every person in two distinct ways. First, every person has a sense of God's existence that comes through the cosmos. Second, a sense of God's existence comes through each person's conscience. Together, the cosmos and the conscience comprise what is known as *general revelation* because it is evidence that God has revealed to all people generally.

The apostle Paul writes this about general revelation:

> *Through everything God made, [people] can clearly see his invisible qualities* (Romans 1:20).

> *Their own conscience and thoughts either accuse them or tell them they are doing right* (Romans 2:15).

In this chapter we're going to take a closer look at the evidence for God through the cosmos and our consciences, two pieces of evidence for the existence of God that have always been available to everyone, including Bertrand Russell.

Evidence for God

_O_ ne of the most common thoughts held by people around the world is both very simple and quite complex. We're referring, of course, to thoughts about God: the Creator, the Almighty, the Holy One. Some people think God is no more than a feeling, a force, or an idea that helps them make sense of the world. Others worship and adore God with every fiber of their being and depend on Him every moment of every day of their lives. He is so real to them that they would give their lives if the alternative were to deny He exists. Still others spend a lifetime denying that God exists. One thing is for sure. Whether they think of God as a force, a personal being, or nothing at all, everybody thinks about God. _Everybody._

We Know Who God Is, but Do We Know God Is True?

That's the simple part about God, that everybody thinks about Him. The complex part about God is that He is, well, complicated. The way God has revealed Himself—through the universe He created (called _general_ revelation) and through both the written word of Scripture and also the living Word of Jesus Christ (called *special revelation*)—tells us that He is much more than an idea, a force, or a feeling. He is the personal, holy, transcendent Creator and Sustainer of the universe. Here are just a few of the characteristics of God that the Bible reveals:

- *God is self-existent.* Everything that exists has a cause, and the first cause of everything is God (Genesis 1:1), who Himself has no cause (more about that in a minute). This is not double-talk or a contradiction in terms. Logic and reason dictate that for anything to exist, there must first be an uncaused, self-existent being.

- *God is eternal.* God is not defined or confined by time. He always was, and He will always be (Psalm 90:2). God is also infinite in that He is above and beyond His finite creation.

- *God is holy.* God is perfect (the Bible term is *righteous*). In the negative context, He has no evil in Him; in the positive context, He is completely pure (Isaiah 6:3).

- *God is unchangeable.* Unlike the gods of other religions, God does not change (Malachi 3:6). He is not capricious (that is, unpredictable). He is the same yesterday, today, and forever (Hebrews 13:8).

- *God is just.* We don't have to worry that God won't be fair with everyone. God doesn't grade on the curve, and He doesn't play favorites (Revelation 15:3).

- *God is all-powerful.* No person, nation, or confederation—whether earthly or from the supernatural world—can conquer Him. God is able to do anything that is consistent with His nature (Revelation 19:6).

- *God is all-knowing.* God knows everything about everything. Nothing exists that He doesn't know, including the details of your life, both good and bad (Proverbs 5:21).

- *God is present everywhere.* God is everywhere, but He is not in everything. God is not the universe; He is transcendent, meaning that He exists apart from His creation. Yet He is near to you every moment of the day (Psalm 139:7-12).

- *God is love.* God's holiness and His justice demand a penalty for imperfection (the Bible word is *sin*). Yet God's love motivates Him to reach out to us even though we are imperfect (Romans 5:8). The greatest demonstration of God's love is Jesus, His only Son, who came to earth to die for our sins (John 3:16).

- *God is personal.* God did not create the universe like a clock maker builds a clock. He didn't wind it up, only to let it wind down on its own. God is personally involved in His creation, holding it together with His power. And He is personally interested in your life. God knows you more intimately and more completely than you can imagine (Psalm 139:1-4).

As powerful and compelling as these descriptions are, how do we know they are true? How do we know God is true? More to the point, how do we know God exists at all? After all, God is a spirit (John 4:24) and cannot be seen (1 Timothy 6:16). He is not composed of matter and does not possess a physical nature. Because He does not have a physical body, He is not limited to our dimensions of geographical location or space. He cannot be measured, calibrated, cataloged, or experienced by the five senses.

Believing Doesn't Make It True, and Disbelieving Doesn't Make It False

God doesn't exist just because you believe He does, nor does He cease to exist just because someone else thinks He doesn't. God isn't Santa Claus or the tooth fairy. He's not a make-believe character. The reason people grow out of their belief in God is not that they once believed in the one true God and now doubt His existence. It's because they once believed in a make-believe god.

We're not saying that childlike belief is impossible. Jesus said, "Let the children come to me. Don't stop them! For the Kingdom of Heaven belongs to those who are like these children" (Matthew 19:14). You can believe in God even if you don't know why you do. But at some point, as you get to know God better and better, you will want to know why believing God exists is reasonable.

Otherwise your faith will get stuck in neutral. More importantly, you will not appreciate the reality, the majesty, and the truth that is God.

How Do We Find the Truth About God?

We've already talked about truth as an objective reality, not a subjective feeling. Therefore, when considering the truth about God, we need to think of Him as an objective reality, not a subjective feeling. But that doesn't mean that you can prove God exists like you can prove the existence of a human being. God doesn't have a driver's license or some other form of I.D. He doesn't show up at parties and say to everyone, "Hi, I'm Jehovah. Remember when we met last year?"

---

*T*he Standard of Proof

J.P. Moreland says that asking whether or not it is possible to prove there is a God is the wrong question because the notion of a proof sets such a high standard. Very few beliefs in the world are bombproof—that is, beyond dispute or disagreement. One exception may be a mathematical equation, but even then there may be people who take exception with "2 + 2 = 4." About the best we can do with 99.9 percent of the beliefs in the world—whether we're talking about belief in the aerodynamics of an airplane or belief in God—is to say, "It's reasonable to believe that," or "A reasonable person would accept that as truth." That's why we've been saying that Christianity is a reasonable faith. That's not to say that God isn't 100 percent true or completely trustworthy. He is. We just can't offer 100 percent proof that He exists.

As we said, God can't be seen. In fact, He can't be detected by any of the five senses (that's why a naturalist has such a hard time believing God exists). But an emotion, such as love, can't be measured by any of the five senses either. Yet we know love exists. How? Because we can see love in action. We can measure the effects of love in ourselves and in other people. So it is with God, only much more so.

Making a Cumulative Case for God

Now we want to give you a summary of the most common (and we think, the most compelling) reasons or evidences for the existence of God. But we want to give you a word of warning. If you're looking for a smoking gun that absolutely proves God's existence, you're not going to find it. If you're looking for bombproof evidence, it's not here.

But what you are going to find is a cumulative case for God's existence. What that means is that even though no one specific piece of evidence proves beyond a shadow of a doubt that God exists, several pieces of evidence together make a reasonable case for the existence of God. Each piece of evidence doesn't have to bear the burden of proof. Instead, the preponderance of the evidence shows the case to be true.

A Rope, Not a Chain

The pieces of evidence in a cumulative case argument are not like links in a chain, where the weakest link can destroy the effectiveness of the entire chain. They are more like different strands in a rope, where several strands help strengthen the rope, and one weak strand doesn't make the rope ineffective. Remember, it's the combined strength of the arguments that matter, not the individual strength or weakness of any one argument.

In the rest of this chapter, we're going to lay out three arguments for God's existence, from the strongest to the weakest:

- *The cosmological argument.* Every effect must have a cause. If the universe had a beginning point (and most scientists now believe this to be true), it must have had an incredibly powerful cause. This argument shows that God is the first cause.

- *The moral argument.* One of the characteristics of humans is that we have a moral code—a built-in sense of right and wrong. How could this moral compass—often called the *objective moral law*—just happen? This argument shows that the sense of right and wrong in the heart of every person is evidence of a moral Creator.

- *The ontological argument.* This argument is based on the notion that every person has thoughts about God. This universal idea points to God's existence.

---

*T*he Hiddenness of God

Two of the more prominent reasons why atheists argue for the non-existence of God have to do with the problem of suffering and evil (we'll deal with that in chapter 7) and the hiddenness of God. They reason that if God existed, He would want to reveal Himself as loving and good, but He doesn't seem to do that. Because He doesn't (according to the atheist), He must not exist. But in fact, God has not hidden himself. As we will see in this chapter and the ones to follow, God has revealed Himself through the world He made, through our own consciences, and through the fact that people think about God (even atheists). And despite the evil and suffering in the world, God has graciously blessed us with many things that display His existence. Speaking to a crowd of unbelievers, Paul and Barnabas say this about God: "In the past he permitted all the nations to go their own ways, but he never left them without evidence of himself and his goodness. For instance, he sends you rain and good crops and gives you food and joyful hearts" (Acts 14:16-17).

The Cosmological Argument

The name of this argument comes from the word *cosmos* (world). This argument has many moving parts, and it can get very philosophical and complex. We're going to do our best to simplify it without oversimplifying it. Make sense? We hope so.

A good place to start with the cosmological argument is to ask a very basic question: Why is there something rather than nothing?

Wow. Talk about a blinding flash of the obvious. At first glance that may seem like a dumb question, but the answer leads to all kinds of serious implications, so we have to start there, whether we're talking about something as basic as a chair or as vast as the universe. If you consider a chair, you might say, "Well, the chair is there because I bought it at Target." That may explain how the chair came to be in your living room, but it doesn't explain how it came to exist.

After thinking a little more, you would probably trace the chair's origin back to a chair designer and builder, who got the pieces of wood from a lumber mill, which in turn got its raw material from a tree that grew in the ground, which was made possible by seeds and dirt and water. Then you would have to ask, where did the seeds come from? (which may actually prompt you to open your high school biology book). You get the point. The chair, which exists in your living room, is there because of a series of events and things, each one dependent on the one before it. This has to do with *contingency*, which is one part of the cosmological argument.

Contingency

As it relates to the universe, *contingency* means dependency. Everything in the universe—a chair, a tree, a sunset, you—is contingent on something else. And here's something about contingent things that may surprise you. Something that is contingent is not necessary. In other words, a chair doesn't have to exist. Neither does a tree. Neither do you. Everything that exists, including the universe itself, depends on something else for its existence. As such, everything is contingent and therefore not necessary.

But this idea of contingency includes a big problem. You can't have an endless series of contingent things. At some point, the process started with something that isn't contingent. If not, you would never arrive at the present moment where the chair, the tree, the sunset, and you exist.

*T*he Impossibility of Crossing Infinity

The reason you can't have an endless series of contingent things is this: Infinite regression is impossible. You can't keep going backward in a series of infinite causes and events for the simple reason that you can't get from minus infinity to zero. It's not possible mathematically. To get to the present thing, you have to have a first thing; to get to the present event, you have to have a first event. In other words, you have to have a starting point.

A Necessary Being

If the universe and everything in it is contingent on something else, then there has to be a "something else" that is not contingent. Philosophers call this something else a *necessary being*. By definition, this being must exist; it cannot not exist. This necessary being stands in contrast to contingent beings, which don't have to exist. By necessity, this necessary being must also be...

> self-existent
>
> eternal
>
> uncaused

The only being that meets these qualifications is God. Doug Geivett, a professional philosopher (yes, there are such people), lists these three major components in the contingency argument for the existence of God:[1]

1. Establish the contingency of the physical universe.

2. Show how the contingency of the universe entails the existence of a necessary being.

3. Show that this necessary being is God.

Causation

Another component of the cosmological argument is the first-cause argument, sometimes known as the *kalam* cosmological argument. *Kalam* is an Arabic word that means speech. At its core, this philosophical idea builds on the contingency argument by saying that because the universe cannot be infinitely old, it must have a beginning. Furthermore, it must have a first cause. Here are the basics of the argument:

1. Whatever begins to exist has a cause.

2. The universe began to exist.

3. Therefore, the universe has a cause.

The goal of the *kalam* argument, which is popular with both Christians and Muslims, is to show that the first cause is God. Let's look at each part of this argument.

1. Whatever begins to exist has a cause. We've already covered this in the contingency argument, but let's throw a little Latin phrase into the mix to make it sound even better: *ex nihilo, nihil fit.* Simply translated, this reads, "From nothing, nothing comes." There isn't really a need to argue with this. As Peter Kreeft writes, "Most people—outside of asylums and graduate schools—would consider it not only true, but certainly obviously true."[2]

2. The universe began to exist. Even though the *kalam* argument is ancient, the actual evidence for this second premise didn't emerge until the last century. Before this evidence for the beginning of the universe came to light, scientists believed the universe was infinite. Then a series of discoveries prompted the vast majority of scientists to come to a new conclusion: The universe had a beginning.

Note to self: Just because science can't prove something to be true—such as the beginning of the universe—doesn't mean it isn't true. Second note to self: Thousands of years before science figured it out, the Bible said the universe had a beginning.

Twentieth-Century Discoveries Prove the Universe Has a Beginning

1914—American astronomer Vesto Slipher studied the galaxies and found that they were moving away from the earth at high speeds.

1922—Alexander Friedmann, a Russian mathematician, speculated that the entire universe was expanding as galaxies moved away from each other.

1927—Georges Lemaitre, a Belgian astronomer, concluded that if the universe was expanding, then it was once much smaller. He also believed that all the material in the universe had once been in a single place.

1929—American astronomer Edwin Hubble used the 100-inch Hooker telescope on Mt. Wilson in California to prove what scientists believed but could not see: Galaxies are rushing away from each other at high rates of speed. His findings meant two things. First, the universe is expanding. Second, everything in the universe came from a single, unbelievably powerful explosion. Astronomer Robert Jastrow called Hubble's discovery "one of the main supporters of the scientific story of Genesis."

1948—George Gamow, a Russian-born scientist, concluded that there had to have been an initial explosion of pure energy in order for matter to exist in the universe. Furthermore, Gamow proposed that this initial explosion was so strong that a "faint glow" of heat should be found everywhere in the universe.

1965—Two radio astronomers, Arno Penzias and Robert Wilson, proved Gamow's proposition. Using equipment built in connection with a communications satellite project by Bell Laboratories, Penzias and Wilson measured the faint glow. The heat they measured was so uniform that it could not have come from any single object in space, such as planets or stars. The entire universe seemed to be the source of this background radiation. The only explanation for this was that the universe was once superheated from the detonation of a primordial bang.

1992—If the universe and everything in it began with a detonation of unimaginable proportions, scientists believed that the ripples from that explosive beginning could be measured. On April 24, 1992, a team of astrophysicists led by George Smoot at the University of California at Berkeley announced that the Cosmic Background Explorer (COBE) satellite had measured the ripples scientists were looking for. Stephen Hawking called this "the discovery of the century, if not of all time." George Smoot declared, "What we have found is evidence for the birth of the universe. If you're religious, it's like looking at God."

The two main components of this series of discoveries—the expansion of the universe and background radiation—are the primary features of the Big Bang theory, now widely accepted by scientists.

$\mathcal{T}$he Big Bang and Creation

The Big Bang has caused some scientists to use words like *created* and *creation* in their description of the Big Bang event. The esteemed astronomer Robert Jastrow, a self-proclaimed agnostic, writes this:

> *The astronomical evidence proves that the Universe was created 15 billion years ago in a fiery explosion...The seeds of everything that has happened in the Universe since were planted in that first instant; every star, every planet and every living creature in the Universe owes its physical origins to events that were set into motion in the moment of the cosmic explosion. In a purely physical sense, it was the moment of creation.*[3]

3. Therefore, the universe has a cause. This is a logical conclusion: If the universe had a beginning, then the beginning of the universe had a cause. Remember, nothing comes from nothing. The only question that remains is whether this first cause is an impersonal event or a personal agent. But it can't be an event, because the Big Bang creation event was the first event in the history of the world. The only other conclusion is that the beginning was caused by a personal agent, or "a personal being, acting with powers and intentions suitable for such an act."[4]

By definition, such a personal being would have to be...

independent of the universe

all-powerful

supremely intelligent

infinite

supernatural

purposeful

Is this personal being God? Earlier in this chapter, we showed that the Bible describes God in these terms, clearly telling us that the God of the Bible fits the profile of the first cause perfectly. And here's something to think about: The Bible's description of God's character traits wasn't developed after computer data from the COBE satellite confirmed the Big Bang. The Bible was written centuries ago, long before scientists developed a profile for the first cause. Beginning in 1500 BC (when Moses wrote Genesis), the Bible has been declaring that God created the universe and that the universe declares God's existence. Now, 3500 years later, findings about the personal nature of the first cause seem to confirm what the Bible has been saying all along.

> *The heavens proclaim the glory of God. The skies display his craftsmanship. Day after day they continue to speak; night after night they make him known* (Psalm 19:1-2).

The Moral Argument

This argument for God's existence follows this line of thinking: Objective moral laws exist, and they must have come from an objective moral lawgiver. There are two parts to this argument. The first has to do with *conception*. The very idea that we as humans can universally conceive of goodness and agree on what is ultimately good (and conversely, what is ultimately evil) means a being must embody this ultimate goodness. The second part of the moral argument has to do with *obligation*. All people have a moral obligation to do good and avoid evil, so a being must have put it there.

Conceiving of Ultimate Goodness

This part of the moral argument goes something like this:

1. It is possible to conceive of an objective moral law that is true for everyone at all times.

2. An objective moral law can exist only if there is an objective moral lawgiver.

3. Therefore, because we can conceive of an objective moral law, an objective moral lawgiver must exist.

The key part of this argument is that all people, regardless of where or when they have lived, have discovered—not devised—almost identical moral standards. In *The Abolition of Man*, C.S. Lewis lists in detail a number of these standards (he calls them "illustrations of Natural Law") from a wide variety of different cultures and traditions through the ages. His point is that people innately know right from wrong, even if they don't always do what's right. And the only explanation for this uniformity is that there is an objective lawgiver.

Having a Moral Obligation

C.S. Lewis approaches the moral argument from a slightly different perspective in *Mere Christianity*. He proposes that an objective lawgiver must exist, not only because we know what is right and wrong, but also because we feel an obligation to do what is right. If this weren't the case...

- moral disagreements would make no sense (but they do),
- all criticism of immoral behavior would be meaningless (which it is not),
- it would be unnecessary to keep promises or legal agreements (which we do), and
- we would not make excuses for breaking the objective moral law (which we do).

Based on these observations, Lewis comes to three conclusions:

- An objective moral law requires an objective moral lawgiver.
- This objective moral lawgiver must be absolutely good. Otherwise all moral effort would be futile in the long run.
- Therefore, there must be an objective moral lawgiver.

We are aware of objective moral law, but not because of the behavior of others informing our actions, nor because society tells us what to do. Yes, society creates laws to manage our behavior, but ultimately each person knows without compulsion what is right and wrong and feels an obligation to do right, even if that doesn't always happen. The bottom line is that we *know* that certain things are right and others are wrong. We don't need laws to tell us that, and we don't need laws to encourage us to do what is right because of this moral obligation, commonly referred to as a *conscience*.

Thomas Jefferson recognized this when he wrote this first line in the Declaration of Independence: "We hold these truths to be self-evident." That means people know certain moral actions to be objectively true and right, and they are internally compelled or obligated to do what is right, not because they have a desire to do what is right, but because they know what is right. Such obligation to objective moral law is rooted in the objective moral lawgiver. It's connected to the fact that the objective moral lawgiver—the Creator God—has made us in His image for a purpose higher than ourselves. Furthermore, having a sense of moral obligation gives us meaning and purpose.

Where Does Our Conscience Come From?

Have you ever thought about your conscience, sometimes referred to as your inner moral compass? Peter Kreeft asks,

> Isn't it remarkable that no one, even the most consistent subjectivist, believes that it is ever good for anyone to deliberately and knowingly disobey his or her own conscience? Even if different people's consciences tell them to do or avoid totally different things, there remains one moral absolute for everyone: never disobey your own conscience.[5]

Where did this conscience come from? It couldn't come from something *less* than us or something *equal* to us. And it couldn't come from just us. The only viable option is that our conscience comes from something *greater* than us, which is God. Kreeft makes this conclusion:

> Thus God, or something like God, is the only adequate source and ground for the absolute moral obligation we all feel to obey our conscience. Conscience is thus explainable only as the voice of God in the soul.[6]

In fact, Kreeft is echoing the apostle Paul, who says this in his letter to the Roman church:

> *Even Gentiles, who do not have God's written law, show that they know his law when they instinctively obey it, even without having heard it. They demonstrate that God's law is written in their hearts, for their own conscience and thoughts either accuse them or tell them they are doing right* (Romans 2:14-15).

This compelling evidence leads Paul Copan to make this conclusion:

> The moral argument does point us to a supreme personal moral Being (1) who is worthy of worship, (2) who has made us with dignity and worth, (3) to whom we are personally accountable, and (4) who may reasonably be called "God."[7]

The Ontological Argument

This is the most controversial (and confusing) of all the arguments for the existence of God, so we aren't going to spend much time with it. The root of the word *ontos* means being, so the argument has to do with God as an absolutely perfect being. Anselm was the originator of this argument, but there have been many variations (and even more objections) through the centuries.

Basically the argument goes something like this (if you can't follow this, don't worry—we can barely follow it ourselves). First, God is the greatest being anyone can think about. If we could think of a being greater than God, then *that* being would be God. Therefore, nothing greater than God can be conceived. So far so good? Hang on, it gets better.

Second, it is greater to really exist than to merely exist as an idea. In other words, you could think about a being like God, but your thoughts about God are not as great as God. Anselm gives the example of a painting. An artist could have an idea for a painting, or he could actually paint something. Which is greater?

The painting, of course, because the painting exists not only as an idea but also in reality.

In the same way, if God existed only as an idea, then something greater could be conceived, namely God existing both as an idea and also in reality. Have we lost you yet? We're almost done. Here's the conclusion: God is the greatest conceivable being, so He must exist not just as an idea but also in reality. Therefore God exists.

*U*ou Cannot Not Think About God

Did you enjoy this little thought experiment? As we said, philosophers have been debating the ontological argument for centuries. But if you never think about it again, that's okay. Plenty of other arguments for the existence of God are available for you to consider. On the other hand, if God exists in reality, you won't be able to *not* think about Him, which in a way proves His existence. Hmmmmm.

Two Extremes to Avoid

We've covered a lot of ground in this chapter, and we're just getting started! As we did in a previous chapter, we want to suggest that you avoid two extremes in this matter of evidence for God. On the one hand, don't get discouraged if you aren't getting all of this the first or even second time around. We've been studying these arguments for years, and we still struggle with certain aspects. Always keep Augustine's quote in mind: "A god you can understand completely is an idol."

On the other hand, if you are really excited about these evidences (and others that will follow), and you think you finally have the ammunition you need to confront your unbelieving friends, always keep Peter's quote in mind: "Do this in a gentle and respectful way." We hope you are encouraged in your own faith by these compelling arguments. You should be! And we pray that you are emboldened to engage others in conversations about faith. That's what God wants you to do! But always remember that God is the one who will change the mind and heart of someone who is sincerely seeking the truth. Your job is simply to present the truth in love.

What's That Again?

1. The way God has revealed Himself—through the universe He created (general revelation) and through both the written word of Scripture and the living Word of Jesus (special revelation) tells us that He is much more than an idea, a force, or a feeling.

2. God is Spirit and cannot be seen. He is not composed of matter and does not possess a physical nature. So how do we know God exists?

3. You can believe in God even if you don't know why, but at some point, as you get to know God better, you will want to know why it is reasonable to believe God exists.

4. A cumulative case for God's existence means that even though no one specific piece of evidence proves beyond a shadow of a doubt that God exists, several pieces together make a reasonable case for His existence. These pieces of evidence include the cosmological, moral, and ontological arguments.

5. The cosmological argument has two major components: contingency and causation. The argument from contingency means that everything in the universe is contingent (or dependent) on something else. This being the case, then "something else" (called a *necessary being*) must not be contingent. The argument from causation (the *kalam* cosmological argument) says that because

the universe cannot be infinitely old, it must have a beginning and therefore a first cause.

6. Evidence for the beginning of the universe did not emerge until the twentieth century, when a series of discoveries by scientists around the world led to the conclusion that the universe began with a bang in a single moment in time.

7. The moral argument says that objective moral laws exist, so an objective moral lawgiver must exist as well.

8. The ontological argument has to do with God as an absolutely perfect being. God is the greatest conceivable being, so He must exist not just as an idea but also in reality.

Dig Deeper

A number of excellent books talk about the three arguments for the existence of God we presented in this chapter. Here are a couple of outstanding ones:

The Case for a Creator by Lee Strobel is written from the perspective of a journalist investigating scientific evidence that points toward God. Includes interviews with some of today's leading philosophers and scientists.

Paul Copan and William Craig are the editors of *Passionate Conviction,* a collection of essays on apologetics and the evidence for God.

We promised to recommend a book to deal with the challenge of the new atheists, and here it is. Alister McGrath and Joanna Collicutt McGrath wrote *The Dawkins Delusion?* as an answer to Richard Dawkins' strident book *The God Delusion.* The McGraths' response is thoughtful and engaging, and it has been praised by theists and atheists alike.

■ ■ ■

Questions for Reflection and Discussion

1. Reflect on the ten characteristics of God listed at the beginning of the chapter. If you never had a Bible to give you these personality traits, would you be able to detect any of them on your own? Which ones?

2. List three reasons why it's important to know *why* it is reasonable to believe God exists.

3. Does it bother you that there is no bombproof argument for God's existence? How can we know that God is 100 percent true and trustworthy without proving with 100 percent certainty that He exists?

4. Love is something we know exists, yet we can't measure love or detect it with any of the five senses. What are some other things all people accept as real even though they can't be measured or detected with the five senses?

5. "Why is there something rather than nothing?" Why is this a good first question to ask when trying to show God exists?

6. Why is it necessary for there to be a necessary being? What is the definition of a necessary being? Why is God the only being that meets this definition?

7. Explain the *kalam* cosmological argument. What is the goal of this argument? Do you think it's effective? Why or why not?

8. Explain what the conscience is and how this points to an objective moral lawgiver. Have you ever done something you knew was wrong? (No need to answer aloud. It's a rhetorical question.) Did you fail to do the right thing because you didn't know what the right thing was, or did you ignore your conscience?

Moving On...

As we continue in part 2, we will consider the fourth classic argument for the existence of God, historically known as the teleological argument. The more current name for this argument is the argument from design, and it includes intelligent design, a scientific enterprise that is gaining more acceptance (and increasing resistance from the naturalist community) for one simple reason. The more science learns about the way our world works, the more the evidence points to an intelligent designer.

Chapter 4

At this moment it seems as though science
will never be able to raise the curtain on
the mystery of creation. For the scientist
who has lived by his faith in the power of
reason, the story ends like a bad dream.
He has scaled the mountains of ignorance;
he is about to conquer the highest peak;
as he pulls himself over the final rock, he
is greeted by a band of theologians who
have been sitting there for centuries.

—*Robert Jastrow*

When it comes to evidence for God, there's no question He has left us plenty. You could even say God has left us two books that reveal a great deal about who He is, what He's done for us, and what He wants from us.

The first book is the book of nature. This is God's world, which declares His glory and tells us who God is. Then there is the book of Scripture, the Bible. This is God's word, which tells us what God has done for us and what He wants us to do.

The book of nature—God's world. The book of Scripture—God's word. Two books worth reading. Let's get started on the first one.

Evidence from the Natural World

$\mathcal{W}$hat's $\mathcal{A}$head

- The Design Argument
- What Is Science Anyway?
- A Brief History of Darwinism
- Specified Complexity: A Perfect Place to Call Home
- Irreducible Complexity: Signs of Intelligent Design
- Biological Information: It's in Our DNA

*I*magine the three of us—you and us—taking a hike in the hills of South Dakota. We're walking along enjoying the natural wonders of the Black Hills, when suddenly you stop in your tracks and stare straight ahead, your mouth agape and your finger pointing. "What is it?" we ask you. "That rock formation on that mountain. It's got four faces on it. I think I've seen them somewhere."

By now we're looking at the formation as well, and we agree with you that the giant rock faces are familiar. In fact, we recognize at least three of the faces as U.S. presidents, mainly because Bruce has matched up three of them with the money in his pocket (Bruce just happens to have exactly $6.05—a one, a five, and a nickel).

At this point, all of us are staring in awe at this sight when you say, "I wonder who carved these formations?" This prompts Stan to reply, "What do you mean? Nobody carved them. That's just a natural occurrence. Over millions of years—no, make that

billions of years—the forces of nature—the wind, water, and ero-
sion—made those rocks appear to look like faces. It's just a coincidence that the natural rock formations look like the actual people
on Bruce's money."

"You can't be serious," you reply incredulously. "I don't care
how much time nature has had, there's no way those rocks look
like real people by accident. The likeness is too *specific* and too *complex* to have been formed by the blind forces of nature. Some guy
with a vision, some dynamite, and really big rock-cutting tools pur-
posely made those rocks to look like George Washington, Abraham
Lincoln, Thomas Jefferson, and that other guy whose name I can't
recall."

The Design Argument

Okay, maybe we went a little overboard with our story, but
we're sure you get the picture. The point of the story and the focus
of this chapter are to lay out the design argument, traditionally
called the teleological argument. The key features of this argument,
which is another in our cumulative case for the existence of God,
include specificity, complexity, and purpose—descriptions normally
assigned to an intelligent agent rather than a natural cause.

We like this argument. It's current. It's compelling. It's controversial. William Dembski, a major voice in the intelligent design
movement (more about that a little later), has this to say about
the design argument:

> The design argument begins with features of the
> physical world that exhibit evidence of purpose. From
> such features, the design argument then attempts to
> establish the existence and attributes of an intelligent
> cause responsible for those features.[1]

Unlike the moral and ontological arguments, which are philosophical, the design argument (like the cosmological argument)
is scientific. So before we go any further, let's look at the nature
of science and see how science and God once went together
like peas and carrots, then split apart like Pamela Anderson and
her latest husband, and are now beginning to once again come
together.

What Is Science Anyway?

Science isn't evil. Science and scientists aren't the enemy. The root word of science—*scientia*—simply means knowledge. Jay Richards makes this comment:

> The essence of natural science is the search for knowledge of the natural world. Knowledge is an intrinsic good. If we are properly scientific, then we will seek to be open to the natural world and not decide beforehand what it's allowed to reveal.[2]

That being the case, we should be able to have productive and civilized discussions with people—scientists, philosophers, theologians, artists, even lawyers—about origins and whether God was responsible for the beginning of the universe. One side would present its arguments for no God being involved, and the other would explain its reasons for believing that God was involved. The question of God's existence would get discussed from both a natural and also a supernatural perspective.

But that's not the way things are. Such discussions usually get a little heated, and they aren't even welcome in the public square, especially public schools. The supernatural explanation for how the universe got here isn't given a fair hearing. In fact, it's decried as superstitious, mythical, and just plain stupid. The only accepted view is the naturalistic worldview.

Science Is King

Theology was once called the "queen of the sciences" because it addresses the whole person—emotional, intellectual, and spiritual—and seeks to bring the natural and the supernatural together. Not anymore. For the past 150 years, science has successfully challenged the notion that there is a God who created the universe. Today, science leads our culture and stands at the forefront of intellectual integrity, while theology has been relegated to the realm of philosophy and personal preference. Science gives us technology and cures our diseases. The findings and benefits of science are universally applicable to peoples of all countries, ethnicities, and faiths. Science seems to be the only universal constant in our lives upon which we can reply. Science is king. Even more, for many people, science is God.

What happened? How did things go from "God" to "no God" so quickly? (A hundred and fifty years in the span of history is pretty quick.) Why can't we raise the notion of God as a legitimate scientific explanation for the origin of the universe?

A Brief History of Darwinism

To get an answer, we have to go back to the mid-nineteenth century, when a relatively obscure English scientist by the name of Charles Darwin became fascinated with his observations from selective breeding experiments. From these observations, he developed a set of innovative theories that formed the basis of two books, *On the Origin of Species* (1859) and *The Descent of Man* (1871). Here are the main theories of Darwinism:

- *Random mutation.* All plants and animals—any organisms that exist—are the products of the random interplay of the known processes of heredity.

- *Natural selection.* Differential reproduction in organisms occurs as weak traits give way to stronger ones (survival of the fittest).

- *Common descent.* All living creatures on Earth (including those that went extinct) share a common ancestor.

- *Abiogenesis.* All life originated from non-life naturally.

To say that these theories were revolutionary for both faith and science is an understatement. Here is what Darwin was saying:

- Life started on its own as a tiny cell that developed over time into all forms of life (including humans).

- Nature acted like a breeding machine and produced biological changes. As useful new traits appeared, they were passed on to the next generation. Harmful traits (or those of little use) were eliminated by Darwin's mechanism of natural selection.

- These changes were small, but over time and generations they accumulated until organisms developed new limbs, or organs, or other body parts. Given enough time, the organisms changed so much that they didn't resemble their ancestors anymore.

A Quick Look at the Terminology

It's important to define the terms we are using in this chapter. Words like *evolution, Darwinism, creationism,* and *intelligent design* carry a lot of baggage and can be misunderstood. Here's an attempt to sort them out.

Naturalism (also known as scientific naturalism) is the philosophy or worldview that denies the supernatural. Scientific laws are adequate to account for all phenomena.

Evolution describes a process (some would say an unplanned and undirected process) that combines elements of random genetic change or mutation that are accumulated through natural selection. It is important to distinguish between the two types of evolution:

Microevolution is evolution at and below the species level. It generally refers to relatively minor variations that occur in a group over time.

Macroevolution is evolution above the species level. It generally refers to major innovations such as new organs, structures, or body plans.

Darwinism (also known as neo-Darwinism and evolutionism) is the belief that undirected mechanistic processes (primarily random mutation and natural selection) can account for both microevolution and macroevolution, and thus for all the complex living organisms that exist. A key philosophical component of Darwinism is the assumption that evolution works without either plan or purpose.

Creationism usually refers to God creating the universe and everything within it. But there are two major views within creationism:

Young-earth creationism (also known as creation science or scientific creationism) says the Genesis account refers to six literal 24-hour days, and the creation event took place 10,000 to 25,000 years ago.

Old-earth creationism holds that the days of Genesis 1 are not six literal 24-hour days. The creation event did occur in the same order specified in Genesis, but it took place billions of years ago.

Intelligent design is a theory that says that the universe and all the life in it owe their existence to a purposeful, intelligent designer.

Darwin couldn't prove his theories because he didn't have the fossil evidence to back them up, but he wasn't worried. He believed that as the science and techniques of paleontology (fossil finding) progressed, the fossils would be found to prove his theory correct. However, he did express his doubts in *On the Origin of Species:*

> The number of intermediate varieties, which must have formerly existed on the earth, [must] be truly enormous. Why then is not every geological formation and every stratum full of such intermediate links? Geology assuredly does not reveal any such finely graded organic chain; and this, perhaps, is the most obvious and gravest objection which can be urged against my theory.[3]

The jury is still out as far as the fossil evidence is concerned, but the central debate over whether Darwinism is a credible theory has shifted from paleontology to other branches of science, especially biology, chemistry, astronomy, and physics (more about that shortly).

Darwin Murders God

Despite Darwin's own doubts, Darwinism was what some people were waiting for. His theories gave scientists and philosophers the ammunition they needed to remove God from the conversation about origins. As you might imagine, people who believed the Bible detested Darwin's theories, but it was very popular with people who wanted an alternate explanation for how the world and the human race came into existence. In England, Thomas Huxley became "Darwin's bulldog" and devised, along with other "brother naturalists," an aggressive campaign to wrest nature from theology and to place scientists at the head of English culture. Huxley coined the term *agnostic* and was instrumental in redefining science. To most people, no longer

> The whole point of Darwinism is to explain the world in a way that excludes any role for a Creator. What is being sold in the name of science is a completely naturalistic understanding of reality.
>
> —Phillip Johnson

did it refer to knowledge. After Darwin and Huxley, science was equal to naturalism.

Darwinism is presented (and believed) as a scientific theory. But it is also a view that explains the world in strictly naturalistic terms. *Time* magazine recognized this when it wrote, "Charles Darwin didn't want to murder God, as he once put it. But he did."

How Do We Get God Back in the Picture?

There's no question that the theistic worldview has been marginalized in a culture that worships at the altar of science, but there's no need to panic for one simple reason. Faith and reason will never contradict each other. Truth will always win out. If science is about knowledge and the truth about the natural world, then it will inevitably point to the one who created it all, despite the efforts of people who want to take God out of the picture.

In fact, remarkable advances in three areas of scientific discovery are pointing to an intelligent designer, and it's all happening right before our very eyes. We're going to look at these three areas, going from the largest to the smallest, from the universe to the microscope. In the process, we're going to find evidence from a fine-tuned universe, from life's intelligent design, and from the molecular level. These evidences show at least three things:

> specified complexity,
>
> irreducible complexity, and
>
> biological information.

The Bible and Science

Some Christians are concerned that recent efforts to bring God back into the scientific conversations about origins (such as intelligent design) don't include the Bible in their discussions. There are two reasons for this. One, intelligent design doesn't concern itself with identifying the identity of the designer. That's up to the theologians. Two, the Bible isn't a scientific textbook. It was written for the primary purpose of revealing God's plan to establish a relationship with humankind. So it is more focused on who God is and who we are from a relational point of view. (That's why the Bible often uses metaphors of a father or a shepherd to explain how God cares for us.) Even though the Bible contains some scientific information—but no scientific absurdities—it isn't intended to explain scientific intricacies and mathematical formulas. You don't expect science to describe the way a shepherd cares for his sheep, and you shouldn't expect the Bible to explain how to clone a sheep.

Specified Complexity: A Perfect Place to Call Home

You know the story of Goldilocks, right? She was the sweet little girl who was looking for something that perfectly suited her needs and desires. Whether it was a chair, a bowl of porridge, or a bed, she settled only for what was just right.

Imagine yourself as a cosmic Goldilocks. You are flying around the universe looking for a planet that is just right for life. Some planets are too cold. Some are too hot. But planet Earth seems to be just right. Now, is it a coincidence that Earth is perfectly suited to your needs and desires? Are there other planets you could choose? As it turns out, the list of what you require for a comfortable existence is quite extensive. And a just-right Earth isn't the only requirement. You also need a special solar system and a fine-tuned universe.

This area of scientific discovery that focuses on specified complexity—that a living system of any kind is specifically designed for life and function—is very new. It's only been in the past 30 or 40 years that scientists have been able to study and measure the parameters of our physical world that make life possible. What they are discovering is extraordinary (you could even say miraculous, but we'll hold that description for later). Let's take a look at some of this evidence of specified complexity from the natural world and then explain how it points to God.

A Fine-Tuned Universe

Scientists have determined that there are more than 100 parameters in the universe as a whole that must be fine-tuned if life is to exist on Earth. Here are just a few:

- *The gravitational force.* If it were stronger than it is, the stars would be too hot, and they would burn up quickly and unevenly. If it were weaker than it is, stars would remain so cool that nuclear fusion would never ignite (and you know the problems that would cause).

- *The ratio of the number of protons to the number of electrons.* If the ratio were either greater or smaller, electromagnetism would dominate gravity, preventing the formation of stars and planets.

- *The expansion rate of the universe.* If it expanded at a faster rate, no galaxies would be able to form. If the rate were slower, the universe would have collapsed prior to star formation.

- *The velocity of light.* If light traveled faster, the stars would be too luminous for us to tolerate. If light traveled slower, the stars would not be luminous enough.

- *The electromagnetic force.* With a force either stronger or weaker, there would be insufficient chemical bonding.

- *The mass density of the universe.* A greater mass density would have produced too much deuterium (a form of hydrogen) from the Big Bang, resulting in stars burning too rapidly. With smaller mass density, there would be insufficient helium from the Big Bang (so too few heavy elements would form).

There are many more parameters in the universe that must be fine-tuned to permit life. And these parameters are very narrow. For example, if the strong nuclear force were just 0.3 percent stronger or 0.2 percent weaker, the universe would never be able to support life. The expansion rate of the universe has even tighter parameters. We have no idea how scientists figure this stuff out, but they have determined that life would not be possible in a universe that had an expansion rate different from ours by more than one part out of 10^{55}.

A Special Solar System

The universe isn't the only aspect of the cosmos that has to be finely tuned to permit life on Earth. Let's get a little closer to home by taking a look at our own solar system. You might think that our sun is just like the billions of other stars in the Milky Way galaxy. Not so. Our sun has a planetary system comprised of eight planets (it used to be nine until they demoted Pluto...poor Pluto), and together our solar system has certain features needed to allow and sustain life on earth. Here's a sampling:

- *Only one star.* It's a good thing our solar system has only one star: the sun. If we had more than one, the tidal interactions would throw Earth's orbit out of whack. This factor alone eliminates 60 percent of the solar systems in the universe as candidates for a place that would support life.

- *The age of the sun.* When stars are newly formed, their burning rate and temperature are not stable. They only begin to maintain a stable burning phase after they have matured a bit. If a star is too old or too young, then the luminosity of the star changes too quickly to allow life.

- *The size of the sun.* If the mass of the star is too large, then its luminosity changes too quickly, and it will burn too rapidly. If the star's size is too small, then you have another set of problems: The range of distances necessary for life would be too narrow, tidal forces would knock the planet's rotational period out of sync, and there wouldn't be enough ultraviolet radiation for plants to make sugars and oxygen. Ninety-nine percent of all stars don't have these characteristics.

- *The sun's distance from Earth.* If a star is too far away from an orbiting planet, the planet temperature is too cool to permit a stable water evaporation cycle. If a star is too close, the climate would be too warm for a stable water cycle. If the distance from the earth to the sun differed by just 2 percent, no plant life would be possible. This parameter alone eliminates 99 percent of all stars from consideration.

Jupiter Is Big for a Reason

A solar system that is conducive for life must have more than just a star. Other planets are necessary and serve a very useful purpose. Take Jupiter as an example. We all know it's the 800-pound gorilla of planets. In fact,

Jupiter is two and one-half times the size of all the other planets combined. Why is it so big? Well, as it turns out, Jupiter is kind of like Earth's protective big brother. Because it's so huge, Jupiter's gravitational force draws comets to it like moths to a flame, or it repels and deflects comets out of our solar system. If it weren't for Jupiter, scientists estimate that comets would strike the earth a thousand times more frequently than they do now.

A Just-Right Earth

We've looked at the parameters that must be met in our universe and in our own solar system. Now it's time to get "up close and personal" and see the permissible parameters for life on the big blue marble we call home. A change in these parameters would either prevent the existence of life on Earth or make it extremely unpleasant.

- *The orbital pattern around the sun.* A change would produce extreme temperature changes that would make life impossible.

- *The tilt of the earth's axis.* The precise angle keeps the differential in the surface temperature from becoming too extreme.

- *The speed of the earth's rotation.* This keeps temperature changes and wind velocities from becoming too great.

- *The age of the earth.* The earth would rotate too fast if it were too young or too slow if it were too old.

- *The ratio of oxygen to nitrogen in the earth's atmosphere.* Life functions would be severely impacted by any change in this ratio.

Even some events on the earth that we consider disasters, such as earthquakes, are actually necessary for sustaining life. Without plate movements that cause earthquakes, essential nutrients on the continents would erode into the oceans (so California does serve a purpose after all). And let's not fail to appreciate the importance of the precise size of our planet. The mass of the earth determines its gravitational force. If the earth were much smaller, the gravitational force wouldn't be strong enough to hold the necessary atmosphere. If it were too much larger, the gravitational force would give each of us an effective weight of 700 to 900 pounds.

*W*hat Are the Odds?

Dr. Hugh Ross, a renowned astrophysicist, has calculated the odds of having all the necessary parameters for life on one planet. He analyzed 41 factors and the probability that each feature would fall in the required range. Then he calculated the probability that all of these factors would occur together so that he could estimate the possibility that a planet would exist capable of supporting life by natural means alone. He concluded that "the probability of finding, without divine intervention, a single planet capable of supporting physical life is much less than one in a trillion, trillion, trillion, trillion, trillion, trillion, trillion, trillion, trillion, trillion, trillion."[4] We're no experts, but that seems like a pretty small probability.

Irreducible Complexity: Signs of Intelligent Design

Arguments for God's involvement in nature have been around for centuries, but these arguments were always in the realm of theology and philosophy. Science wasn't yet able to demonstrate any connection between God and the natural world.

As far back as the fourth century, guys like Minucius Felix reasoned that nature exhibits features that nature itself cannot explain and that require an intelligence beyond nature. Arguments for intelligent design were articulated by the likes of Thomas Aquinas in the thirteenth century. Perhaps the most famous intelligent design argument belongs to William Paley from his book *Natural Theology*, published in 1802. Paley came up with the analogy of the watch and the watchmaker.

Suppose you are walking through a field and find a watch, which has a function (telling time). You can be sure that the watch is the result of an intelligence (a watchmaker) and not the result of undirected natural processes. The watch, with all of its intricate, delicate parts, didn't just fall into place by itself. Paley saw the watch as analogous to the eye in a mammal. The eye has a specific function, which must be the result of an intelligent designer because the parts are too intricate and delicate to have fallen into place by themselves.

This concept, known as irreducible complexity, lies at the heart of the theory of intelligent design. An irreducibly complex system is one that cannot be reproduced directly by gradual, successive modifications or refinements. In a biological system, an irreducibly complex system cannot be reproduced gradually; it would have to arise as a completed unit, or it couldn't exist in the first place. The best explanation for such a system is that it was designed.

ᗪarwin's Wager

In *On the Origin of Species,* Darwin made a wager of sorts when he wrote about his concern for "specific function" and what came to be known as irreducible complexity, a feature of intelligent design. Here's his wager:

If it could be demonstrated that any complex organ existed, which could not possibly have been formed by numerous, successive, slight modifications, my theory would absolutely break down.[5]

The arguments of Aquinas and Paley were theological and philosophical, so when naturalism became the predominant worldview of science in the mid-nineteenth century, the theory of intelligent design was kept out of the scientific mainstream because there were no precise methods for distinguishing intelligently caused objects from unintelligently caused ones. That is, until the second half of the twentieth century, when discoveries in the scientific disciplines of chemistry, physics, astronomy, and biology clearly showed that complex systems were at work that could not necessarily be explained by natural causes.

In 1953, Francis Crick and James Watson discovered the now-famous double helix of deoxyribonucleic acid (DNA), where the "language of life" is stored. Nearly half a century later, Francis Collins, head of the Human Genome Project, would refer to DNA as "the language of God."

In the 1960s and 1970s, scientists working in the area of physics began uncovering data that suggested certain universal constants of physics seemed to be "finely tuned" for the specific purpose of maintaining complex life. Upon seeing some of these results, Fred Hoyle, an astrophysicist and ardent atheist, grudgingly said, "a super intellect seems to be monkeying with the physics."

In the 1990s, Michael Behe, taking on Darwin's wager in his book *Darwin's Black Box,* demonstrated the fundamental claim of intelligent design: that intelligent causes are necessary to explain the complex, information-rich structures of biology and that these causes are empirically detectable. There exist well-defined methods for observing the world and reliably distinguishing intelligent cause from undirected natural causes.

Intelligent design approaches science from the opposite perspective of Darwinism. Darwinism is all about undirected natural causes rather than intelligent causes. Intelligent design is concerned with demonstrating that intelligent causes can do things that undirected natural causes cannot (such as carving Mt. Rushmore or making a watch).

What Intelligent Design Is

One of the leading scientific scholars involved with intelligent design is William Dembski. Here is how he describes the role of intelligent design:

> Intelligent design is the science that studies signs of intelligence. Note that a sign is not the thing signified. Intelligent design does not try to get into the mind of a designer and figure out what the designer is thinking. Its focus is not a designer's mind (the thing signified) but the artifact due to a designer's mind (the sign).[6]

Intelligent design is controversial because it proposes to find signs of intelligence in biological systems. This puts intelligent design theory in direct competition with the prevailing naturalistic theories of Darwinism, which explains how "the organized complexity of organisms could be attained without a designing intelligence."[7]

It's important to note that the scientists supporting intelligent design do not oppose Darwinism because it contradicts the Bible or challenges Christianity. For these scientists and philosophers, it is not about religion (some of them, in fact, describe themselves as agnostics).

The intelligent design scientists do not think that Darwin was totally out to lunch. They acknowledge that Darwin's mutation-selection mechanism constitutes a respectable concept in biology that merits continued investigation. But Darwinism is so much more than just the random mutation–natural selection mechanism. Darwinism is the all-encompassing claim that this undirected mechanism accounts for all the diversity of life and the common descent of all life forms. The intelligent design movement contends that the evidence does not support this broad claim. In their examination, intelligent design scientists find that...

- The evidence of naturalism supports only limited variation within fixed boundaries (microevolution).

- The random ability of organisms to diversify across all boundaries (macroevolution) even if it's true—cannot be attributed solely to the mutation-selection mechanism.

What Intelligent Design Is Not

Intelligent design does not speculate or theorize about the nature, character, or purposes of the intelligence responsible for the design. Intelligent design leaves to theology the task of figuring out who the intelligence is (whether the God of the Bible, some other god, or some other type of intelligence). Intelligent design examines the evidence for design and from this evidence infers a designer. It doesn't try to figure out the designer's profile or who the designer is.

This is similar to what happens when archaeologists find a tool crafted by some unknown tribe. They can easily identify that intelligence was involved without knowing the purpose for which the tool was made. They may speculate that the tool was designed as a weapon or for agricultural purposes. The fact that the purpose is unknown doesn't detract from the determination that intelligence was responsible for the object.

Nonetheless, the scientific community has resisted intelligent-design theory, primarily because of at least three misconceptions about intelligent design as it relates to science: that it stifles scientific investigation, that it is an unscientific activity, and that it is outside the scope of science. Nothing could be further from the truth.

Intelligent Design Does Not Stifle Scientific Investigation

Darwinists are quick to claim that intelligent design flies in the face of extensive scientific investigation. Why do research when you know that some intelligent designer is responsible? But Darwinists are wrong. The answers don't stop when it is determined that an object was intelligently designed. If anything, the issue of how something works stimulates investigation.

William Dembski uses the illustration of a Stradivarius violin to explain how intelligent design actually encourages in-depth scientific investigation. We know that a Stradivarius violin was designed, and we know who the designer is (luckily, he put his name on the final product). But we don't know *how* Antonio Stradivari did it, which is a shame, since no one today can manufacture a violin as nearly perfectly as he did.

> Intelligent design is one intelligence determining what another intelligence has done.
>
> —*William Dembski*

Because we know the Stradivarius was designed, we can employ reverse engineering to figure out how it was designed. If we assume that the violin fell together by random chance, we have no need for reverse engineering. Therefore, the criticism that intelligent design stifles scientific inquiry is unjustified.

Searching for Design Is Not an Unscientific Activity

Darwinists like to attack intelligent design on the basis that looking for design is unscientific. Really? Science recognizes the search for intelligent design in many fields:

- Many industries depend on being able to distinguish accident from design: insurance fraud investigation, criminal justice, cryptography, patent and copyright protection. No one accuses these industries of being unscientific simply because they look for evidence of design.

- Some scientific disciplines such as anthropology and

archaeology could not exist without the detection of intelligent design.

- NASA's $100-million SETI project (Search for Extra-Terrestrial Intelligence) searched for signs of intelligence in outer space. Your tax dollars paid for the world's largest satellite dish in an attempt to pick up any communication from intelligent life forms in the cosmos.

Intelligent Design Is Not Outside the Scope of Science

Darwinists contend that intelligent design doesn't belong in the scientific sphere because it's a theory more suited to theology. They believe the theory of evolution addresses a scientific question, whereas intelligent design addresses a religious question. This false distinction is the reason Darwinism is taught in the schools, but intelligent design (although it promotes no religion) is prohibited from classroom instruction on the fallacious argument that it constitutes the establishment of religion by the State, which is prohibited by the Constitution. By defining science as a form of inquiry restricted solely to what can be explained in terms of undirected natural processes, the Darwinian establishment has ruled intelligent design to be outside of science and therefore an unacceptable scientific theory that cannot be taught in public schools.

By contrast, intelligent design views science as broad enough to seek an explanation that may involve intelligent input and direction in addition to—not instead of—undirected natural causes. There is no danger that science will get sidetracked with arguments about religion from the intelligent-design scientists. Darwinists are the ones who raise the issue of religion in the debates with intelligent-design supporters. They are the ones who ask questions like these:

- Do you really believe that the whole universe was created in six 24-hour days?
- Could Jesus really have been God?
- If there is a God, why does He allow evil?

Intelligent design tries to keep everything on a scientific level. There is no talk about the character and nature of the designer. As

William Dembski says, "It detects intelligence without speculating about the nature of intelligence."

*I*ntelligent Design—Expelled!

The current climate in the scientific and academic communities is hostile to the theory of intelligent design and the intelligent-design proponents, to the point that legitimate scientists and professors are being pressured to keep their ideas out of the public conversation. Some credentialed professors have been denied tenure at public universities because of their views on intelligent design.

Biological Information: It's in Our DNA

So far we have looked at two components of the design argument—specified complexity and irreducible complexity—both of which seem to point to an intelligent designer. When you seriously consider the fine-tuning of the universe (not to mention its origin), it seems a bit far-fetched to conclude that undirected mechanistic causes were responsible for its specified complexity. When you look at the interlocking intricacies of biological systems, it seems unsatisfying to conclude that the only option for their irreducible complexity is random mutation and natural selection. If anything, it seems more reasonable to conclude that there was an intelligent agent behind the design of the universe and the life it contains.

Now we're going to look at a third component of the design argument: biological information. Specifically, we want to talk about DNA. Remember when we referred to Stephen Hawking's exclamation that the confirmation of the Big Bang creation event was the most important discovery of the twentieth century? Well, the discovery of the double helix of deoxyribonucleic acid, which contains the unique genetic information, would give that one a run for its money.

DNA is formed by pairing up two of the four nucleotides found in DNA (nucleotides are molecules containing nitrogen). In order for DNA to work, the nucleotides must be arranged in a precise and incredibly complex way so that the information contained in

DNA is meaningful. From a natural perspective, the only explanation for how DNA generates and stores this information is through a series of physical occurrences and chemical reactions. This may explain the information, but not the meaning it conveys. Nor can the laws of physics and chemistry explain the origin of DNA. The information contained in the DNA genetic code of a single human being is staggering. J.P. Moreland (who has an advanced degree in chemistry as well as a doctorate in philosophy) suggests that the amount of information is more than all the information in all the books in the Library of Congress combined.

The bottom line is that the information contained in DNA is too specific, too complex, and too ordered to have come about through undirected mechanistic and chemical causes. A more satisfying explanation is that DNA was intelligently designed.

The Validity and the Power

We've thrown a lot of information at you in this chapter, and we've just scratched the surface! If this is an area that interests you, there are many valuable resources you can read and study. Just keep in mind that mere information can take people only so far in their search for true faith. Remember, all of these scientific data are part of general revelation, or the book of nature. To find out more about God's plan to bring people back into a right relationship, it's necessary to access God's special revelation (that's coming in the next two chapters).

At the same time, the design argument can be very effective in moving people along in their search for truth. One of the more prominent examples was the movement of Antony Flew, a professor from Oxford who for the past half-century has been one of the world's most eloquent and persuasive defenders of atheism. His argument was essentially unchanged during that time. Flew didn't believe there was enough evidence to believe in God.

Then in 2004, at the age of 81, Flew acknowledged that he had been persuaded to move from atheism to a mild form of theism. He stated that he didn't know what to make of Jesus, and he wasn't even sure that God relates to the world on a personal level, but he was convinced that there was an intelligent designer behind the universe.

Specifically, Flew pointed to the three "cumulative case" arguments presented in this chapter as the reasons for his change: the fine-tuning of the universe (specified complexity), the intricacy of biological systems (irreducible complexity), and information-rich DNA (biological information). As expected, his intellectual shift was met with skepticism by the naturalistic community, in particular the ardent atheists who once considered him a role model. But there's no denying that the design argument had a major influence on one of the world's foremost intellects. That in itself speaks volumes about the validity of the argument and the power of the Designer behind it all.

What's That Again?

1. The key features of the design argument include specificity, complexity, and purpose—descriptions normally assigned to an intelligent agent rather than a natural cause.

2. For the last 150 years science has successfully challenged the notion that there is a God who created the universe. Today, science leads our culture and stands at the forefront of intellectual integrity, while theology has been relegated to the realm of philosophy and personal preference.

3. Darwinism was what some people were waiting for. Darwin's theories, first proposed in 1859 in his landmark book *On the Origin of Species,* gave scientists and philosophers the ammunition they needed to remove God from the conversation about origins.

4. If science is about knowledge and the truth about the natural world, then it inevitably will point to the one who created it all, despite the efforts of people who want to take God out of the picture.

5. Remarkable scientific discoveries in specified complexity, irreducible complexity, and biological information are pointing to an intelligent designer.

6. A fine-tuned universe, a special galaxy, and a just-right earth are examples of specified complexity. That our planet is perfectly suited for life is best explained by an intelligent designer.

7. Intelligent design examines the evidence for design in the natural world, and from this evidence it infers a designer. It doesn't try to figure out the designer's profile or who the designer is.

8. Unlike Darwinism, intelligent design views science as broad enough to seek an explanation that may involve intelligent input and direction in addition to—not instead of—undirected natural causes.

9. The information contained in DNA is too specific, too complex, and too ordered to have come about through undirected mechanistic and chemical causes. A more satisfying explanation is that DNA was intelligently designed.

Dig Deeper

As we said, many really good books give great information on the design argument. Here are several we like:

The Creator and the Cosmos by Hugh Ross is extremely helpful in listing the fine-tuning parameters. Dr. Ross is great about updating this book, so look for the latest edition.

William Dembski has written a number of books on intelligent design. Our favorite is *The Design Revolution,* in which Dembski answers the toughest questions about this ever-expanding theory.

If you want something a little easier to read, pick up a copy of *Understanding Intelligent Design* by William Dembski and Sean McDowell. This is as close to a user-friendly book on the subject as you will find.

Speaking of user-friendly, we would be remiss if we didn't recommend our own book on this subject, *Creation & Evolution 101.*

■ ■ ■

Questions for Reflection and Discussion

1. Summarize the design argument. Even though it's been around for centuries, why do you think this argument is stirring up so much interest these days? Why is it so controversial?

2. Why are so many Christians suspicious of science and scientists? Why are so many scientists skeptical of Christians? What are some specific things you could do to foster civil and productive dialogue between these two groups?

3. What are the main points of Darwinism? What are the implications for the Genesis creation story? Why has the scientific community been so quick to adopt these principles without considering any alternate views?

4. Despite the prominence of the naturalistic worldview in the field of science, why is there hope that science will inevitably point to God?

5. What is specified complexity? How do our universe, our solar system, and our planet show evidence that they have been designed specifically for life on Earth? How strong is the theory that this evidence points to an intelligent designer?

6. What is irreducible complexity, and how does it point to an intelligent designer? Why does naturalism not adequately explain irreducible complexity?

7. Why is intelligent design a legitimate scientific enterprise? Give some examples that are based on distinguishing between accident and design. Why has the Darwinian establishment fought so hard to keep intelligent design out of the mainstream of public education?

8. Why does naturalism fail to adequately explain the existence of DNA?

Moving On...

A few years ago we were doing research for a book, and we ended up in the office of a prominent scientist who had worked on the research team responsible for developing the Cosmic Background Explorer (COBE), which proved beyond doubt that the universe had a beginning. We had a great discussion about this evidence and whether or not it pointed to an intelligent designer. We didn't say a word about faith in God, but as we were leaving his office, this very thoughtful man asked us a profound question about the way God saves people. "Help me to understand something," he said. "How is it that someone can live a rotten life, and then at the end accept Jesus and go to heaven?"

Do conversations about God's general revelation lead people to think about God's special revelation? You bet they do. That's where we're going next.

Chapter 5

> The Bible is alive, it speaks to me; it has feet, it runs after me; it has hands, it lays hold of me.
>
> —*Martin Luther*

The Bible is an amazing book. From a purely statistical perspective, no other book comes close to the Bible's popularity. Year after year it is the bestselling book in the world. Since it was first printed in 1455, more than six billion copies of the Bible have been published. Yet statistics don't begin to describe the miraculous nature of a book that originated in the mind of God, was written by human authors who were divinely inspired by the breath of God, and can now be read by ordinary people with access to the Spirit of God.

In a physical sense, the Bible you read is like any other book, with words on a page (or a screen if that's your preference). But in a spiritual sense, the Bible is much more than words. This is what the writer of Hebrews says:

> *For the word of God is alive and powerful. It is sharper than the sharpest two-edged sword, cutting between soul and spirit, between joint and marrow. It exposes our innermost thoughts and desires* (Hebrews 4:12).

In this chapter we will consider how the Bible came to be and why you can trust it completely.

Evidence for the Bible

What's Ahead

- Why Is the Bible So Important?
- The Utter Uniqueness of the Bible
- Evidence from the Bible
- Evidence for the Bible
- How to Read the Bible

We've written a lot of books about God, probably more than two guys with marginal writing skills and a lack of scholarly credentials should be allowed to produce. But people like you keep reading our books (thank you very much), so we're going to keep writing them.

Actually, the reason we write books and produce content for online access is very simple. We have a great desire to enter into conversations about God with other people (we get tired of talking to each other). Even more, we have a passion to communicate the truth about God in a correct, clear, and casual way. (We realize that a book is a form of one-way communication—us to you—but we don't want to stop there. That's why we invite you to e-mail us directly with your questions or comments, or go online and join a community of people who are connecting faith to news and culture in creative and dynamic ways.)

In this particular book, our primary objective is to *show* how you or anybody can really *know* the truth about God by adding trust and commitment to your belief in God. Then, in the process of knowing God better and better, we want to walk alongside you as we uncover the evidence for your faith. We've already looked at evidence for God as found in the *world*. Now it's time to look at evidence found in the *word*—more precisely, God's word, the Bible.

Why Is the Bible So Important?

The Bible is an essential component of the Christian faith. You could even say, as Tim Keller writes: "The Christian faith requires belief in the Bible."[1] What's the big deal? How can one book be so important? What makes it so special? And do you need to believe in the Bible in order to be a Christian?

---

*T*he Bible Is Not the Object of Our Faith

As important as the Bible is, the Bible is not the object of our faith. That may sound rather obvious, but it's easy to place the Bible in the same category as God—something holy to be worshiped and glorified. God and only God is the object of our faith. The Bible is God's special revelation to us, but it is not God. Just as God is distinct from all He created, God is distinct from all He has said.

Here are some reasons why the Bible is important and why it's necessary to believe that the Bible is truly God's word:

1. The Bible claims to be the word of God. This is an astounding claim. Think about it. A written book contains the very message of the invisible God. Yet that's exactly what the Bible is: the verbal and written revelation of God. In the Old Testament, Moses and the prophets claimed *verbal* inspiration from God. Here's what God said to Moses:

> *I will raise up a prophet like you from among their fellow Israelites. I will put my words in his mouth, and he will tell the people everything I command him* (Deuteronomy 18:18).

Moses also presented the *written* revelation from God in the form of the Ten Commandments, written on stone tablets by God.

> *When the LORD finished speaking with Moses on Mount Sinai, he gave him the two stone tablets inscribed with the terms of the covenant, written by the finger of God* (Exodus 31:18).

In the New Testament, the words of Scripture are attributed to God revealing His words though the Holy Spirit:

> *Above all, you must realize that no prophecy in Scripture ever came from the prophet's own understanding, or from human initiative. No, those prophets were moved by the Holy Spirit, and they spoke from God* (2 Peter 1:21).

The apostle Paul confirms that God's word is literally His word:

> *Therefore, we never stop thanking God that when you received his message from us, you didn't think of our words as mere human ideas. You accepted what we said as the very word of God—which, of course, it is. And this word continues to work in you who believe* (1 Thessalonians 2:13).

---

*D*id You Know?

The word *Bible* never appears in the Bible. The word is derived from the Latin word *biblia,* which means a book.

---

2. The Bible gives us God's plan for humanity and the world. The Bible not only gives an account of God's creative act in bringing the universe into existence but also describes in detail His creation of people who carry His divine imprint and can relate to Him personally (Genesis 1:26-27). The Bible then describes the rebellion of the human race, followed by God's loving efforts to restore a relationship with fallen humanity. Henrietta Mears eloquently describes the Bible this way:

> The Bible is one book, one history, one story, His story. Behind 10,000 events stands God, the builder of history, the maker of the ages. Eternity bounds the one side, eternity bounds the other side, and time is in between: Genesis—origins, Revelation—endings, and all the way between, God is working things out. You can go down into the minutest detail everywhere and see that there is one great purpose moving through the ages: the eternal design of the Almighty God to redeem the wrecked and ruined world.[2]

3. The Bible tells us about Jesus Christ. The central figure in the Bible is Jesus Christ, the living Word of God (John 1:1), who came to earth in human form (John 1:14). He lived a perfect life (Hebrews 4:15) and revealed the true nature and character of God (John 14:9). Most important, the Bible gives us the words of Jesus, who clearly explained why He came:

> *God sent his Son into the world not to judge the world, but to save the world through him* (John 3:17).

4. The Bible gives us instructions for living every day. The Bible is *descriptive* in that it tells us about God and His plan to restore our relationship with Him. And it is *prescriptive* in that it tells us how God wants us to live:

> *All Scripture is inspired by God and is useful to teach us what is true and to make us realize what is wrong in our lives. It corrects us when we are wrong and teaches us to do what is right* (2 Timothy 3:16).

The Utter Uniqueness of the Bible

In the view of believers and non-believers alike, the Bible is considered the most remarkable book the world has ever seen. Consider these facts:

- *The Bible is made up of 66 books written by 40 different authors.* There are 39 books in the Old Testament and 27 in the New Testament. The subject matter of this anthology includes thousands of topics, many of them controversial. Yet the authors, who for the most part didn't know each other or live at the same time, wrote in complete harmony with each other.

- *The Bible was written on three continents over a span of centuries.* Starting with Moses and Job, and ending with the apostle John, the Bible was written over a period of 1600 years on the continents of Asia, Africa, and Europe.

- *The Bible was written in two languages.* Hebrew is the original language of the Old Testament. The New Testament was written in Greek (the international language at the time of Christ).

- *The Bible records thousands of prophecies.* These concern nations, cities, national and world leaders, and the coming of Jesus Christ. Nearly every fulfilled prophecy recorded in the Bible can be verified by historical records outside the Bible—and not one prophecy has been proven wrong.

- *The Bible has one theme and one message throughout.* From Genesis to Revelation, the books of the Bible record one internally consistent point of view about God and humankind.

*A*mazing Prophecies

Hugh Ross, one of those guys who just loves to calculate probabilities, says that approximately 2000 of the 2500 prophecies in the Bible have been fulfilled to the letter with no errors (the remaining 500 concern events that have not yet occurred).

According to Dr. Ross, the probability of any one of the prophecies coming true is less than one in ten. The chances that all 2000 prophecies could have been fulfilled by chance without error is less than one in 10^{2000}. Since any probability less than 1 in 10^{50} is considered impossible, the only reasonable explanation for the complete accuracy of the prophecies found in the Bible is this: God made them, and God fulfilled them.

It's Got Everything You Could Want

You won't find anything to read more unique, more interesting, and more valuable than the Bible. No other book ever written is like it. The Bible uses many literary styles: poetry, musical lyrics, historical narration, instruction, biographies, and even a few dream sequences. In terms of content, it's got everything you could want in a page-turning book:

- *High drama.* The Bible is the story of God creating human beings in His image, followed by humankind rebelling against God and God's plan to restore a relationship with His created beings. It includes an interesting subplot of Satan's failed mutiny and his continued attempts to thwart the human race's reconciliation with God. The stories, plots, and characters are timeless and present the full range of human emotions.

- *Great adventure.* The Bible contains political intrigue, travel on the high seas, and episodes in which men are pitted against the elements of nature. Those *Survivor* episodes have nothing on the Bible.

- *Incredible action.* You'll find true-life stories of wars and battles within the pages of the Bible. Whether reporting man-to-man combat or gigantic massacres, the Bible tells these stories in graphic detail.

- *Tender romance.* As the inventor of love and sex, God knows how to write a good love story. The Bible includes stories of romantic relationships and love poetry.

- *Lofty philosophy.* The wit, wisdom, and philosophical ruminations of the world's wisest people are contained within the Bible.

- *Intricate science.* Although it is not a science textbook, it touches on the sciences of astronomy, geology, biology, and physiology, to name just a few.

- *Comprehensive history.* The Bible covers the spectrum of history, reaching back to a time before the universe began. You can't get much more historical than that. The progress of humankind from Adam to the first century AD is covered in detail.

- *Apocalyptic prophecies.* The Bible doesn't stop with just a past historical perspective. It projects forward with prophecies about how the present world will end and how a new world will begin.

Most importantly, the Bible stands out as a holy book. More than any other religious text ever written, the Bible is read by people looking for spiritual answers to their deepest questions.

---

*E*vidence *from* the Bible and Evidence *for* the Bible

The reason we are making a distinction between these two kinds of evidences is very simple. The Bible tells us a lot about God and how He relates to the world He created. It gives us information about God that is consistent with what we know from the natural world, but it goes much further and tells us things about God that can't be known any other way. But the evidence and information about God in the Bible is good only if we can trust the Bible to be a true and trustworthy document. You could say the evidence *from* the Bible is dependent on the evidence *for* the Bible.

Evidence from the Bible

The Bible is not just the musings of human authors writing on their own. As we said, the Bible contains the verbal and written revelation of God given to men (called *prophets*).

Long ago God spoke many times and in many ways to our ancestors through the prophets (Hebrews 1:1).

But how did the Bible get here in the first place? How did God's revelation get from His mind to your Bible? In his book *A General Introduction to the Bible,* Norman Geisler explains that God's word passed through three "links" in the chain from God to you: inspiration, canonization, and transmission.[3] Each of these in their own way gives evidence for the reliability and accuracy of the Bible.

Together they present a compelling cumulative case for the Bible's truthfulness and trustworthiness.

Inspiration

The first link in the chain is *inspiration*. In the literal sense of the word, *inspire* means to breathe or blow into, and that's what God did. Using the Holy Spirit, God literally breathed His message into 40 different human writers (2 Peter 1:20-21). Even Webster's dictionary acknowledges the uniqueness of inspiration, defining it as a "divine influence." Because of this process, you can trust the Bible completely, even if you don't understand everything about it. God, who is perfect, used a foolproof means to get His message into print. God breathed in what He wanted. Nothing more, nothing less. And all of it is inspired and valuable.

*G*od Isn't a Dictator

When God inspired the human authors to write down His message, He didn't speak into some kind of divine Dictaphone. Instead, the Holy Spirit communicated the message of God through each human writer, who then wrote down the words using his own style and personality. That's why different books of the Bible have different writing styles and perspectives.

Canonicity

The second link in the chain is *canonicity,* which is the process by which church leaders recognized individual books of the Bible as being inspired by God. The *canon* is the collection of books that make up the Bible we use today. (The word comes from the root word translated *reed*. Reeds were used as measuring sticks in ancient times.)

When applied to the Bible, *canon* indicates the measure or the standard used to evaluate which books were inspired and which ones weren't. The final book of the Bible to be inspired by God was the book of Revelation. The apostle John, who was the human author, finished writing Revelation at the end of the first century. For the next few hundred years, several church councils met to determine which books should be included in the canon of Scripture. Their main task was to evaluate books written during and after the time of Christ (the Old Testament canon had already been determined). According to Dr. Geisler, the councils followed strict guidelines in order to determine whether or not a book was inspired by God. They asked these questions:

1. Does it speak with God's authority?

2. Is it written by a man of God speaking to us as a prophet of God?

3. Does it have the authentic stamp of God?

4. Does it impact us with the power of God?

5. Was it accepted by the people of God?

It is important to know that the canon councils did not declare a book to be from God. They simply recognized the divine influence that was already there.

Transmission

The third link in the chain has nothing to do with your car. *Transmission* describes the total process of transmitting the Bible from the early writers to us today using the most practical and reliable methods and materials available. According to Geisler, "The Scriptures had to be copied, translated, recopied, and retranslated. This process not only provided the Scriptures for other nations, but for other generations as well."

---

*I*nfallibility and Inerrancy

When we say the Bible is infallible or inerrant, we mean that it is completely true. This is because God, who is the author, is incapable of error. However, this doesn't mean that today's Bible translations are completely without error. Only the original manuscripts were absolutely correct.

The whole Bible didn't come at one time. As we said before, God inspired 40 different authors over a period of 1600 years to write the Bible. With all of the materials and people involved, how did God make sure that His word was transmitted accurately from one person to the next, from one generation to the next, and from one century to the next? Since there were no Xerox machines or printing presses back then, there had to be a reliable way to copy the Scriptures so God's word could be accurately transmitted and preserved.

From the earliest times, Jewish scribes (you could call them professional human copiers) had to follow detailed procedures and rules for copying Scripture. These rules helped ensure complete concentration and accuracy. Their meticulous approach set the standard for monks and other scholars who transcribed the Bible through the ages. Here are just three rules for scribes (Jewish scholar Samuel Davidson lists dozens) that will give you some idea as to the painstaking detail involved in copying God's word:

1. No word or letter or any other mark may be written from memory. The scribe must look directly at the original scroll for every stroke.

2. Between every letter, the space of a hair or thread must intervene.

3. Should a king address him while writing the name of God, the scribe must take no notice of the king until finished.

The Language of God's Word

The materials used to write down God's word were important, and so were the detailed methods of transcribing the words. But what about the means of communication? What about the words themselves, which are at the heart of God's word? Once again, God was involved in this tool, which we call *language*.

The two original languages of the Bible are Hebrew (Old Testament) and Greek (New Testament). God didn't choose these languages at random, but rather for specific purposes, including accuracy, reliability, and understanding. The languages God chose were the best possible for communicating His message to us.

- *Hebrew*—Language experts agree that Hebrew, the principle language of the Old Testament and of the Jewish (or

Hebrew) people, is precise, pictorial, and personal. Hebrew has been called the perfect biographical language because it describes a God who is very much involved in the lives of people, especially His chosen people, the Jews.

- *Greek*—One of the reasons God chose Greek as the language of the New Testament is that this was the language spoken by most of the world at the time Jesus Christ lived on Earth. Greek has been called the perfect intellectual language, which is ideal for expressing the propositional truth of the New Testament.

Translating the Original Languages

Translating simply means changing from one language to another while retaining the meaning of the original language. The first translation of the Bible came in the third or second century BC, when the Hebrew Old Testament was translated into Greek so more people could read it (it was called the Septuagint because 70 scholars worked on the translation). The entire Bible was translated into Latin in AD 405 (it was called the Vulgate), and that remained the authoritative Bible translation for the next thousand years.

The first English version of the Bible didn't come until 1384, when John Wycliffe translated the Bible from the Latin Vulgate. In 1530 William Tyndale finished translating the Bible from the original languages into English. The Geneva Bible (also known as the Puritan Bible because this is the Bible the Pilgrims brought to America on the Mayflower in 1620) was produced in 1560. The King James Version, the most popular English translation ever, was first published in 1611. Many of the modern English translations we read today were produced in the twentieth century.

The Bible and the Printing Press

As recently as the fifteenth century, it took ten months to copy the Bible by hand, and a single copy cost more money than the average person made in a lifetime. Besides that, few people knew how to read. Then came Johannes Gutenberg and his printing press, generally acknowledged to be the most significant invention of the past thousand years. The first book

Gutenberg printed in 1455 was a Latin version of the Bible. Within 50 years, hundreds of Gutenberg presses were producing thousands of Bibles. The price of a Bible dropped dramatically, people learned how to read, and the world has not been the same since.

Evidence for the Bible

Now it's time to turn our attention to evidence *for* the Bible. There is so much we could cover in this section because there's so much evidence. Here are just a few pieces of evidence that will help you understand why the Bible can be trusted.

The Bible Can Be Trusted for Its Reliability and Accuracy

Scholars have a way of determining if ancient documents are reliable and accurate. First, how many copies exist of a document? The more copies there are, the more chance you have to compare the copies and test the accuracy. Archaeologists have uncovered more copies of ancient Bible manuscripts than of any other document of antiquity. There are more than 5000 various manuscript fragments of the New Testament Scriptures alone!

Second, how close to the date of the first manuscript are the copies? The Bible shines in this area as well. In 1947 some Bedouins found ancient scrolls in a cave in Jordan. Scholars drooled over this magnificent discovery (although they were careful not to drool on the scrolls), which they called the Dead Sea Scrolls. Before the discovery of these scrolls, the oldest complete copy of the Old Testament was dated 1400 years after the Old Testament was completed. The Dead Sea scrolls closed the gap by a thousand years, and they showed that the Bible text had been transmitted accurately.

The third test of reliability and accuracy has to do with the corroborating evidence. In other words, do any other historical documents confirm the claims of the Bible? The answer is a resounding yes. Not every person, date, or fact in the Bible has been verified by outside sources, but many have, and not one has been shown to be false. The evidence for the accuracy of the Bible from sources outside the Bible is nothing short of miraculous.

The Bible Can Be Trusted Historically

The critics of the Bible generally say that it is not a historically trustworthy document, but instead a collection of legends and myths. Most of the criticism centers on the New Testament, in particular the four Gospels. If the four biographies of Jesus can be discredited as historically inaccurate, then the subject of these "eyewitness" accounts—the person of Jesus—can be discredited as well.

A group of scholars working under the umbrella of the Jesus Seminar has discredited all but 20 percent of the sayings and actions of Jesus, including all of Jesus' miracles and His resurrection (the biggest miracle of all). We're going to deal with the Jesus Seminar, the miracles of Jesus, and the resurrection in the next chapter. Right now we want to focus on the Bible as a historical document. Can we trust what it says? Are the four Gospels accurate in their portrayal of Jesus, or did the four biographers try to create a legend and make Jesus into someone He wasn't? Are the letters of Paul consistent with the rest of Scripture, or did he have a personal agenda? Limitations of space don't allow us to dig too deeply into these two important issues, but we do want to give you some general responses.

The Four Gospels

Tim Keller offers three excellent reasons why Matthew, Mark, Luke, and John are not legends, but in fact accurate and historically reliable.[4]

1. *The timing is far too early for the Gospels to be legends.* Critics claim that the four Gospels were written too long after the actual events they describe to be truly accurate. In fact, the Gospels were written sometime in the second half of the first century—at the latest, 40 to 60 years after Jesus' death. This means the writings were in circulation well within the lifetimes of people who were eyewitnesses of the people, places, and events described in the Gospels, in particular the person of Jesus and all He did.

And it wasn't just the people who supported Jesus who were still alive when the Gospels were first being circulated. His enemies would have been around as well. If the Gospel accounts were inaccurate, you can be sure people would have offered a challenge. But such challenges do not exist. What does that mean? The Gospel accounts are true.

2. *The content is far too counterproductive for the Gospels to be legends.* Many critics today contend that the Gospels were deliberately written to promote Christianity. But this idea doesn't make sense. For one thing, the stories in the Gospels, such as the crucifixion of Jesus and the persecution of the early Christians, don't portray Christianity as a very attractive belief. Jesus was executed as a criminal, and His followers were marginalized and killed. Hardly the kind of information you'd put on a recruitment brochure.

For another thing—and this is very important—if the Gospels were written to promote Christianity and its central figure, Jesus Christ, why were women the first witnesses of the resurrected Christ? In the Roman world of the first century, women were so low on the social ladder that their testimony wasn't admissible as evidence in court. If the Gospel writers had wanted to sell their religion to the public, they would have written the resurrection story with men as the first eyewitnesses. There's only one reason why the story is the way it is: It's true.

3. *The literary form is too detailed to be legend.* The style of writing at the time the Gospels—indeed, until about 300 years ago—didn't focus on details. Literary works weren't realistic the way novels are today. The Gospels aren't fiction, but they are written in a detailed style that is unique for the time. The authors of the Gospels reveal little details about the characters that only an eyewitness could know. These details are included in all four Gospels simply because the writers actually saw them.

The Letters of Paul

The apostle Paul wrote more New Testament books than any other writer, and as we have already seen, he is very important from the standpoint of apologetics. But he has come under fire for a couple of reasons.

The church has always accepted Paul as an apostle (that is, an eyewitness of Christ), but critics of Christianity often attack Paul and blame him for turning the simple faith of Jesus into a religion. His themes are blamed by atheists and agnostics alike for distorting the person and message of Christ (who they say was nothing more than a very tragic human figure).

The truth is that Paul did a great deal to explain the meaning of Christ's death and its meaning for salvation, but he didn't invent it. For example, Paul's statement that Christ died according to the Scriptures (1 Corinthians 15:3-8) is based on literature that pre-dates Paul. And the idea of Christ's atonement for our sins isn't Paul's original idea. He got it from Jesus!

Other critics contend that Paul isn't a credible witness of the risen Christ. They say his conversion was a hallucination. But this doesn't line up with the facts. When Paul does convert, he doesn't become just another Christian. He becomes an ambassador for Christ to the world. Paul doesn't just follow Jesus and remain in the circle of converted Jews in Jerusalem. He takes the message to the Gentiles, whom the Jews considered second-class. Hallucinations don't normally produce this kind of dramatic result.

*W*hat About The Lost *Gospel of Thomas*?

Much of the current criticism of the Bible (mostly from popular culture and not from scholars) has come from *The Da Vinci Code,* the blockbuster book by Dan Brown that undermines the credibility of the four Gospels. Brown based some of his research on legend and some of it on the work of Elaine Pagels, a professor of religious history whose book *Beyond Belief* became a bestseller in its own right. Pagels has spent her academic career looking for the truth about Jesus and Christianity outside the New Testament canon, mostly to the writings contained in *The Gospel of Thomas,* a so-called "lost" gospel written in the second century.

Pagels has rejected the conclusion of the Gospels, in particular the Gospel of John, that the only way to God is through Jesus Christ. For Pagels the correct view of Jesus—the one presented in *The Gospel of Thomas*—is that "the divine light Jesus embodied is shared by humanity."[5] To Pagels, the message of the New Testament canon, in particular the Gospel of John, is a distorted and too narrowly defined way of believing. In order to truly experience all that God offers, we must move beyond belief to find what lies hidden in each one of us.

In fact, *The Gospel of Thomas* and all of the "lost" gospels are "obviously inferior theologically and historically to the four accounts that eventually came to be regarded as the only canonical Gospels."[6] Only the four Gospel writers correctly understand the gospel—or good news—message of Christ, because only these historic writers portray Jesus as He really is: the embodied and living God who speaks with divine authority.

How to Read the Bible

All the evidence in the world doesn't amount to much unless you actually read and study the Bible. As you do this, the most valuable thing you can do is to bring out the meaning. This is also known as *interpretation*. When you interpret something, you make it plain and understandable. Gordon Fee and Douglas Stuart write that the interpreter (that's you) has two tasks:

- The interpreter needs to be engaged in "careful, systematic study of the Scripture to discover the original, intended meaning" (this is called *exegesis*). You don't read the Bible only when you feel like it or only on Sundays. As an interpreter, you are in the word of God daily.
- The interpreter needs to seek "the contemporary relevance of ancient texts" (this is called *hermeneutics*). In other words, you learn to apply what the Scripture says without contradicting the original meaning.[7]

Principles of Interpretation

There are no two ways about it. If you want to be a good Bible interpreter, you need to work at it. You need to be a skilled and accurate interpreter. Many people think that if they just read the Bible casually, all of these amazing insights will come into their heads, but it doesn't work that way. Yes, the Holy Spirit will guide you into all truth (John 14:17), but you can't remain a passive bystander. You need to engage the brain God gave you, and that means developing your interpretation skills.

Getting good at Bible interpretation is no different from getting good at business, sports, science, or music. If you want to be a success, you have to observe the rules and follow the principles. R.C. Sproul lists three important principles for making the Bible plain and understandable.[8]

1. Interpret the Bible by the Bible. "What is obscure in one part of Scripture may be made clear in another," writes Sproul. "To interpret Scripture by Scripture means that we must not set one passage of Scripture against another passage." This also means that you always read Bible verses and passages in context.

Context is a lot like character. Just as we can be tempted to jump on a rumor about someone even if it's totally out of character, we can also be tempted to take something in the Bible out of context. In both cases, all that does is make us feel better, even if we're wrong. Here's a guideline: When it comes to people, consider the character before making a conclusion. When it comes to Scripture, consider the context before making an interpretation.

---

*T*he Rules of Context

Gordon Fee and Douglas Stuart talk about two kinds of context: historical and literary. Each book of the Bible has a different historical context, which has to do with the time and culture of the author and his readers. You have to ask why and when the book was written. What was going on in the culture at the time, and who were the major historical figures involved? To get a general sense of the historical context, read the introductory notes to the book in your Bible (if you have a study Bible), or look up the information in a trustworthy Bible handbook.

The literary context of the Bible refers to the words themselves. All words have meaning, but they take on different meanings in a sentence or paragraph. For example, if Stan said the word *lawyer,* you would probably have negative thoughts. But if he said, "Bruce is a lawyer," then you would think happy thoughts. The word takes on a different meaning in context.

---

2. Interpret the Bible literally. This means that you should interpret the Bible as it is written. The Bible is a miraculous book but not a magical book. God used the rules of grammar to communicate His message, which means a noun is always a noun and a verb is always a verb. "To interpret the Bible literally is to interpret it as *literature,*" Sproul writes. This means you have to look at literary form or style, such as poetry, prophecy, and historical narrative (we do this with everything we read). Is the author using a metaphor (figurative language) or hyperbole (deliberate exaggeration used for effect) to make a point? For example, when Jesus said your faith could move a mountain (Matthew 17:20-21), He didn't mean that you could literally move Mount Everest. Jesus was using a literary expression to show us just how potent our faith really is.

3. *Interpret the Bible objectively.* It's easy to interpret the Bible subjectively, according to our own viewpoints and desires. This is where people can get into serious disagreements, both with the Bible and with each other. As you read and study the Bible, focus on what it says rather than on what you already believe. You must first ask what a given Scripture was intended to mean to the people for whom it was originally written before you can ask what it means to you personally.

Avoid the temptation to stamp your own impressions or feelings on Scripture before you discover the objective truth it contains. This doesn't mean that you shouldn't come to your own conclusions about what the Bible means. You aren't obligated to follow someone else's viewpoint. However, your own private interpretation will only be meaningful with the guidance of the Holy Spirit combined with your own diligent study. Remember that the Bible bears the authority of God. Trust God's word to mean what it says.

By following these principles, you will become a person who "correctly explains the word of truth" (2 Timothy 2:15).

ⓊⓎour Secret Weapon

There are several advantages to being a Christian. First of all, there's that whole eternal life thing. How wonderful and comforting to know that because you have put your trust in God through the person and work of Jesus Christ, you won't die spiritually, but will have eternal life (John 3:16). But as important as your eternal destiny is, that's not all there is. The Christian life is more than having a spiritual fire-insurance policy. Jesus said that He came to give us life "in all its fullness" (John 10:10 GNT). This includes the life you live in the here and now, not just in the hereafter. The most effective way to enjoy life in all its fullness is through the power of the Holy Spirit (in fact, it's the *only* way). "So I say, let the Holy Spirit guide your lives," writes the apostle Paul (Galatians 5:16).

When you live in the Spirit's power, you will be led by the Holy Spirit (Romans 8:13-14) and you will follow the Spirit (Romans 8:4). You will also desire to study God's word. This makes perfect sense because the Holy Spirit is God's Spirit in person—in you! When you invite God into your life by faith in Jesus, the Holy Spirit enters your life in order to help you live the Christian life. And one of the most important things the Holy Spirit does is help you understand God's personal message to you, the Bible.

The Holy Spirit is your secret weapon—your inside source—helping you to understand the things of God as you study His word.

What's That Again?

1. The Bible is an essential component of the Christian faith. You could even say that the Christian faith requires belief in the Bible.

2. Believing that the Bible truly is God's word is important for at least four reasons: (1) the Bible claims to be the word of God, (2) the Bible gives us God's plan for humanity and the world, (3) the Bible tells us about Jesus Christ, and (4) the Bible gives us instructions for living every day.

3. The Bible is the most remarkable book in history. It was written by 40 authors over a span of 1600 years in two languages, yet it has one consistent message.

4. Evidence *from* the Bible depends on evidence *for* the Bible for one simple reason: The evidence and information about God in the Bible is good only if we can trust the Bible to be a true and trustworthy document.

5. The key components of evidence from the Bible are inspiration, canonicity, and transmission.

6. The pieces of evidence for the Bible include these: (1) There are more than 5000 various manuscripts of the New Testament, (2) the ancient manuscripts

upon which the Bible is based are amazingly con-sistent, and (3) the evidence for the Bible's accuracy from sources outside the Bible is miraculous.

7. There is ample evidence to show that the four Gospels, which give us the story of Jesus, are accurate and historically reliable. The so-called lost gospels, including *The Gospel of Thomas,* have never been accepted as part of the New Testament canon.

8. The evidence for the Bible doesn't mean anything unless you read it. The most valuable thing you can do is to interpret the Bible accurately, using these principles as guidelines: interpret the Bible by the Bible, interpret the Bible literally, and interpret the Bible objectively.

Dig Deeper

There is no shortage of helpful books on the Bible. Here are three to get you started:

The New Testament Documents: Are They Reliable? by F.F. Bruce is a little book packed with information that will give you the confidence you need to believe that the New Testament—the primary source for the claims and life of Jesus—is reliable.

What the Bible Is All About by Henrietta Mears offers a brilliant summary of each book of the Bible. This is an essential book for your library.

When Skeptics Ask by Norman Geisler and Ron Brooks is a handbook for Christian evidences. The chapter on the Bible is worth the price of the book.

Here we go again, plugging away. *Knowing the Bible 101* is vintage Bruce & Stan. In fact, it's the bestselling book in the Christianity 101 series.

■ ■ ■

Questions for Reflection and Discussion

1. Why do you read the Bible? What benefits do you experience when you're consistent in your reading and study? Why does your faith require that you believe the Bible is true?

2. In what ways does the Bible claim to be the word of God? According to the Bible, what is God's plan for humanity? How does the Bible tell us about Jesus?

3. Read 2 Timothy 3:16. Describe the ways the inspired word of God...

   > teaches us what is true
   >
   > makes us realize what is wrong in our lives
   >
   > corrects us when we are wrong
   >
   > teaches us to do what is right

4. In what ways does the inspiration of Scripture demonstrate that the Bible is true? How does the process of canonicity give you confidence that the Bible you read is the actual word of God? How does the transmission of the Bible text assure you that the Bible you read is the same as the Bible as it was written?

5. Why does the existence of more than 5000 manuscript fragments give the Bible a stamp of authenticity?

6. Of the three reasons Tim Keller gives for the accuracy and reliability of the Bible, which one is the most compelling to you? Which one is the least compelling?

7. Why do you think our culture is so eager to embrace the "truth" of a book of fiction like *The Da Vinci Code?* Why might Elaine Pagels be so intent on finding what lies hidden in all of us rather than what is in plain sight in the Bible?

8. Review the three principles of Bible interpretation. Give a one-sentence reason for the importance of each of these.

Moving On...

We've taken a fairly detailed look at God's written word, the first part of God's special revelation. Now it's time to turn our attention to God's living Word, Jesus Christ, the second and most important component of God's special revelation.

Chapter 6

Christianity in its radical form, its apostolic form, is a dynamic story, a powerful force that shaped Western civilization. In prisons, what resonates is the story of Jesus, a poor man riding on a borrowed donkey, born in a borrowed manger. That's the story that's resonating in the Third World. In South America, Africa, Asia, they're preaching the real thing.

—Charles Colson

Everybody wants a piece of Jesus. The majority of the people in the world know the name of Jesus, and at least a third of them—those who call themselves Christians—identify with Jesus personally. Muslims respect Jesus as a prophet and someone who lived a sinless life. Even Jews call Jesus "one of us," a rabbi who preached love and tolerance. Everybody wants a piece of Jesus because they want Him on their side.

But what Jesus do they want? Do they want the Son of God, who came to seek and to save those who are lost, or do they want a great teacher? Do they want the Jesus who died to free them from the bondage of sin and self-centeredness, or do they want a revolutionary figure who will free them from political oppression?

There's no disputing Jesus' popularity. The issue these days isn't whether you believe in Jesus. Now, the question is, which Jesus do you believe in? In this chapter we're going to consider the evidence for the biblical Jesus, portrayed as God in human form, who came into our world for one purpose: to make it possible for people alienated from God because of sin to enter into a new relationship with Him by putting their faith in Jesus alone for salvation.

Before we get to the portrait of the real Jesus—the one who is—we need to first take a look at some pictures of the other Jesus—the one many people want.

Evidence for Jesus

*W*hat's *A*head

- Alternate Views of Jesus
- The Jesus We Want
- The Jesus Who Is
- The Deity of Jesus
- The Humanity of Jesus
- The Death of Jesus
- The Resurrection of Jesus

*R*ecently the television program *Faith Under Fire* featured a debate between Marianne Williamson, the popular spiritualist and the author of *A Return to Love,* and Craig Hazen, one of the world's foremost Christian apologists.[1] Lee Strobel, host of *Faith Under Fire,* served as the moderator, giving both guests the opportunity to answer the question, how do we get to heaven? Dr. Hazen was clear and objective, suggesting that an investigation of the truth would lead to a belief in the resurrected Christ as the only way to heaven. But Williamson was vague and subjective, insisting that there's no single truth except for the divine light in each of us. "We're all going to get to heaven in the end," she said.

For viewers predisposed to a Christian worldview, Hazen's remarks are familiar and reassuring. Truth can be known. All you have to do is engage in an honest intellectual pursuit, and you will discover the historic Jesus as revealed in the Bible. By contrast,

Williamson teaches that the resurrection of Jesus is a symbol that we are all sons of God who need to be awakened.

Alternate Views of Jesus

The Hazen–Williamson debate illustrates the enormous challenge the follower of Christ faces when attempting to present the truth claims of the Bible in contemporary culture, especially those claims that involve the person of Jesus Christ and His resurrection from the dead. Many voices are competing for the true picture of Jesus. Some of these voices, like Williamson's, are coming from contemporary culture. Far from being passing fads, these perspectives are enormously popular, capturing the imaginations of tens of millions of spiritual seekers.

We've already talked about Dan Brown's book *The Da Vinci Code*, the fastest-selling novel in history. Drawing in part upon *The Gospel of Thomas*, Brown proposes that Jesus didn't die at all, but got married and raised a family. That this book is a work of fiction is lost on many people who have bought into the alleged hidden truths Brown says have been kept from the public.

The Jesus Seminar

Other voices are coming from the field of academics, in particular a group of scholars writing and lecturing under the umbrella of a theological think tank called the Jesus Seminar. Allegedly, the purpose of the seminar is to recover the authentic Jesus by peeling back the layers of supernatural myths and legends that are presented in the Gospels and believed by Christians today.

And just who was this authentic Jesus? Here is a sampling of quotes from a few of the Jesus Seminar participants:

> Jesus was a charismatic Jewish peasant "spirit person" like Buddha or Lau Tzu, combining qualities of sage and prophet, who sought to reform Jewish society and was killed for it (Marcus Borg).

> Jesus was a peasant philosopher-poet like the Cynics, wandering around Galilee and preaching freedom and love—a kind of first-century Jewish hippie (John Dominic Crossan).

The Gospel of Mark created a myth based on the beliefs of the "Jesus movement," which saw him as a Jewish reformer, and the "Christ cult," which had reinvented Jesus as a divine being (Burton Mack).

The Jesus Seminar even published its own version of the Gospels called *The Five Gospels,* given that title because it includes *The Gospel of Thomas* along with Matthew, Mark, Luke, and John. The words of Jesus in *The Five Gospels* are in red (as they are in many Bibles). But as it turns out, less than 20 percent of the sayings traditionally attributed to Jesus are in red. That's because the Jesus Seminar scholars have determined that the other 80 percent aren't authentic.

So what does this alternate portrait of Jesus look like? Here are the main features:

- Jesus was a kind of itinerant social critic and Jewish philosopher.
- He never claimed to be the Son of God.
- He never claimed to forgive sins.
- He never claimed to be the only way to God.
- His crucifixion was an accident.
- His corpse was thrown into a shallow grave, where it rotted away or was eaten by wild animals.

A Useless Faith

If you are a Christian who believes the truth claims of the Bible, including the things the Bible says about Jesus and the things Jesus said, this alternate portrait probably seems pretty bizarre. But if you are unfamiliar with the Bible and aren't sure about Jesus, the Jesus Seminar Jesus probably doesn't seem too far-fetched. The issue, of course, isn't what seems to be true about Jesus, but what *is* actually true. In other words, what matters is the truth, the whole truth, and nothing but the truth.

If you don't have confidence that the things the Bible says about Jesus are true, your faith is going to be in question. In fact, if Jesus was not resurrected, as the members of the Jesus Seminar and other contemporary voices are saying, then your faith is absolutely useless, and your belief is pitiful. That's not us talking. The apostle Paul says it:

> And if Christ has not been raised, then your faith is useless and you are still guilty of your sins. In that case, all who have died believing in Christ are lost! And if our hope in Christ is only for this life, we are more to be pitied than anyone in the world (1 Corinthians 15:17-19).

Now, do you think Paul would have said this if he didn't believe the resurrection of Jesus Christ was an actual historical event? Not on your life. Paul would not have hung the Christian faith on such a thin thread unless it was, as Dr. Hazen has said, an impervious titanium thread that can stand up to all scrutiny and doubt.

The Christian life is built on the good news that Jesus lived a perfect life, that He died for your sins, that He was buried, and that He was raised from the dead on the third day, just as the Bible says (1 Corinthians 15:3-4). You need to know these events aren't part of a myth or legend, and you need to be able to show them to be true to someone who would like a reasonable explanation.

We're going to help you do just that in a little while, but first we want to explore some reasons why some people are so willing to embrace the alternate view of Jesus rather than the true biblical portrait of Jesus.

The Jesus We Want

Pat Morley made a statement that has stuck with us like glue. It has to do with the way people—Christians and non-Christians alike—think about God: "There is the God we want, and there is the God who is, and they are not the same God."

We can just as easily apply that statement to Jesus, who claimed to be God. There is the Jesus our culture wants, and there is the Jesus who is, and they are not the same. The alternate views of Jesus proposed by the Jesus Seminar are all about the Jesus we want. Let's look at three reasons why this is the case.

1. *The Jesus our culture wants is natural.* The first thing the alternate views of Jesus do is to strip Him of His supernatural power. Remember the worldview of naturalism? This is the view that the

universe and everything in it—every person and event—have a natural cause. There are no supernatural people or events. Miracles can't happen. In this worldview, things like God coming to Earth in human form, the virgin birth, and the resurrection aren't possible. According to the Jesus Seminar, the historical Jesus must be by definition a non-supernatural figure. Of course, if this is the case, then what do you do with God? By definition, God is supernatural. So if you eliminate the supernatural, you automatically take God out of the picture as well (more about this later in the chapter).

The people who take this alternate view of Jesus have no proof for their claim. It's just assumed because they don't want a supernatural Jesus. Why? Because a supernatural Jesus is God in human form. A supernatural Jesus can forgive sins. A supernatural Jesus died on the cross and rose from the dead. Humankind is not the center of the universe or the highest form of life. People are sinners in need of salvation, and Jesus is the Savior they need.

The problem with the naturalistic assumption about Jesus—and we call it that because no proof is offered—is that it is not based on evidence, but on desire. It represents the Jesus our naturalistic culture wants—a Jesus who doesn't demand that people turn from their sin toward God—not the Jesus who is.

2. *The Jesus our culture wants lives in everyone.* The second characteristic of the alternate Jesus is that He lives in every person as a kind of divine light. Clearly this assumption comes from *The Gospel of Thomas,* a text favored by the Jesus Seminar in general and by the Princeton scholar Elaine Pagels in particular. In *Beyond Belief,* she offers this saying from Jesus as recorded in *The Gospel of Thomas:* "If you bring forth what is within you, what you bring forth will save you." Pagels makes this conclusion:

> The strength of this saying is that it does not tell us what to believe but challenges us to discover what lies hidden within our selves; and, with a shock of recognition, I realized that this perspective seemed to me self-evident.[2]

This form of Christianity is not based on belief in what is true, but on personal preference. It is a view that presents, in the words of New Testament scholar Ben Witherington III, "a reconfigured form of Christ—reconfigured as self-actualization."[3]

Pagels and the members of the Jesus Seminar view *The Gospel of Thomas* as the primary source for what we know about Jesus, but the vast majority of scholars believe this gospel wasn't written until the middle of the second century (which means it wasn't written by Thomas at all). And rather than giving a true portrait of Jesus, it reflects the philosophy of second-century Gnosticism, a philosophy that teaches that salvation comes through secret knowledge of the spiritual realm.

The idea that *The Gospel of Thomas* or any lost gospel gives us a new and correct version of Jesus is, in the words of one prominent New Testament critic, "largely fantasy." The truth is that your Bible contains the most reliable and trustworthy account of the life of Jesus.

3. The Jesus our culture wants is politically correct. When you put religious pluralism together with political correctness, you end up with the view that all religious views about the nature of God and Jesus are valid—except, of course, for the view that Jesus is the only way to God! William Lane Craig writes:

> If you insist on being politically correct, then somehow you've got to get Jesus out of the way. For his radical, personal claims to be the unique Son of God, the absolute revelation of God the Father, the sole mediator between God and man, are frankly embarrassing and offensive to the politically correct mindset.[4]

The problem with the politically correct picture of Jesus is that it doesn't correspond with reality (remember, by definition truth corresponds with reality). Rather than shaping a portrait of Jesus based on who He is, Marianne Williamson, Dan Brown, and members of the Jesus Seminar have shaped a portrait of Jesus based on what they want.

Okay, enough about the Jesus we want. Now it's time to turn our attention to the true Jesus who is. To do this, we want to explore briefly the life and work of Jesus, starting with the historical Jesus as seen through the eyes of those who knew Him. Then we will look at His unique God-man nature and His central reason for coming into this world—to seek and to save those who are lost (Luke 19:10). Finally, we will evaluate the resurrection of Jesus, the remarkable historical event the Christian life depends on.

The Jesus Who Is

To get to the heart of the historical Jesus, we need to find out what His contemporaries thought and wrote about Him. These eyewitness accounts tell us a great deal about who Jesus was and what He did.

The Disciples

The people who knew Jesus best were His disciples, handpicked by Jesus (the word *disciple* means a learner or follower). All but one of these 12 ordinary men followed Jesus wholeheartedly. Jesus recruited "the Twelve" after His baptism, which marked the beginning of His public ministry. For the next three years—up until the time He ascended into heaven—Jesus taught this ragtag group, and gradually they learned. More importantly, they came to believe in Him as their Savior.

Two of Jesus' disciples, Matthew and John, were also biographers of Jesus. There were four biographers in all (they wrote the four Gospels), and all were trustworthy eyewitnesses of the life of Jesus. Craig Blomberg, one of the most respected authorities on the biographies of Jesus, has this to say about their credibility: "In terms of honesty, in terms of truthfulness, in terms of virtue and morality, these people [the biographers] had a track record that should be envied."

The Opposition

If anyone had reason to discredit Jesus, it was the people who opposed Him, such as the religious leaders. If there had been any doubts that Jesus spoke with authority, or that His followers were exaggerating His claims, the religious leaders would have jumped on the opportunity to expose Jesus as a fraud. But that never happened. No one ever contradicted the claims and teachings of Jesus. No one ever successfully argued with Jesus and proved Him wrong. All His enemies could do was silence Jesus by putting Him to death, which only served to validate the prophecies concerning the Messiah and accomplish what Jesus came to do.

The Historians

Even though the Bible is the most reliable and trustworthy ancient document ever written, some people want more evidence for the existence of Jesus. "Show me outside the Bible where it says Jesus lived and walked the earth in first-century Palestine," someone might say. Here's how you can respond. Josephus was a Jewish historian who lived and wrote in the first century. His writings, which are respected by scholars as trustworthy, mention Jesus several times. Other ancient secular writers—including Cornelius Tacitus and Plinius Secundus—made references to Christ, Christians, and historic events mentioned in the Bible. For example, the first-century historian Phlegon wrote about the darkness that came upon the earth at the time of Christ's crucifixion.

Criteria of Authority

How do we know that Jesus said and did the things He did? Can we really trust the testimony of His biographers? Here are three criteria proposed by scholars that validate the eyewitness accounts of the Gospel writers:

1. *The criterion of embarrassment.* If a Gospel writer recorded something embarrassing about Jesus, especially something Jesus said, then it's more likely to have stemmed from the historical Jesus. Jesus did and said plenty of things that embarrassed His followers. He mixed with prostitutes, tax collectors, and beggars, something no self-respecting rabbi would ever do. He was baptized, which was something associated with purification and cleansing. Why would Jesus need to be purified? And then there are all those hard sayings of Jesus that surely embarrassed His followers. For example, He told them they had to eat His flesh and drink His blood (John 6:53). And Jesus told the men closest to Him that they had to hate their families in order to be His disciples (Luke 14:26). The fact that the Gospel writers left all this stuff in lends credence to their truth.

2. *The criterion of dissimilarity.* If Jesus uses words and phrases that nobody else uses, we would expect the content to be true. For example, Jesus talked a lot about the kingdom of God. Even though Jesus used this phrase deliberately, nobody else used it in His day. Another is Jesus' own use of "the Son of Man," His favorite self-descriptive term. The early church didn't use this title to allude to Jesus. The fact that He used it showed that He

was using it deliberately, and it shows that these phrases really go back to Jesus.

3. The criterion of multiple attestations. Gospel scholars use this criterion to show the truth of Jesus' statements. If independent testimonies agree on what He said, it lends credibility. Many of the sayings the Jesus Seminar has gotten rid of have multiple attestations.

The Deity of Jesus

One thing separates Jesus from every other religious leader in history: He claimed to be God!

Jesus didn't say He was *like* a god. He said that He *was* God. When referring to God the Father, Jesus said it bluntly: "The Father and I are one" (John 10:30). Surely Jesus didn't make this bold statement in jest or in a desperate attempt to get attention. He said it because it was true. The religious leaders certainly knew what Jesus meant, and they plotted His death because of it (John 5:18).

Jesus wasn't the only one who believed that He was God. John the Baptist recognized the deity of Christ (John 1:29), and the apostle Paul wrote this about Jesus: "For in Christ lives all the fullness of God in a human body" (Colossians 2:9). This single distinction—the claim of Jesus to be God—is the foundation of Christianity. And we can believe it for at least three reasons: Jesus had the proof to back up His claim, He fulfilled Old Testament prophecy to the letter, and He had His Father's endorsement.

Jesus Had the Proof to Back Up His Claim

Jesus not only claimed to be God; He also played the part. He assumed the role that only God could fill when He forgave people of their sins. One day He was preaching in a house to a standing-room-only crowd when several men lowered their paralyzed friend down through the roof to be healed by Jesus (Mark 2:1-12). The first thing Jesus did was to tell the man, "My child, your sins are forgiven." Some religious leaders who were in the house were outraged. "This is blasphemy!" they exclaimed. "Only God can forgive sins!"

We know what you might be thinking: Claiming to possess the power to forgive sins doesn't prove that Jesus was God. Anyone can say that he is forgiving sins. We agree. That's a good objection, except that Jesus then healed the paralyzed man, showing that He had supernatural powers that only God possesses. The healing of the paralyzed man wasn't a fluke. Jesus consistently exhibited supernatural powers that could only belong to God:

> He gave sight to the blind (Mark 8:22-26).
>
> He cured the lame (John 5:1-9).
>
> He healed the sick (Luke 7:1-10).
>
> He raised the dead to life (Matthew 9:18-26).
>
> He fed thousands with only a boy's lunch (Matthew 14:14-21).
>
> He calmed a raging storm with one command (Matthew 8:23-27).

Besides having these supernatural powers, Jesus had supernatural qualities that only God can possess. Various passages throughout the New Testament describe Jesus this way:

> eternal (John 17:5)
>
> all-knowing (John 16:30)
>
> all-powerful (John 5:19)
>
> unchangeable (Hebrews 13:8)
>
> the Creator of the universe (Colossians 1:16)

Jesus Fulfilled Prophecy Concerning the Messiah

Throughout the Old Testament, God promised the Jews that He would send a king who would establish God's kingdom on earth. This king was referred to as the Messiah. He would be God coming down to earth. There was a big mystery surrounding the Messiah. Although they knew He was coming (because God had promised), the Jews weren't sure how they would know who He was, and they didn't know when He would arrive. But through the predictions in the Old Testament (called *prophecies* because the prophets were the ones that announced them), the Jews had some fairly specific clues about this Messiah. Here is a portion of the checklist they were working from:

- *City of birth.* He was going to be born in the little town of Bethlehem (Micah 5:2).
- *Parentage.* He would be a direct descendant of the famous King David (Isaiah 11:1).
- *Distinguishing characteristics.* As strange as it seems, the Messiah would be born to a virgin (Isaiah 7:14). How inconceivable!
- *Childhood.* Although born in Bethlehem, He would spend His childhood in Egypt (Hosea 11:1).
- *Notoriety.* He would have a ceremonial entrance into Jerusalem on a donkey (Zechariah 9:9). A rather humble and inauspicious ceremony for a Messiah, don't you think?
- *Death.* He would die by crucifixion, the method of death reserved for the most heinous criminals (Psalm 34:20).
- *Famous last words.* Even the Messiah's dying words were predicted (Psalm 22:1).
- *Resurrection from the dead.* As if the immaculate conception thing weren't enough, the Messiah was predicted to come back to life after His death (Psalm 16:9-10).

Over the centuries, as the list of prophecies about the Messiah became longer, the pool of potential candidates got smaller. That doesn't mean that the Jews didn't have their share of Messiah impostors. Similar to Elvis impersonators, the counterfeits were easy to spot. Oh, maybe they could fake a few of the criteria (like forging a birth certificate to show Bethlehem or riding a donkey into Jerusalem), but the impostors weren't willing to be crucified, and none of them could pull off the "come back to life after death" prediction. But along came Jesus Christ. He claimed to be the long-awaited Messiah. And He had the résumé to back it up:

born in Bethlehem (Luke 2:4,6-7)

a descendant of King David (Luke 1:31-33)

born of a virgin—which was very hard to fake (Matthew 1:18,22-23) raised in Egypt (Matthew 2:13-21)

rode into Jerusalem on a donkey (Matthew 21:1-11)

famous last words (Mark 15:34)

died on a cross (Matthew 27:32-35)

came back to life—perhaps the hardest to fake (John 20–21)

No person before or after Christ has been able to pass the Messiahship test—only Christ.

Jesus Had the Endorsement of God the Father

With a booming voice from heaven, God the Father announced that Jesus was His Son when Jesus was baptized by John the Baptist.

> *After his baptism, as Jesus came up out of the water, the heavens were opened and he saw the Spirit of God descending like a dove and settling on him. And a voice from heaven said, "This is my dearly loved Son, who brings me great joy"* (Matthew 3:16-17).

This scene is phenomenal for two reasons:

- It reveals the three persons of the Trinity present in one place at one time, distinct yet united: God the Father's voice is heard, Jesus Christ the Son is being baptized, and the Holy Spirit descends just as a dove would.

- Most pertinent to our discussion, God the Father is identifying Jesus as His Son. You can't get a better endorsement than from God Himself.

$\mathcal{T}$he Mystery of the Three-in-One

Please excuse us if our discussion of Jesus being God and the Son of God seems a little confusing. It isn't our fault. Any discussion on this topic involves the mysterious concept of the Trinity—the three-in-one nature of God. The word *Trinity* doesn't even appear in the Bible, but it is an important aspect about God. The Trinity refers to the three distinct persons that make up God: God the Father, Jesus Christ the Son, and the Holy Spirit.

Trinity does not mean that there are three gods who exist together to make up one God. There is only one God, but within that unity are three eternal and coequal persons—all sharing the same essence and substance, but each one having a distinct existence.

Now, the doctrine of the Trinity may be biblical, but does it make sense? There's no question that the Trinity is a difficult idea to grasp. In fact, if you use common sense, it won't make sense. But that doesn't mean the concept is nonsense. The Trinity is hard to think about, not because it is incoherent or illogical, but because it is so dense. Like God Himself, it packs a lot of information into one truth. That doesn't mean you shouldn't do your best to understand it, because as you come to a greater understanding of the Trinity, you will better understand God, Jesus, the Holy Spirit, and the Bible.

The Humanity of Jesus

Even though Jesus declared Himself to be God, the Bible describes Jesus Christ as being all man. In fact, Jesus referred to Himself as "the Son of Man" (Luke 19:10). He frequently used this phrase in reference to Himself because He saw Himself as the representative for the human race. He identified Himself as being human. Jesus also identified His ancestry as human. He referred to Himself as the son of David because He was born into the bloodline of Israel's famous king.

But the greatest evidence of His humanity is not what He said about Himself. His humanity is revealed in His life. Jesus Christ had traits that proved His humanity. Most significantly, He had a body. This is obvious because so many people saw Him and touched Him. They couldn't nail a spirit to the cross. And His body had all of the traits that come with a human body (and that don't belong to a spirit):

Jesus got hungry (Matthew 4:2).

He got thirsty (John 19:28).

He grew weary (John 4:6).

He experienced human love and compassion (Matthew 9:36).

He cried (John 11:35).

He was tempted (Hebrews 4:15).

These are the characteristics of a human. If Jesus was all God and just stuffed into human skin, He could have existed on earth as a type of cyborg in human form without human feelings. But that isn't how it was. He had all of the human emotions and was just like we are—except for one major difference.

Everything About Jesus Was Human—Except for the Sin Part

Yes, Jesus was all human, with one major—very major—distinction from the rest of us. He was sinless. That means that He never did anything that displeased God or violated the Mosaic law. At every stage of His life (infancy, boyhood, adolescence, and manhood), He was holy and without sin.

Jesus must have considered Himself to be sinless. He was a Jew, and it was customary for all Jews to offer sacrifices for their sins. But there is no record of Jesus ever offering a single sacrifice, even though He was frequently in the temple. He didn't need to. He was without sin. Perhaps the best proof of His sinlessness was demonstrated at the trials preceding His crucifixion. The religious authorities would have loved to present evidence that He had broken a law—religious or civil—but He hadn't. He was declared innocent 11 times:

> six times by Pilate (Matthew 27:24; Luke 23:14,22; John 18:38; 19:4,6)
>
> once by Herod (Luke 23:15)
>
> once by Pilate's wife (Matthew 27:19)
>
> once by the repentant thief (Luke 23:41)
>
> once by a Roman centurion (Matthew 27:54)
>
> once by Judas (Matthew 27:4)

There is further reliable proof that Jesus was without sin: He died for our sins. He could only be an acceptable sacrifice if He was sinless. All of Christianity is premised on that fact. The disciples—who knew Christ better than anyone—would not have been willing to be persecuted for their faith if they knew Christ was guilty of sin and if Christianity was based on a faulty premise. But these disciples declared Christ's holiness. Peter said it plainly: "He [Jesus] never sinned" (1 Peter 2:22). The disciple John echoed the same truth: "And you know that Jesus came to take away our sins, and there is no sin in him" (1 John 3:5). And the apostle Paul summed it up this way:

> *For God made Christ, who never sinned, to be the offering for our sin, so that we could be made right with God through Christ* (2 Corinthians 5:21).

*I*s Jesus God or Man—or Both?

We have shown evidence for both the deity and the humanity of Christ. But how do these two natures—the divine and the human—come together in one person? Is Jesus all God, all man, or both? The answer is yes—to all three options. From our human perspective, this is a difficult concept to grasp, but like the concept of the Trinity, it is not impossible or illogical. The person of Christ contains the union of His divine and human natures in one being. Jesus is all God and all man at the same time. When Jesus lived on earth, He demonstrated an interesting balance:

- His deity wasn't limited by His humanity. He was always God, as evidenced by His sinlessness and supernatural powers.

- His humanity wasn't overshadowed by His deity. Jesus didn't use His God powers to make His life easier. He experienced all the emotions we have. He even endured the pain and suffering of the cross. Jesus didn't give up His godly attributes. He simply took on human attributes as well (Philippians 2:6-7).

In His earthly body, Jesus voluntarily chose not to use all His godly powers. When He was hungry, He didn't turn the stones into bread. But He could have. When He was crucified, He didn't call down angels to rescue Him. But He could have. Choosing not to use an ability is different from not having it. And Jesus had it all: all God and all man.

The Death of Jesus

Why did Jesus have to die? He died to earn our salvation. As sinners, we deserve the penalty for sin, which is death (Romans

6:23). Because God is holy and just, He demands a punishment for sin. A penalty must be paid, and we aren't capable of paying the penalty because we are sinners. The only one who could offer an acceptable payment is Jesus, because only He lived without sin.

The Bible clearly tells us it was love that caused God to send Jesus to pay the penalty for our sin:

> *This is real love—not that we loved God, but that he loved us and sent his Son as a sacrifice to take away our sins* (1 John 4:10).

The work that Christ did in His life and in His death to earn our salvation is called the *atonement*. The death of Jesus by crucifixion was the pivotal event that allowed sinful humankind to get back into a right relationship with the holy, almighty God. The crucifixion of Christ wasn't a tragedy. It wasn't a series of events gone out of control. It was the divinely designed plan of God. Here is an abbreviated list of some of the fundamental accomplishments achieved by Christ's death on the cross. Each one is a vital part of God's plan of salvation for humankind:

Substitution. Christ died so that we don't have to. This is what Christianity is all about, and it required the death of Christ on the cross. It boils down to three basic points:

- All humans are sinful (Romans 3:23).
- The penalty for our sin is eternal death (Romans 6:23).
- Jesus was the ultimate human sacrifice. He died in our place (Romans 8:3-4).

Propitiation. If you're like us, the word *propitiation* doesn't find its way into your everyday vocabulary. Theologians use it to explain that Christ's death on the cross turned God's wrath away from us. Because God is so holy, He hates sin and is radically opposed to it. As sinful beings, that would place us as the objects of God's wrath. But Christ's death on the cross appeased God's wrath.

> *For God presented Jesus as the sacrifice for sin. People are made right with God when they believe that Jesus sacrificed his life, shedding his blood* (Romans 3:25).

Reconciliation. Humankind was alienated from God because of sin. That alienation was removed when Christ died on the cross. Reconciliation between God and humanity was made possible.

> *For since our friendship with God was restored by the death of His Son while we were still his enemies, we will certainly be saved through the life of His Son. So now we can rejoice in our wonderful new relationship with God because our Lord Jesus Christ has made us friends of God* (Romans 5:10-11).

Redemption. Before Christ died on the cross, we were slaves to sin. We were in bondage. We couldn't escape sin's snare. Think of it as if Satan had kidnapped you and was holding you as a hostage. Your release depended on someone paying a ransom. That's exactly what Christ did on the cross. He paid the ransom to redeem you (literally, to purchase you back) from the slave market of sin. The ransom price was high. It cost Christ His life (1 Peter 1:18-19).

Destruction. Satan was behind all of this sin stuff from the beginning. (Remember the serpent in the Garden of Eden?) Christ's death on the cross not only freed us from Satan's bondage but also demolished Satan in the process (Hebrews 2:14-15).

Perfection. In the Old Testament times, the priest had to offer a sacrifice on behalf of the people each year (in a ceremony referred to as the Day of Atonement). When Christ died on the cross, His sacrifice was enough to cover the sins of all people—past, present, and future.

> *Now, once for all time, he has appeared at the end of the age to remove sin by his own death as a sacrifice. And just as each person is destined to die once and after that comes judgment, so also Christ died once for all time as a sacrifice to take away the sins of many people* (Hebrews 9:26-28).

Salvation comes from what Jesus did without any help from us. He did everything that was necessary. Nothing else is required of us but to accept what He did for us.

*W*hat Does the Cross Say?

To God the cross says "enough" because God is satisfied. To humankind the cross says "forgiven" because we are. To Satan the cross says "shut up" because it puts God and us on the same side.

—*Fred Sanders*

The Resurrection of Jesus

The death of Jesus on the cross for you is central to your Christian life, and it is central to a larger story, one that includes the resurrection. Without the resurrection of Jesus, the cross would be meaningless because without the resurrection, there would be...

No Messiah. The true Messiah must fulfill every single prophecy, including the prophecy that the Messiah would die for the sins of the world (Isaiah 53:7-8) and that God would raise Him from the dead (Psalm 16:9-10). If Jesus did not come back to life after dying, He wasn't the Messiah. And if Jesus wasn't the Messiah, both Jews and Gentiles alike (any non-Jew is a Gentile) are still waiting for salvation.

No eternal life. Jesus didn't just say He would be resurrected. He also said we would be resurrected too:

> *I am the resurrection and the life. Anyone who believes in me will live, even after dying. Everyone who lives in me and believes in me will never ever die* (John 11:25-26).

If Jesus wasn't raised from the dead, He was a big fat liar, and we have no hope of enjoying eternal life.

No heaven. Do you think about heaven? We human beings can have no loftier thought. Now think about this: Without the resurrection of Jesus from the dead, we'll never get there. Jesus made it very clear that He is our connection to heaven. He not only is designing and building a place in heaven for all who believe in Him but also has promised to take us there personally (John 14:1-4). As wonderful and amazing as heaven sounds, it doesn't mean a thing if Jesus is still dead.

No hope. The bottom line is that without the resurrection, we're sunk. Oh yeah, we can appreciate the teachings of Jesus, we can do our best to imitate the life of Jesus, and we can feel good about living good lives here on earth. But what good is that if we have no hope of a life with Jesus beyond this one? If Christians are merely putting their faith in a dead guy, they are just what Ted Turner once called them—a bunch of losers. Or as the apostle Paul put it, we are to be pitied (1 Corinthians 15:19).

Let's Talk About Miracles

Miracles in the Bible—especially the miracle of the resurrection of Jesus Christ from the dead—are a problem for many people, including many Christians. To those who operate within a worldview of naturalism or relativism, a miracle is a violation of natural law (remember, naturalism by definition excludes the supernatural). They discount the testimony of the eyewitnesses because the events happened so long ago during a time when people were more prone to believe myths and fables. (However, they don't seem to question the eyewitness accounts of other people who lived in ancient times, such as Julius Caesar.) Even some theists would rather not bother with any proofs for miracles because they don't consider them convincing. They would rather accept the miracles and the resurrection of Jesus by faith without any corroborating evidence.

So how should we appeal to miracles to argue for the existence of God and Jesus? According to our philosopher friend Doug Geivett, when offering a defense of the life of Christ, it's not a good idea to put a lot of weight on just one kind of evidence (in this case, miracles) for the simple reason that it's hard to overcome "worldview commitments" people have that exclude supernaturalism.

A preferred approach is to use a cumulative case approach. (Sound familiar?) Start with the probability that God (who is supernatural) exists and then look for *anomalies* (another word for miracles) that cannot be explained naturalistically (such as the resurrection of Christ). If you start with the premise that God exists, you can then proceed to the idea that miracles are not only possible, but exactly what you would expect from a supernatural being. For if a supernatural being wanted to reveal Himself to His created beings, would He not do so in the form of miracles, which are by definition supernatural events? When you look at miracles in this way, they act like a kind of "divine signature, confirming God's actual sponsorship of a particular revelation claim."[5]

Did the Resurrection Really Happen?

The resurrection is so important to your faith that you need to know that it's reasonable to believe the resurrection happened, just like the Bible said. Yes, you can take God's word for it, but you can also investigate the facts for yourself and see that they support what the Bible says. That way, if you are ever asked about your Christian hope (and we hope that you are), you will be ready to explain it (1 Peter 3:15).

Here are three proofs for the resurrection of Jesus Christ. Again, look at these pieces of evidence like strands in a rope, each one working together with the others to present a cumulative case for the miracle of the resurrection.

1. The Proof of the Empty Tomb

Ever since the resurrection, people who oppose Christianity have disputed the empty tomb. Here's the reasoning: If you disprove the resurrection by showing that the tomb wasn't really empty—or that it was empty for a reason other than the resurrection—then you can discredit Christianity. We don't disagree. So let's look at the three most popular explanations for the empty tomb (other than the resurrection) and see if they hold water.

Explanation 1: Jesus didn't really die. There are those who believe that Jesus merely "swooned" from the torture, pain, and exhaustion of the crucifixion, and then He was buried alive. After three days, He was revived by the cool air of the tomb, and He walked out under His own power. Of course, if you believe that, you also believe that Jesus not only survived the crucifixion but also was able to extricate Himself from 70 pounds of tightly wound grave clothes, knock down a 1000-pound rock, and overpower a bunch of armed Roman guards—all without the benefit of food and water for three days.

⏀esus Can't Lie

Max Anders adds one more objection to this theory. "If Jesus had somehow recovered from a deathlike swoon, He would have been a liar." This would have been completely inconsistent with His character. "Would a person of the integrity revealed in the Gospels have encouraged His followers to preach and base their lives on a lie?" Besides, Jesus is God, and God cannot lie (Titus 1:2).

Explanation 2: The disciples stole the body. This theory was first proposed by the religious leaders (the very same ones who ordered the crucifixion). Knowing that the resurrection would ignite the Christian movement, they bribed the Roman soldiers assigned to guard the tomb to spread the rumor that the disciples stole the body of Jesus (Matthew 28:12-15). This theory is weak for a couple of reasons. First, it's unlikely that the religious leaders could have convinced all the guards to go along with their little scheme. Second, some of the guards would have certainly noticed the commotion caused by the disciples trying to pry back a huge stone and steal a corpse.

Even if the disciples were able to pull off this amazing feat of strength and daring, why would they die for a lie? Paul Little writes, "Each of the disciples faced the test of torture and martyrdom for his statements and beliefs. People will die for what they *believe* to be true, though it may actually be false. They do not, however, die for what they know is a lie."

Explanation 3: The disciples were hallucinating. They wanted so much to believe that Jesus was alive that they saw something (or someone) that wasn't really there. This theory has a couple of problems. First, the disciples weren't expecting Jesus to rise from the dead. In fact, when reports of the resurrection first came to the disciples, they didn't believe them (Mark 16:11). Second, the same hallucination could not possibly occur to hundreds of people in several locations over a period of 40 days. If anything, such a consistent report from that many people is a proof for the resurrection, not a refutation.

2. The Proof of Hundreds of Eyewitnesses

Jesus clearly wanted people to see Him after His resurrection, and hundreds did. The Bible records ten different appearances from the time He rose from the dead until His ascension into heaven 40 days later. He appeared to individuals (such as Mary Magdalene— see John 20:11-18); He appeared to two men walking to Emmaus

(Luke 24:13-32); He appeared to the disciples, who couldn't believe their eyes (Luke 24:35-43); and He appeared to more than 500 people at one time (1 Corinthians 15:6).

3. The Proof of Transformed Believers

Once Jesus convinced the disciples that He wasn't a ghost, that He was alive, and that He was going to heaven to prepare a place for them, they went from being frightened to being fearless. This is what happens when the living Jesus truly gets ahold of ordinary people, and it's one of the major proofs of the resurrection. The book of Acts tells the dramatic story of these transformed disciples. The Holy Spirit came upon them in power as Jesus promised (Acts 1:8), and they proclaimed the message that Jesus was alive. The power of the resurrection didn't stop with just those who saw Jesus for themselves. In the 2000 years since, it has been the power to change lives.

Where Is Jesus Now?

Jesus is in heaven now, "in the place of honor next to God, and all the angels and authorities and powers are bowing before him" (1 Peter 3:22). Does this mean Jesus is no longer here on earth with us? Not in body, but He is here spiritually, living in all who have invited Him into their lives (Colossians 1:27).

What Is Jesus Doing?

Just because Jesus is at the right hand of God doesn't mean He is sitting around, biding His time until He returns to earth in the second coming. Jesus is engaged in at least three different very important activities, all of which concern you:

- *Preparing a place for you.* You can be sure that Jesus is engaged in the most spectacular construction project in the history of the universe: He's preparing heaven—for you (John 14:2).

- *Praying for you.* Actually, the Bible says that Jesus is pleading to the Father on your behalf (Romans 8:34). Who better to plead your case before God? No one knows you better than Jesus (Hebrews 4:15-16).

• *Keeping the universe going for you.* There's a reason why the universe functions so beautifully: Jesus is holding all creation together (Colossians 1:17).

Jesus Is Coming Back

There's one final thing Jesus has promised to do, and that's to come to Earth a second time (that's why they call it the second coming). Jesus said, "When everything is ready, I will come and get you, so that you will always be with me where I am" (John 14:3). This isn't a fairy tale. This is real. And it's the most exciting prospect you could ever have in life, made possible by the resurrection of Jesus Christ.

> *God raised Jesus Christ from the dead. Now we live with great expectation* (1 Peter 1:3).

What's That Again?

1. Many voices are competing for the true picture of Jesus. These perspectives are enormously popular, capturing the imaginations of tens of millions of spiritual seekers.

2. One of the more popular voices is the Jesus Seminar. The purpose of the seminar is to recover the authentic Jesus by peeling back the layers of supernatural myths and legends that are presented in the Gospels and believed by Christians today.

3. These alternate views of Jesus present Him as natural, living in everyone as a kind of "divine light," and they are politically correct. However, these views do not correspond with the reality of who Jesus is.

4. The evidence that Jesus is the person the Bible portrays Him to be is corroborated by His disciples, by

the people who opposed Him, and by historians. We can trust these eyewitnesses because of three criteria: embarrassment, dissimilarity, and multiple attestations.

5. Jesus made a remarkable claim for Himself—that He was God—and backed it with miracles. Jesus also fulfilled many prophecies made about Him hundreds of years before He appeared on Earth. And He had the endorsement of God.

6. Even though Jesus declared Himself to be fully God, there is ample evidence that Jesus was also fully human, except that He lived a sinless life.

7. The idea that Jesus is both divine and human is difficult to grasp, but not impossible or illogical. When Jesus was on earth, His deity was not limited by His humanity, nor was His humanity overshadowed by His deity.

8. The resurrection is the central event in the life of Christ and the single most important event in the life of the Christian. If the resurrection did not happen, the Christian faith is useless. On the other hand, because the resurrection did happen, we have hope of eternal life.

9. The proofs for the resurrection of Jesus Christ are like strands in a rope, each one working together with the others to present a cumulative case for this miracle.

10. Jesus is no longer on Earth physically, but He is here spiritually, living in all who have invited Him into their lives.

Dig Deeper

At the end of his Gospel, John talks about the things Jesus did. He concludes, "If they were all written down, I suppose the whole world could not contain the books that would be written" (John 21:25). What a great statement! No doubt more books about Jesus have been written than about any other person in history. Unfortunately, we only have room for three suggestions:

The Case for Christ by Lee Strobel is quickly becoming a classic. Lee uses the format of an investigator checking out the evidence for Jesus. In the process, he interviews some of the most respected and trustworthy Jesus scholars in the world today.

Jesus Under Fire, edited by J.P. Moreland and Mike Wilkins, is a collection of essays by scholars who critique the modern scholarship that has reinvented the historical Jesus.

Perhaps the most popular and user-friendly book ever written about Jesus (other than the Bible) is *More Than a Carpenter* by Josh McDowell. This book includes some of the evidences for Jesus, but even more compelling is Josh's personal focus on the person who changed his life.

■ ■ ■

*Q*uestions for *R*eflection and *D*iscussion

1. What do you think of the Jesus Seminar? Had you ever heard of this group of scholars? If someone were to cite a member of this group as a credible resource for information about Jesus, what would you say in response?

2. Read 1 Corinthians 15:17-19 again. Why should this bold statement by Paul give you confidence that the resurrection of Jesus actually happened? Why should this statement give you hope for your own future in Christ?

3. Why do you think it is so appealing for people to accept Jesus as a "divine light" present in all people rather than the second person in the Trinity? What is it about the Jesus of

the Bible that offends people and prompts them to develop these alternative portraits of Him?

4. Of the three groups of eyewitness to the life of Jesus—the disciples, the opposition, and the historians—which one carries the most weight for you? Why is the cumulative effect of all three groups more credible than any one group standing on its own in terms of giving us an accurate portrayal of Jesus?

5. Have you ever struggled with the so-called "hard sayings" of Jesus? When you encounter one in your reading of Scripture, what do you normally do? Do you overlook these portions of Scripture, or do you try to find out what they mean? Where can you go for help?

6. Why is it so important that Jesus claimed to be God? What if He had never made this claim? What proof did Jesus offer to back up His claim?

7. Why is it so important that Jesus was fully human as well as being fully God? What proof do we have that Jesus never sinned? Briefly explain how Jesus' deity wasn't limited by His humanity. Why wasn't His humanity overshadowed by His deity?

8. Did our little talk on miracles help you understand how and why miracles are possible? Explain why miracles are what you would expect from God.

9. Which of the proofs for the resurrection of Christ is the most convincing to you? Why does it help to see these proofs as strands in a rope rather than links in a chain?

Moving On...

We've come to the end of part 2 in our study on the evidence for your faith. We've pretty much covered the basics, and in one sense you could probably stop here and feel like you've gotten your money's worth (especially if someone gave you this book). But in another sense our journey is incomplete for one simple reason: Some difficult and nagging questions confront the Christian faith, and often these questions, if left unanswered, can negate all of the evidence we've already talked about.

So in part 3, we want to address some of the more common questions and objections that keep many people from even considering the possibility that God exists or, if He does exist, that He is worth knowing.

Part III
Faith and Doubt

Introduction to Part III

*D*oubt is a tangible and real human emotion, as real as love or fear. Like fear, doubt can keep you from doing certain things. That's both good and bad. It's good when doubt prevents you from doing something you probably shouldn't, like buying an extended warranty on a $50 electronic device (that's a good thing to doubt). But doubt can be bad when it keeps you from doing something you probably should.

When it comes to God, doubt can also be both good and bad. It's a good thing when you doubt or question something you hear or read about God that just doesn't seem right, so you take it upon yourself to verify the truthfulness of the statement. When the apostle Paul and his ministry partner came to the region of Berea to do some teaching, the people "listened eagerly to Paul's message." But they had some doubts, so "they searched the Scriptures day after day to see if Paul and Silas were teaching the truth" (Acts 17:11). Rather than take offense, Paul and Silas commend them. Just because someone claims to have the truth doesn't mean they do. Doubt motivates you to sort truth from error.

But doubt can also play a negative role if it keeps you from doing an investigation into the claims of Christianity. If the Bereans had simply said to Paul, "We don't believe you," and then failed to do their due diligence, their doubt would have been counterproductive.

Reasons for Doubting God

Why do you have doubts about God in the first place? We can think of a few reasons. Here are some common doubts in two categories: intellectual and emotional.

Intellectual Doubts

- *Knowing God.* Very often you doubt God or something He has said in His word because you don't have enough information or knowledge. You haven't studied and you haven't done your due diligence, so you form opinions rather than doing your homework.

- *Understanding God.* You may have knowledge about God, but you don't understand certain things, such as how a loving God could allow suffering and evil. Other specific things about God (like the Trinity) may not make sense to you, so you have doubts about your faith.

- *Believing God.* This was Adam and Eve's problem. They doubted that God's word was true. The same may be true for you. You may doubt something in God's word because you don't believe it or because you don't think it applies to you. Sometimes you say, "I don't believe you," not because you don't know or understand, but because you prefer something else. It's the same way with God. Some of your doubts are there because you don't really want to do what God says.

Emotional Doubts

- *Disillusionment.* Sometimes other people let you down (it's inevitable), and you feel deeply hurt or wounded. When this happens, you may choose doubt over the possibility of being disappointed again. Some people doubt God because of a strained relationship with their fathers. If they can't trust their father on earth, how can they trust their Father in heaven?

- *Fear.* You may have a tendency to focus on your own weakness rather than God's strength. You may not feel up to the task God has called you to do, so instead of stepping up to the challenge, you hide in your doubts.

- *Discouragement.* You may be weary from the cares and pressures of life, so you get to a place where you doubt the very one who can help you overcome your problems.

Overcoming Doubt

If the issue is a lack of information or knowledge, you need to do some study (which is what you are doing by reading this book—good for you!). The next four chapters deal with questions that can cause you to doubt or question your faith if they are not resolved. You may not be able to resolve every problem or answer every question, but you will make progress if you stay at it and gain knowledge about God and your faith. Faith includes more than knowledge, but without knowledge, your faith will be overly dependent on your feelings. As the saying goes, "feed your faith, and your doubts will starve to death" (or at least be less hungry).

If the issue is a lack of understanding, ask God to give you wisdom. Guess what? He will do it (James 1:5). Spiritual understanding is a little different from knowledge in that you don't get it by cracking open a book or doing a search on the Internet. It comes through the Holy Spirit, and that means we have to ask for it (Colossians 1:9).

If the issue is unbelief, you need to ask God for help. Once a man brought his son to Jesus for healing. He wanted so much for Jesus to heal his son, but he struggled to believe it was possible. "Anything is possible if a person believes," Jesus told him. And the man replied, "I do believe, but help me overcome my unbelief!" (Mark 9:23-24).

If the issues are disillusionment, fear, or discouragement, you may need spiritual refreshment. Often a spiritual retreat or conference can be just what you need when your spiritual gas tank is low. Or you may need to simply ask some stronger and more mature Christians to help you. We can't do this thing called the Christian life on our own. We need other people to encourage us and pray for us, we need teachers who will instruct us, and we need mentors who can inspire us. You need to be proactive in finding encouragers and mentors. Don't be afraid that you are going to bother people with your requests for encouragement, prayer, teaching, and mentoring. You will be surprised at how willing people are to help, especially if you approach them with humility and respect.

Most of all—and we can't emphasize this enough—ask God for help. He is the ultimate encourager, prayer partner, teacher, and mentor. When you have doubts about God, seek Him all the more. We alluded to James 1:5 earlier. Here it is in case you didn't look it up:

> *If you need wisdom, ask our generous God, and he will give it to you. He will not rebuke you for asking* (James 1:5).

Chapter 7

The fact of suffering undoubtedly constitutes the single greatest challenge to the
Christian faith, and has been in every generation. Its distribution and degree appear
to be entirely random and therefore unfair.
Sensitive spirits ask if it can possibly be
reconciled with God's justice and love.

—*John R.W. Stott*

Open any newspaper, turn on your television, check the headlines on Google or Yahoo, and in between the celebrity gossip, sports scandals, and economic woes you'll find stories of war, ethnic cleansing, shootings, torture, kidnappings, terrorism, rape, and child abuse—in short, *evil*. On top of that, from time to time you'll be confronted with the news of yet another natural disaster— a hurricane, tornado, tsunami, earthquake, or fire—that destroys untold lives. As if that weren't enough, you are constantly being reminded that vast numbers of people in certain parts of the world are afflicted with poverty, disease, and starvation.

How do you account for this seemingly endless supply of evil that produces human suffering on such a massive scale? How do you explain it? We'll be honest. Those are very difficult questions with no easy answers. But you can take one approach that will help you sort through the problem of evil and the suffering it produces. That's what this chapter is all about.

Evil and Suffering

John Marks started out life like many believers. He was born in the Bible Belt and was born again as a teenager. He went to a faith-based college with the intention of serving the Lord, but shortly thereafter abandoned his faith. It wasn't a dramatic turn-around as much as a drift into disillusionment, mainly because of the other Christians he encountered.

After graduating from college, John became a journalist, working first as a reporter for *U.S. News & World Report* and then as a producer for Morley Safer on *60 Minutes*. While he was on a special assignment for the legendary television program, his life took a dramatic turn. "I interviewed a couple for a piece on the Left Behind series, the bestselling novels about the apocalypse," he says. "At the end of that meeting, they asked me a question: Would I be left behind? In other words, had I accepted Jesus as my savior, or would I go to hell?"

After that fateful meeting, John embarked on a personal quest to understand both the meaning and the object of faith. He even wrote a book called *Reasons to Believe*. The book's subtitle, *One Man's Journey Among the Evangelicals and the Faith He Left Behind,* tells you that his motivation for writing it came from the question posed by the well-meaning couple. Being a good reporter, John interviewed dozens of people of faith. At times he was moved by their sincerity of heart and their desire to help make the world a better place. In the end, however, neither the positive experiences of faith professed by some Christians nor the evidences for faith offered by others were enough to nudge him back to the belief he once embraced.

The final statement of John's book speaks volumes about his decision to no longer believe. For him, the reasons to believe aren't good enough to overcome a problem that is for him—as it is for many people—insurmountable. Here are his words:

> The twentieth century, my century, asks its own terrible questions. Bosnia? Hiroshima? Rwanda? Armenia? So many people, and so many Christians, looking away when the Jews of Europe were led to their deaths? So many people, and so many Christians, embracing racist policies all over the world during the era of colonialism, policies that led to murder and catastrophe on a cosmic scale? One species allowed its full, unfettered measure of violence for so long? A god has overseen this nightmare? A god whose divine plan accounts for all the torment, horror, and loss visited upon ourselves over the course of this century, and all centuries? And it's not over yet, surely. Someone else, some other nation, is already preparing itself for the next slaughter, in which I do not want to voluntarily, unnecessarily implicate myself. A god who can't stop it has no right to my loyalty or my belief.[1]

The Problem of Evil

We mentioned earlier in the book that the two most vexing issues that keep people from believing in God are the hiddenness of God and the problem of evil. For the first issue, the question is this: If God exists, why doesn't He show Himself more plainly? We think you will agree that the cumulative case arguments for God, the Bible, and Jesus provide a reasonable answer: God has revealed Himself through His world and His word.

But even if you are confident that God exists and has revealed Himself, the question generated by the other issue—the problem of evil—can stop you cold: If God is loving and powerful, why does He allow evil?

That's just one version of the question prompted by the problem of evil. For a former believer turned skeptic (like John Marks), the question goes deeper: Why should I believe in a God that would allow evil and suffering?

And for the atheist, the question turns into a negative conclusion about God's very existence: It is impossible for a loving and all-powerful God to co-exist with evil. Evil exists, so God does not.

*T*hree Faces of Evil

Theologians and philosophers generally distinguish between three kinds of evil: *metaphysical evil* (the lack of absolute perfection in created things), *moral evil* (caused by the free choices of moral agents), and *natural evil* (brought about by natural causes). In this chapter we're going to deal with all three kinds of evil, although our main emphasis will be moral evil.

The questions about evil and God are no longer confined to theology. The problem of evil today is philosophical, political, moral, and spiritual. And people are no longer content to focus only on how we can stop evil (although that remains an important issue). Today the bigger focus is on trying to respond to evil.

Various Worldview Perspectives on Evil

The Christian, the skeptic, and the atheist approach the problem of evil from different perspectives, mainly because each one operates from a different worldview. (Aren't you glad we talked about worldviews early in the book?) Here is the perspective each worldview offers:

Christians and Other Theists

These people take evil very personally because they believe in a personal God. They often have a hard time understanding how a loving and powerful God would allow evil to take place, especially when Christians find themselves as victims of horrific evil or when they witness evil happening to someone else. Without an adequate response to evil, a Christian's faith can be damaged or destroyed.

How do you respond to the Christian who is dealing with evil? The proper response involves love, care, and empathy—not philosophy or theology. We will expand on this response at the end of the chapter.

ℒousy Christian Responses to Evil

If you are a Christian, you have plenty of opportunities to respond to the problem of evil. Whenever someone asks you why a friend has cancer, you have an opportunity to respond. Whenever people wonder why innocent children in Africa have to suffer disease and starvation, you have an opportunity to respond. Whenever the people in your workplace talk about the latest school shooting, you have an opportunity to respond. We haven't yet given you any positive responses to evil (that's coming), but we can give you some responses that are downright lousy:

"Evil is necessary." This response comes out of the idea that a diamond sparkles when placed against a black background. In other words, good looks better when evil things happen. Or to push it further, good could not exist without evil. This is a really dumb response because it's based on a totally false premise. Good is an absolute property, and it *can* exist without evil. On the other hand, evil could not exist without good. Therefore, evil is unnecessary.

"This is the best of all possible worlds." This is like saying, "Well, at least you have your health," to people who have just lost their jobs, their marriage, their house, and their dog. This is definitely *not* the best of all possible worlds. According to Norman Geisler, it's actually the worst of all possible worlds. It's as bad as God will let it be.

"Evil is a punishment for sin." Unfortunately, this lousy response comes out of the mouths of way too many Christians, including some high-profile Christians who undoubtedly make God cringe every time they say this. Jesus refuted this response when His disciples asked Him if some people died because of their sins. "No way, no how," Jesus replied. (That's our paraphrase. You can read the story yourself in Luke 13:1-5.)

"God is using this horrible thing for your own good." This is the number one worst response a Christian can give to anyone going through a difficult time. It's true that God uses all things—even the bad things—for the

ultimate good of those who love Him (see Romans 8:28), but this is a lousy response to anyone in the middle of a very difficult situation.

Skeptics

These people look at all the evil in the world and come to the conclusion that the existence of God is highly improbable. This is a common perspective that can be fatal to faith if it's not dealt with.

How do you respond to the skeptic who is dealing with evil? Ask this very important question: Might the cumulative evidence for the existence of God possibly outweigh the negative evidence against the existence of God? If the answer is yes, then God might exist, even though there may not be an immediate explanation for the existence of evil.

Atheists

Naturalists argue that the existence of evil proves the Christian God is logically impossible, mainly because the Christian God is by definition all-good, all-powerful, and all-knowing.

How do you respond to the atheist who is dealing with evil? We're going to devote an entire section to this response because it deals with the question that all three kinds of people—Christians, skeptics, and atheists—are asking about God and evil: Why doesn't He stop it?

> Because evil is atheism's greatest objection to the existence of God, evil is theism's greatest problem.

Why Doesn't God Stop Evil?

This question goes to the heart of all three worldviews because people with all three worldviews ask it. Ironically, thoughtful skeptics and atheists are confident they have an answer, but most Christians struggle to come up with one (you would think it would be the other way around).

To illustrate what we mean, here is the classic argument offered by many skeptics, moral relativists, and former believers like John Marks:

An all-powerful God would be able to eliminate evil.

> An all-good God would want to eliminate evil.
>
> An all-knowing God would know how to eliminate evil.
>
> But evil exists.
>
> Therefore, God is not all-powerful, all-good, nor all-knowing.

Notice that this conclusion leaves the door open for God to exist. But it's a cynical conclusion because a God who is not all-powerful, all-good, nor all-knowing is just a god and not really God.

The classic argument offered by atheists follows the same logical sequence, only with one additional line:

> An all-powerful God would be able to eliminate evil.
>
> An all-good God would want to eliminate evil.
>
> An all-knowing God would know how to eliminate evil.
>
> But evil exists.
>
> Therefore, God is not all-powerful, all-good, nor all-knowing.
>
> Therefore, the God of Christianity does not exist.

A Reasonable Response

So how should Christians respond to this argument? For starters, they should start with the points they agree with:

> An all-powerful God would be able to eliminate evil.
>
> An all-good God would want to eliminate evil.
>
> An all-knowing God would know how to eliminate evil.
>
> But evil exists.

Then it's a matter of looking at the premises connected to the first three statements and see if they hold water. Let's take them one at a time.

An all-powerful God would be able to eliminate evil. This statement assumes that God can do anything, but that's a false premise. To say God is all-powerful isn't to imply He can do something that violates His character or a defining quality. For example, God can't lie (because He is holy). God can't make a mistake (because He is perfect). And God can't cease to exist (because He is eternal).

Here's something else God can't do: God cannot make free moral agents who can never go wrong. This statement is part of a relatively recent argument, called the free-will defense, developed by the philosopher Alvin Plantinga. It goes like this:

> A world with moral good is better than a world with no moral good.
>
> Only free agents can do moral good.
>
> Even God cannot create free moral agents who can never go wrong.
>
> Therefore, to create a world with moral good but no moral evil is not within God's power.

At the heart of this argument is the idea that God cannot create truly free moral agents who do not have the freedom to do wrong. If they didn't have that freedom, they wouldn't be free moral agents. To put it another way, even an all-powerful God "cannot forcibly prevent sin without removing our freedom."[2]

An all-good God would want to eliminate evil. This statement fails to recognize the true definition of good as it relates to God. Goodness is more than kindness. It's more than trying to make people happy. As Wayne Grudem defines it, "The goodness of God is the final standard of good, and all that God is and does is worthy of approval."[3] When God created the universe, He pronounced it good at every stage. When He was finished, "God looked over all he had made, and he saw that it was very good!" (Genesis 1:31).

This goodness includes God's creation of free moral agents, people who have the freedom to do wrong along with the freedom to do good. And what is the highest good for all free beings? It's love (Matthew 22:36-40), which is impossible without freedom, whether we freely love God or our fellow human beings. Peter Kreeft puts it this way:

> Why didn't God create a world without human freedom? Because that would have been a world without humans. Would it have been a place without hate? Yes. A place without suffering? Yes. But it also

would have been a world without love, which is the highest value in the universe. That highest good never could have been experienced. Real love—our love of God and our love of each other—must involve a choice. But with the granting of that choice comes the possibility that people would choose instead to hate.[4]

An all-knowing God would know how to eliminate evil. This statement assumes that God doesn't know how to stop evil. Isn't that a bit arrogant of someone to think that they know what God knows or doesn't know? Think about yourself for a moment. The fact that you don't do something doesn't mean you don't know *how* to do something. The same principle applies to God. He doesn't eliminate evil, but that doesn't mean He doesn't know how.

God Is Being Patient

Is it possible that God, who knows how to eliminate evil, is holding off for our sake? That's exactly what Peter says:

> *The Lord isn't really being slow about his promise, as some people think. No, he is being patient for your sake. He does not want anyone to be destroyed, but wants everyone to repent* (2 Peter 3:9).

Here's the deal. God knows how to deal with evil, but He is being patient "for your sake." He is choosing not to act on His knowledge of how to destroy evil because He loves us, and He knows that destroying evil would mean destroying us. God wants us to exercise our freedom—the freedom He gave us—to turn away from sin toward Him (that's what repentance is). Because God is good, and because His goodness is tied to His love, God is giving humankind more time until He deals with evil once for all.

> *But the day of the Lord will come as unexpectedly as a thief. Then the heavens will pass away with a terrible noise, and the very elements themselves will disappear in fire, and the earth and everything on it will be found to deserve judgment* (2 Peter 3:10).

God isn't eliminating evil right now, but that doesn't mean He never will. At some point in the future, God will deal with evil once for all. "If we restate the argument to correct this oversight in temporal perspective," write Norm Geisler and Ron Brooks, "it turns out to be an argument that vindicates God."[5] Here's what that argument looks like:

> If God is all-good, He *will* defeat evil.
>
> If God is all-powerful, He *can* defeat evil.
>
> Evil is not *yet* defeated.
>
> Therefore, God *can* and *will one day* defeat evil.

Can you live with that future promise? Admittedly, it takes faith because you can't yet see when that will happen. But it will happen. Evil will be defeated. Geisler and Brooks make this conclusion:

> There is no question here that if it has not yet happened and God is as we suppose Him to be, then we simply haven't waited long enough. God isn't finished yet. The final chapter has not been written. Apparently God would rather wrestle with our rebellious wills than to reign supreme over rocks and trees. Those who want a quicker resolution to the conflict will have to wait.[6]

What About Natural Evil?

Act of God is the phrase we often use to describe natural disasters. Even insurance companies use the term to designate major natural catastrophes: hurricanes, earthquakes, tsunamis, and the like. Is that accurate? Does God act to bring them about? Does He actually cause natural evil?

Interestingly, one answer lies in a variation of the free-will defense we just discussed. It's called the free-process defense. Just as God cannot make free moral agents who can never go wrong, God cannot make a dynamic world in which natural evil can never occur. Why? Because free moral agents can make free moral choices only in a dynamic world where natural elements interact in a dynamic way. If the natural world were static, free moral choices would not be possible.

In a dynamic world, God grants a qualified self-sufficiency to nature to operate according to the laws He designed. This means that even though God is sovereign (nothing happens outside of His control), He created an open system of causes and effects. (An example of this is gravity. If you jump off a cliff—the cause—you will feel gravity's effect when you hit bottom.)

God's transcendence means that He is *super*natural—or above nature. God is not nature (or Mother Nature), nor is He bound by natural law. But God can intervene in nature supernaturally with a *miracle*. Scripture offers us several examples of God acting miraculously in nature. Noah's flood may be the most striking example, but a more personal incident occurred when Jesus calmed the stormy sea simply by saying, "Silence, be still." This scared the you-know-what out of His disciples, who happened to be in the boat during the storm. "Who is this man?" they asked each other. "Even the wind and waves obey him!" (Mark 4:39-41). They weren't terrified so much of the miraculous act as they were of the realization that they were in the presence of the living God.

Sin and Natural Evil

Finally, what about sin and natural evil? Is there a connection between the two? Paul seems to make the connection when he writes:

> The creation looks forward to the day when it will join God's children in glorious freedom from death and decay. For we know that all creation has been groaning as in the pains of childbirth right up to the present time. And we believers also groan, even though we have the Holy Spirit within us as a foretaste of future glory, for we long for our bodies to be released from sin and suffering (Romans 8:21-23).

Even creation is under the weight of sin and suffering, brought into this world by rebellious acts of free moral agents. It isn't that God has lost control. He is merely allowing the natural world He created to operate in a dynamic way. Despite the natural evil that does occur from time to time, our finely tuned world functions superbly 99 percent of the time, allowing us not only to survive but also to thrive. We may never fully understand the reason why God allows natural evil to happen, but we can take comfort in the fact that He is still in control, still offering His mighty hand to those who put their trust in Him.

> *The Lord rules over the floodwaters. The Lord reigns as king forever. The Lord gives his people strength. The Lord blesses them with peace* (Psalm 29:10-11).

Satan and Sin and Natural Evil

Dr. Gary DeWeese offers an interesting take on the topic of sin and its relationship to natural evil.[7] He starts with the idea that God's creation itself was very good. The dynamic system of the natural world was in equilibrium. Then Satan, the powerful angel who rebelled against God, was cast out of heaven and exiled to earth along with one-third of the heavenly host—thereafter known as demons—who followed Satan's rebellion.

We know that spiritual beings (demons and angels) can have an effect on the natural world. According to DeWeese's theory, Satan and his demonic horde may have upset the equilibrium of nature when they arrived on earth, and this dis-equilibrium already could have been in effect when Adam was created. Indeed, God told Adam and Eve to "fill the earth and subdue it" (Genesis 1:28 NIV). If the earth were still in perfect equilibrium, why would God tell Adam to subdue it?

To summarize, a free-process argument is a logically possible explanation for why God allows natural evil, just as a free-will argument is a logically possible explanation for why God allows moral evil. In both cases, evil ultimately may be due to sin. Because God created free moral agents in a dynamic natural world, evil exists. But that evil doesn't rule out the possibility of a loving, powerful God.

Why Does God Allow Evil and Suffering?

God may not cause evil, but He allows it, which begs the question why. What possible purpose could God have for allowing bad things to happen to good people? Well, for one thing, that statement—made famous by Rabbi Kushner in his book *Why Bad Things Happen to Good People* (his basic answer, by the way, is that God can't stop evil)—assumes that people are good. People are capable of doing good things, but the Bible clearly shows that all people are sinners (Romans 3:23). So the first thing we need to acknowledge in this discussion of why God allows evil is this: Sinful people are not only capable of doing evil, but are also responsible for the moral evil in the world. C.S. Lewis makes this point in his book *The Problem of Pain:*

> When souls become wicked they will certainly use this possibility to hurt one another, and this, perhaps, accounts for four-fifths of the sufferings of men. It is men, not God, who have produced racks, whips, prisons, slavery, guns, bayonets, and bombs; it is by human avarice or human stupidity, not by the churlishness of nature, that we have poverty and overwork.[8]

In Lewis's paradigm, the other "one-fifth" of human suffering is caused by natural evil, which includes disease. That doesn't make the suffering caused by human wickedness any more tolerable, but it helps us make some sense of the source. Still, it all adds up to human suffering, and it cries out for an answer to our question: Why does God allow evil?

God's Purpose for Evil and Suffering

We will be the first to admit that we don't have some kind of special insight into the mind of God and know what His purpose is. We just believe that as a holy, loving, all-powerful, all-good, all-knowing God, He does have a good reason for allowing evil to exist in our world and inflict the suffering it does.

Here are some possible purposes God may have for allowing evil and the suffering it produces. See if you don't identify with one or more of these.

Suffering Can Make Us Stronger

You've no doubt heard the expression, "No pain, no gain." We're not trying to reduce the nature of pain and suffering to a mere slogan, but we think you get the point. Something about hardship, difficulty, and pain can sometimes strengthen us. Suffering and setbacks can also bring us closer as families, friends, and communities. On the one-year anniversary of the Virginia Tech massacre, the worst shooting

> Complete success alienates a man from his fellows, but suffering makes kinsmen of us all.
>
> —*Elbert Hubbard*

in United States history, more than 30,000 people gathered for a candlelight vigil to honor the victims. Evil and the suffering it produces can make us stronger.

Some Evil Helps Bring About Greater Good

We can find many examples of this principle at work in Scripture. In one of his letters to the Corinthian church, the apostle Paul recounts the pain and suffering in his life, including a nagging thorn in his flesh, yet he knows that his troubles have made him stronger.

> *That's why I take pleasure in my weaknesses, and in the insults, hardships, persecutions, and troubles that I suffer for Christ. For when I am weak, then I am strong* (2 Corinthians 12:10).

Joseph was sold into slavery by his own brothers and then suffered in prison after being falsely accused. But eventually he was elevated to a position of power and influence, and when he was finally reunited with his brothers, he uttered these immortal words:

> *You intended to harm me, but God intended it all for good. He brought me to this position so I could save the lives of many people* (Genesis 50:20).

And in the greatest example of pain and suffering bringing about greater good, Jesus suffered on the cross and died so that all who believe in Him can have eternal life (John 3:16).

Suffering Can Point Us to God

Have you ever noticed that when things are going well, you have a tendency to drift away from God, and when things are going badly, you get closer to God? You would think that pain and suffering would drive us away from God—and for some people they do. But most people, even hardened cynics, seem to seek God like never before when they are going through terrible suffering and unbearable grief. C.S. Lewis expresses this concept eloquently when he writes: "God whispers to us in our pleasures, speaks in our conscience, but shouts in our pains: it is His megaphone to rouse a deaf world."

*A*ll Will Be Well

A few years ago we took part in a healing service for a dear friend with a deadly brain tumor. He was scheduled for surgery, so a few close friends, including two ministers, gathered at his home. One of the ministers read a well-known passage from the book of James that gives instructions for healing (James 5:14-15). Following the instructions, the ministers anointed our friend with oil, and we all prayed for God's healing. None of us had any doubts that God *could* heal our friend. Still, there were those of us who wondered if God *would* heal him.

The surgery was performed, and the outlook was grim. We continued to pray, hoping for a miracle, but it was not to be. Within five months, our friend passed into eternity. We were sad, of course, but we also had hope. Though God had not healed our friend physically, He had actually done much more. We know this because we visited our friend one month before he died. Physically, he was deteriorating, but there was a sparkle in his eye. As we talked, we asked if he was disappointed that God had not healed him. "Oh, but He has," our friend replied, sitting up as straight as he could. "God has healed me in ways you can't imagine. I don't want you to worry about me. God is in control. All will be well."

Seeing the puzzled expressions on our faces, he continued. "This is how God has healed me. He is using my life to touch others with His love. As long as I live, I want God to use me." Indeed, God used our friend to shine on hundreds of people who saw him in the last weeks of his life. God had healed him, and through that healing, God showed us how much He cares for us all, especially in the middle of our pain and suffering.

God's Answer for Human Suffering

We've examined the argument that Christian theism can't explain why a good and loving and all-powerful God would allow evil. Even though no final answer could satisfy everyone's desire to know why evil and suffering exits, some evidence indicates that evil and suffering do have some benefits. The Christian faith doesn't always give us a reason for each experience of pain and suffering, but it does give us a way to face our difficulties with hope rather than despair.

God Knows What It's Like to Suffer

We may feel like shaking our fists at God when something extraordinarily painful happens to us. The most natural question to ask is, where is God in all of this? On a very personal level, you want to know where God is in your cancer, or your father's stroke, or your baby's birth defect. Or maybe you're going through a painful divorce, or one of your children may be putting your family through hell, or you are at the end of your financial rope. Where is God when it hurts? Does God even care?

Yes, God cares, and He demonstrated just how much He cares when He sent Jesus to enter our world in the form of a human. Here is the text of a hymn sung by the early church that tells us just why Jesus came:

> *Though he was God,*
> *he did not think of equality with God*
> *as something to cling to.*
> *Instead, he gave up his divine privileges;*
> *he took the humble position of a slave*
> *and was born as a human being.*
> *When he appeared in human form,*
> *he humbled himself in obedience to God*
> *and died a criminal's death on a cross*
> (Philippians 2:6-8).

When we think that God neither cares about us nor identifies with us when we suffer and hurt, we forget that the Son of God suffered beyond what any of us can even imagine. From the beginning of His ministry on earth, Jesus knew what He had to do: bear the cumulative sin and sickness and evil and disease and pain of the entire human race. This was the incredible burden Jesus carried. It was His mission, and He knew it (Matthew 16:21).

When we ask, where is God when we suffer? we need only look to Christ, who suffered for us so that ultimately, in the life that follows this temporal existence, we won't have to suffer. Meanwhile, we live imperfectly in an imperfect and sometimes cruel world. And when we suffer, we can take comfort in knowing that we are "partners with Christ" in His suffering (1 Peter 4:13).

> The problem of evil isn't merely a theoretical problem but an intensely practical one. It is not merely the alienation between two concepts, God and evil, but the alienation between a little child and her father when she looks up through tears and asks him, "Why did you let me hurt so bad?" The heart of the problem is not found in words like ours, in a book, but in the words from the cross: "My God, my God, why have you forsaken me?" It is a problem not on paper but on wood.[9]
>
> —*Peter Kreeft*

The Promise of a World Set Free

Knowing that God personally identifies with us in our suffering is just one part of the hope. The other part is the promise that one day, all of the pain and difficulties of this world will give way to a world set free, where "there will be no more death or sorrow or crying or pain" (Revelation 21:4). That is not wishful thinking. That is a hope you can count on. If you have good reason to believe in a God who has revealed Himself through His world and word, and who has promised to deal with evil and suffering once for all, then you can have confidence that what you hope for will actually happen.

What's That Again?

1. The questions about evil and God are no longer confined to theology. The problem of evil today is philosophical, political, moral, and spiritual. People are looking for ways to respond to evil, not just defeat it.

2. The problem of evil is a difficult one for Christians, skeptics, and atheists alike. For the Christian, unanswered questions about evil can damage or destroy faith. For the skeptic, the problem of evil can lead to doubts about God's existence. The atheist uses the problem of evil to prove that God does not exist.

3. People with all three worldviews ask the question, why doesn't God stop evil? That's because all people wonder why an all-powerful God would not be able to eliminate evil, why an all-good God would not want to eliminate evil, and why an all-knowing God would not know how to eliminate evil.

4. The free-will answer to the question of evil hinges on this premise: Even God cannot create free moral agents who can never go wrong. Therefore, to create a world with moral good but no moral evil is not within God's power.

5. The goodness of God includes the creation of free moral agents who can do wrong as well as good. The highest good is love, which is impossible without freedom, whether we freely love God or our fellow human beings.

6. God knows how to deal with evil, but He is being patient for our sake because He loves us.

7. A dynamic natural world is necessary in order for free moral agents to make free moral choices. God is not bound by natural law, but He can intervene in nature supernaturally.

8. We can't see into the mind of God, but He seems to have some purposes for evil: Some suffering makes us stronger, some evil brings about greater good, and suffering can point us to God.

9. God's answer to suffering lies in these two truths as recorded in Scripture: God has suffered in the

> person of Jesus Christ, and God has promised a
> world where there will be no more death or sorrow
> or crying or pain.

Dig Deeper

The best book we have encountered that deals with the problem of evil from a philosophical, political, moral, and spiritual perspective is *Evil and the Justice of God* by N.T. Wright. However, before you dive into that one, we would suggest that you consider these three books that deal with the problem of evil and suffering from a more personal and devotional perspective:

Where Is God When It Hurts? by Philip Yancey has helped millions of people deal with their own suffering as well as the suffering of our world.

The Problem of Pain by C.S. Lewis is a little more difficult to read, but the payoff is more than worth the effort.

God Is in the Hard Stuff by Bruce & Stan (yes, another plug) is devotional in nature, with 42 short chapters that deal with many different kinds of evil, suffering, and garden-variety difficulties that affect us all.

■ ■ ■

Questions for Reflection and Discussion

1. Can you identify with John Marks' journey of faith? Do you know people who are currently on a similar path? Could you do anything to bring them back to faith in God?

2. Why do Christians take evil more personally than skeptics and atheists? How have you dealt with this problem in the past?

3. Have you ever been guilty of using any of the four "lousy" responses to the problem of evil in order to help someone

through a difficult situation? Even though Romans 8:28 is true, why is that not a good verse to use when someone is in the middle of something terrible?

4. What is your response to the free-will explanation? Is this just a bunch of philosophical mumbo jumbo, or does it have a practical application for real life?

5. What kind of people would we be if we were forced to love God? Why do you think God would not—even if He could—create human beings who had no choice but to love Him?

6. What comfort can you take in knowing that God can and will one day defeat evil? If this is true, how should knowing this affect your relationship with non-Christians?

7. Which explanation for natural evil seems more reasonable to you: (1) Adam's sin corrupted the perfect order of the natural world, or (2) Satan and his demons disrupted the equilibrium of the natural world?

8. Has suffering ever made you stronger? Have you ever seen evil bring about a greater good? Has your own personal suffering ever brought you closer to God?

9. How does the Christian faith offer hope and comfort to people who are suffering? Is this a "wishing" hope or a real hope?

Moving On...

Congratulations! You've begun to work through one of the more thorny issues of the Christian faith. You will never have all the answers to the questions we've considered in this chapter (and probably many more we haven't covered), but at least you have a path to follow. Now it's time to turn our attention to two more issues that prompt all kinds of questions about the Christian faith: sin and salvation. In this age of religious pluralism, how can Christianity claim to have the only answer to the sin problem? And how can the death of one person cover the sins of people for all time? We're going to deal with those questions and more in the next chapter.

Chapter 8

God loves us *in* our sin, and *through* our sin, and goes on loving us, looking for a response.

—*John Coggan*

Three things are necessary for the salvation of man: to know what he ought to believe, to know what he ought to desire, and to know what he ought to do.

—*Thomas Aquinas*

In *The Problem of Pain,* C.S. Lewis writes that we humans are responsible for 80 percent of the evil in the world. Even though Lewis didn't conduct a scientific study to arrive at that number, you probably won't find too many people who would disagree with his conclusion. We see the evil that people can do. It's all around us.

So we can agree that evil exists. No disagreement there. Things get controversial when the discussion shifts to the origin of evil. Why do humans do bad things? Where do our evil impulses come from? Depending on your world-view, you might have a different answer than someone else has. For the Christian, the answer is clear: Evil comes from sin, which comes out of a sinful nature. But where did sin come from, and what can we do about it?

Well, in a word, there's nothing we can do, because God already has a plan in place to deal with our sin problem. But is that plan valid? Is it reasonable? Let's find out.

Sin and Salvation

*K*ing David was one of history's most insightful observers of human nature, particularly as he thought about humans and their relationship to God. In Psalm 8, David reflects on the great Creator God and wonders why He bothers with us mere mortals:

> *When I look at the night sky and see the work of your fingers—*
> *the moon and the stars you set in place—*
> *what are people that you should think about them,*
> *mere mortals that you should care for them?*

Then David considers the value and dignity that God has assigned to His created beings:

> *Yet you made them only a little lower than God*
> *and crowned them with glory and honor* (Psalm 8:3-5).

On the one hand, David is aware of the insignificance of the human race when compared with the awesomeness of God. On

199

the other hand, he understands that we are not insignificant to God for one simple reason: God has made us in His image.

What It Means to Be Human

When you read the opening chapter of the Bible and see how God created humankind, you get a clear and dramatic sense that humans matter immensely to God:

> *Then God said, "Let us make human beings in our image, to be like ourselves. They will reign over the fish in the sea, the birds in the sky, the livestock, all the wild animals on the earth, and the small animals that scurry along the ground." So God created human beings in his own image. In the image of God he created them: male and female he created them* (Genesis 1:26-27).

In the Image of God

We can't emphasize enough the uniqueness and the significance of God creating humankind "in his own image." Human beings bear the divine imprint—the *imago dei*—of God and His design. In the Garden of Eden before sin entered the world, the image must have been very pronounced. God and humanity must have enjoyed an intimacy (even though humanity was just a party of two at the time) that was beyond description.

$\mathcal{A}$ Picture of Intimacy

Genesis doesn't tell us much about the relationship Adam and Eve had with God in the Garden of Eden, so we can only speculate. However, the last book of the Bible gives us a clue of what it will be like when God and His created human beings are once again in perfect harmony with one another, when the perfect conditions that existed before sin stained humanity and our planet will be restored. In his vision of a new heaven and new earth, John hears a loud voice from God's throne proclaiming, "Look, God's home is now among his people! He will live with them, and they will be his people. God himself will be with them" (Revelation 21:3).

Even after sin entered the world, God's imprint remained. Many years after Adam and Eve were expelled from the Garden, God says this to Noah:

> *If anyone takes a human life, that person's life will also be taken by human hands. For God made human beings in his own image* (Genesis 9:6).

From this truth come some extremely important beliefs concerning the continued dignity and value of humanity. *All* human beings have dignity because of God's divine imprint. Human life is to be respected and preserved, whether it is very young or very old, strong or weak. "And from each man..." God says in Genesis 9:5 (NIV), "I will demand an accounting for the life of his fellow man."

Unique Qualities

Humans are the only beings personally and lovingly crafted by the Creator. God made everything else by calling it into existence: "Let there be light," "Let the waters swarm with fish and other life," and "Let the earth produce every sort of animal," and so forth. Not so with humans. God took a hands-on approach. He "formed the man from the dust of the ground" (Genesis 2:7) and "made a woman from the rib" of the man (Genesis 2:22). As a result, we have several unique qualities:

- We alone can communicate with God.
- We alone have been given the right and the responsibility to manage the earth's resources and all living things (Genesis 1:26,28-30).
- We alone are morally responsible to obey God.
- We alone have both a physical and a spiritual dimension. In addition to our physical bodies, we have a heart, soul, mind, and will.

1. The human heart. In everyday speech, we use the word *heart* in a variety of ways, usually having nothing to do with the organ that pumps blood through our bodies and keeps us alive. We talk about getting to the heart of the matter, or we commend someone for having a lot of heart. In similar ways, the Bible talks about the human heart in these nonphysical ways:

> The heart has emotion (Psalm 37:4).
>
> The heart has a will (Exodus 7:22).
>
> The heart has thoughts (Matthew 15:19).

What the writers are saying is that the heart is the human control center for emotions and deep desires. In Proverbs, Solomon tells his son, "Guard your heart above all else, for it determines the course of your life" (Proverbs 4:23).

2. *The human soul.* Heart and soul sometimes go together in music and literature, but there is a distinction between the two. The soul, which is sometimes referred to as spirit, is the eternal essence of a person, the part that never dies.

- We are commanded to love God with all our soul (Deuteronomy 6:5; Matthew 22:37).

- King David loves to praise the Lord with his soul (Psalm 103:1 NIV).

- Jesus tells His disciples not to fear those who "want to kill your body" because "they cannot touch your soul" (Matthew 10:28).

Because the soul is eternal, people often say that your soul is the "real you." The soul is also something that can be lost in the spiritual sense. Jesus talks about forfeiting the eternal soul in exchange for what this temporal world has to offer:

> *And what do you benefit if you gain the whole world but lose your own soul? Is anything worth more than your soul?* (Matthew 16:26).

The implication is clear. A soul can be lost eternally if a person does not entrust his or her soul to God. On the other hand, the soul cannot exist without the power of God (Acts 17:28).

3. *The human mind.* The mind of a person is capable of many positive things:

> loving God (Mark 12:30)

understanding God's will (Ephesians 5:17)

praising God (1 Corinthians 14:15)

being renewed (Romans 12:2)

But a human mind is also capable of many negative things:

depravity (Romans 1:28 NIV)

futility (Ephesians 4:17 NIV)

darkness and ignorance (Ephesians 4:18 NIV)

being blinded by Satan (2 Corinthians 4:4)

4. *The human will.* The will is another essential but intangible part of all humans. This quality usually shows up early in life and never goes away. We often talk about the will to win. In a contest between two people, we may refer to a battle of the wills. The human will—the ability to choose and pursue desired goals—is a powerful drive.

The will has played a major role in humanity's spiritual development. In fact, it has shaped the human condition, beginning with Adam and Eve. God created our first parents as free moral agents. They had the freedom and the power to make their own decisions, including the decision that would change the human race forever.

*S*o Why Are We Here?

Why did God create humanity, especially since He knew how we would respond to His command to obey Him? And why does He put up with us now? The "why are we here" question got its best-known answer in the Westminster Confession of Faith (a church creed from 1646): "The chief end of man is to glorify God and enjoy Him forever." God loves His creation, especially those special creatures He made in His image. He desires nothing more than for us to glorify Him in all we do and to truly enjoy everything about Him.

Sin: One Strike and You're Out

Isn't it interesting that nobody uses the word *sin* anymore, at least not in popular culture? In fact, you rarely hear people admit to being wrong. If someone is caught lying or cheating, they will say something like, "I'm sorry if I offended anyone," or "mistakes were made." People these days—especially people with a public profile—just don't seem to admit they were wrong or, heaven forbid, that they sinned.

Ironically, the evidence of sin is all around us. If we know anything about history, we can't deny the wars, racial hatred, oppression, and injustice that characterize the human race. If we know anything about culture, we can see the evidence of sin every day in news reports about murders, robberies, rapes, greed, and cheating. And if we know anything about ourselves, we are aware of the hatefulness, deceit, pride, jealousy, and selfishness in our own lives. Yet we just can't seem to bring ourselves to admit that we've sinned.

The Bible doesn't dance around the issue like that. Look what David, a very public person and a national leader, has to say about sin:

> *How can I know all the sins lurking in my heart? Cleanse me from these hidden faults. Keep your servant from deliberate sins! Don't let them control me. Then I will be free of guilt and innocent of great sin* (Psalm 19:12-13).

So what is sin exactly? Sin is anything that is contrary to God's nature. If God's perfection is the target, then sin is anything that misses the target. Both our nature and the actions that come from our nature are sinful. The Bible gives us a whole glossary of synonyms for sin. Let's call this the language of rebellion:

transgression (trespasses)—crossing the boundary (Ephesians 2:1 NIV)

unrighteousness—not hitting the target (Romans 3:5 NIV)

lawlessness—breaking accepted rules (1 John 3:4)

rebellion—going beyond a limit (Numbers 14:18)

godlessness—no reverence for God (Romans 1:18 NIV)

wickedness—evil deeds (Romans 1:18)

evil (Matthew 7:11 NIV)

Why Sin Matters

Sin matters to God, and it should matter to us. It matters to God because it saddens Him, because sin brings consequences to His beloved children, and because it separates us from Him. Sin should matter to us because we are accountable to God, because sin brings us consequences, and because it separates us from Him. The common thread, of course, is that sin *separates* us from God. Sin isn't just a theological concept. Ultimately sin is about breaking the most important relationship in our lives.

Sin was not in God's plan for humankind. Man and woman were created just the way God wanted them to be: free moral beings living in an ideal environment. There was only one rule, and God made it very clear what would happen if Adam and Eve broke it:

> But the LORD God warned him, "You may freely eat the fruit of every tree in the garden—except the tree of the knowledge of good and evil. If you eat its fruit, you are sure to die" (Genesis 2:16-17).

*D*id God Set Us Up?

A common objection to the biblical concept of sin is that God set us up for the fall. We were entrapped, as it were, by Satan's temptation. This is not what the Bible teaches, and it's not the position of historic Christianity. In the fifth century, Augustine taught that Adam was created as a free moral agent who was not under the control of outside coercion. In other words, nobody—not God, not Satan, not even Eve—forced him to sin. He made the choice to sin out of his nature.

And just what was Adam's nature prior to the fall? He was able to sin and able not to sin. (Just in case you ever want to impress your friends, the Latin term for this condition is *posse peccare et posse non peccare*.) By contrast, God is not able to sin (*non posse peccare*). As a free moral agent, Adam chose sin, and as a result his nature became one in which he was not able not to sin (*non posse non peccare*), which is the nature of the human race after the fall.

When the Sin Virus Invaded Earth

Genesis 3 tells us what happens next. Along comes Satan (having been kicked out of heaven and allowed to roam the earth). Satan takes on the form of a serpent and talks to Eve. You may find it surprising that she wasn't shocked by a talking snake. Maybe that's because everything was new to her, and she had never before heard a lie. But here's the real surprise: Eve believed the snake and doubted God. Here's how the conversation went in Genesis 3:1-3:

> Snake: Did God really say you must not eat the fruit from any of the trees in the garden?
>
> Eve: Of course we may eat fruit from the trees in the garden. It's only the fruit from the tree in the middle of the garden that we are not allowed to eat. God said, "You must not eat it or even touch it; if you do, you will die."
>
> Satan: You won't die! God knows that your eyes will be opened as soon as you eat it, and you will be like God, knowing both good and evil.

This dialogue between Eve and Satan marks the beginning of Satan's great struggle for the ruin of humankind. His deceptive questions and statements were intended to get her to disobey God's rules. Notice the progression of lies he told Eve and how familiar this dark logic is to us today:

- God is placing an unreasonable restriction on you.
- This restriction is bad because you would be better off without it.
- Therefore, God's rule is bad.
- You would be better off if you didn't pay attention to the restriction.

This was the big test. Would Adam and Eve believe and obey God, or would they believe Satan's lies? As we all know, they bought into Satan's argument and flunked the test. The interesting thing is that as soon as they both ate the forbidden fruit, "their eyes were opened" (Genesis 3:7). They knew they had sinned by breaking God's standard.

This darkest day in the history of humankind has been known ever since as the fall. It was the day on which the sin virus invaded Earth and infected humankind with deadly consequences.

---

*W*hat's the Big Deal?

It's tempting to trivialize this story and ask, "What's the big deal? It's only a piece of fruit, for goodness sake." But the fruit isn't the issue. The fruit isn't what's offensive to God. Adam and Eve's great offense was the act of deliberate disobedience, or sin. Whether it's a disobedient act in a small or large issue doesn't matter. Regardless of the form it takes, sin violates God's nature and separates us from Him.

The Consequences for Us

The consequences of Adam and Eve's sin were not limited to them. The sin virus is too infectious for that. Because of that first sin, we are sinners in three critical ways:

1. We inherit a sin nature. The sin nature is inherited at birth and passed from one generation to the next—sort of like a genetic trait. The sin nature is so pervasive and corruptive that a parent (no matter how good) is incapable of giving birth to anything but a sinful child (no matter how cute). David reflects,

> For I was born a sinner—yes, from the moment my mother conceived me (Psalm 51:5).

2. We carry a sin debt. Sin is directly charged against us—like a bad debt—because Adam was a representative of humankind. As our representative, when he sinned, we sinned. Theologians call this *imputed* sin. In other words, the blame of Adam's sin carries forward to us. Here's how Paul explains it:

> When Adam sinned, sin entered the world. Adam's sin brought death, so death spread to everyone, for everyone sinned (Romans 5:12).

3. We suffer sin's penalty. As soon as Adam and Eve sinned, God issued a series of consequences:

- For Adam and Eve: physical death (Genesis 2:17), spiritual death (Romans 6:23), and expulsion from the Garden of Eden (Genesis 3:23).

- For Eve and all women who follow her: pain in childbirth and submission to her husband (Genesis 3:16).

- For Adam and all men who follow him: a lifetime of struggle to make a living (Genesis 3:17).

- For the serpent: cursed to forever crawl on its belly (Genesis 3:14).

- For Satan: He would strike the heel of woman's offspring, but her offspring would crush his head (Genesis 3:15 NIV). This is the first Bible reference to the future events when Satan's evil influence over humankind would bring about the crucifixion of Jesus (the woman's offspring), followed by Jesus eventually crushing Satan.

The Bad That We Do (and the Good That We Don't)

We can't simply blame Adam and Eve for our sin. We are guilty of sin all on our own because of three things: the things we do, the things we don't do, and the things we think:

- *Sinful acts.* We sin when we commit acts that are contrary to God's holy standard of righteousness: lying, stealing, anger, gossip, and the like. Theologians call these *sins of commission.*

- *Sinful failures to act.* We sin when we fail to do what we know is the right thing to do: failing to speak the truth when we know it, failing to help others when we know we should. Theologians call these *sins of omission.*

- *Sinful thoughts.* We sin when we have unrighteous attitudes: jealousy, pride, hate, greed. These are referred to as *sins of the heart.*

Diagnosing the Sin Virus

Unlike popular culture, the Bible doesn't hold back on the subject of sin. It speaks clearly about the terrible nature of sin and how it affects every person. Sin is pervasive on two counts: Sin affects *every one* of us (Romans 3:23), and sin affects *every part* of us. It taints our mind, our emotions, and our actions. With respect to spiritual and moral issues...

> We aren't sinners because we sin; we sin because we are sinners.

- Our mind and our conscience are corrupted (Titus 1:15).
- Our will is stubborn, rebellious, and defiant (Romans 1:32).
- Our desires are selfish and base (Colossians 3:5).
- Our thoughts are evil (Genesis 6:5).

And with respect to our relationship with God...

- We are hostile to God (Romans 8:7).
- We don't understand truth about God (1 Corinthians 2:14).
- We can't see the light of the good news of Christ (2 Corinthians 4:4).

---

*T*otally Depraved?

One of the big philosophical and theological debates concerns the question of sin and its effect on the human race. Are people basically good or basically evil? With phrases such as "nobody's perfect" and "to err is human" in our vocabulary, it seems as though people agree with the Bible's assessment that "all have sinned." But how sinful are we? The Bible teaches the "total depravity" of the human race, but that doesn't mean we are as bad as we could possibly be. As R.C. Sproul explains, that would be *utter* depravity. According to Sproul, total depravity means that we are "depraved or corrupt in the totality of our being. Our minds, our wills, and our bodies are affected by evil. We speak sinful words, do sinful deeds, have impure thoughts. Our bodies suffer from the ravages of sin."[1]

Salvation

Salvation describes how each of us can be "saved"—saved *from* the penalty of sin, and saved *to* eternal life in God. Essentially, salvation restores the relationship between sinful humans and a holy God. It is initiated and arranged for by God, accomplished by Christ, and applied by the Holy Spirit. All three persons of the Godhead are involved in the process of salvation.

On one level, it is almost impossible to understand how and why a perfect God would sacrifice His own Son on behalf of a rebellious humanity. But on another level, God has made understanding salvation so simple that it can be received by anyone. Nobody is excluded. That's the promise of salvation. But with that promise comes a responsibility. Its very simplicity means that people have no excuse for rejecting God's offer of salvation because they don't understand it. Nobody will ever be able to say, "It wasn't my fault. I just didn't get it."

---

*F*our Losing Ways to Save Your Life

The very quality that got the human race into trouble in the first place—the desire to go its own way—can keep people from finding their way back to God. The prophet Isaiah writes, "All of us, like sheep, have strayed away. We have left God's paths to follow our own" (Isaiah 53:6). Sadly, people think their own paths will save them. These paths should sound familiar:

Salvation by doing good works. Many people live by the mistaken belief that salvation is like a big scale, where their evil deeds are on one side and their good deeds are on the other. If they do more good things than bad in their lives, they will make it to heaven. Good deeds are great, and they can have a beneficial impact on culture, but they are meaningless as far as salvation is concerned. Compared to God's righteousness, any good deed we do is worthless (Isaiah 64:6). Because of our sin nature, we can't do anything to earn God's favor (Ephesians 2:8-9).

Salvation by being religious. Sometimes people think that religious activities—going to church, teaching a Bible class, praying the rosary—can earn them salvation. But living religiously doesn't bring you salvation any more than clucking like a chicken can bring you an egg. Many religious leaders in Jesus' time taught that observing religious rituals would earn people good standing with God. Jesus taught that a person's relationship with God, not observance of rituals, brings salvation (Titus 3:5).

Salvation by keeping tradition. Some people believe that because they have been born into a particular culture or family, they get an automatic free pass to heaven. The Bible is clear that salvation through Christ is available to all people (Galatians 3:26-28), and it's not something you inherit (John 1:12-13).

Salvation by believing God exists. The vast majority of people in the world believe God exists, and many think that belief alone will get them to heaven. However, as we have already discussed, when the Bible talks about believing in Jesus Christ, it means more than just intellectual understanding. Faith is more than belief.

God's Grace and Our Faith

Salvation does not come from doing good works, being religious, keeping tradition, or even believing God exists. Pure and simple, salvation comes from God, and He offers it to us as a gift by His grace. Our task is to understand the gift and accept it by faith. Here's what that looks like:

1. God offers His grace freely to humankind. Grace is unmerited favor. Here is another way of saying it: We experience grace when *we get what we don't deserve.* We don't deserve God's favor and His salvation, but He gives it to us anyway, "not because of the righteous things we had done, but because of his mercy" (Titus 3:5).

> God saved you by his grace when you believed. And you can't take credit for this; it is a gift from God. Salvation is not a reward for the good things we have done, so none of us can boast about it (Ephesians 2:8-9).

The gift is free, but just like any gift, salvation is meaningless unless we receive it by faith.

2. Faith in Jesus Christ brings salvation. Belief that Jesus Christ paid the penalty for the sins of humankind is required for salvation. We can't receive God's great and graceful gift of salvation through Jesus without it.

$\mathcal{W}$e Can't Add Anything

God's plan to save us contains a series of "alones." We are saved by the grace of God alone through faith alone in Christ alone. We can add nothing to grace, nothing to faith, and nothing to Christ. All we have to do is believe that God's plan *alone* is the one that can save us.

This Great Salvation

The writer of Hebrews talks about "this great salvation" (Hebrews 2:3). That's absolutely the way to see this beautiful truth, succinctly expressed in the most famous verse in the Bible.

> For God loved the world so much that he gave his one and only Son, so that everyone who believes in him will not perish but have eternal life (John 3:16).

This single sentence, spoken by Jesus to an earnest seeker who wants to know what it means to be born again, helps us understand salvation.

"For God so loved the world so much..." Ever since humanity rebelled against God in the Garden of Eden, God has longed to restore the relationship He once had with His created beings. Because of our sin, we are unable to reach God on our own. Paul writes, "But God showed his great love for us by sending Christ to die for us while we were still sinners" (Romans 5:8).

"...that he gave his one and only Son..." God allowed His Son, Jesus Christ, to die a painful and humiliating death on the cross to pay the penalty for our sins. Jesus took on Himself the wrath of God against sin. Paul continues: "And since we have been made right in God's sight by the blood of Christ, he will certainly save us from God's condemnation" (Romans 5:9).

"...so that everyone who believes in him..." We can accept or reject salvation. Accepting salvation requires a conscious step of faith where we add trust and commitment to belief. When that happens, God exchanges our old sin nature for Christ's new nature. This is what it means to be in Christ or to belong to Christ. Paul explains: "This means that anyone who belongs to Christ has

become a new person. The old life is gone; a new life has begun!" (2 Corinthians 5:17).

"...will not perish but have eternal life." Without salvation we will spend eternity in hell. Salvation gives us eternal life that begins the moment we receive Christ by faith. Paul tells us, "For the wages of sin is death, but the free gift of God is eternal life through Christ Jesus our Lord" (Romans 6:23).

*W*ords That Can Save Your Life

God has blessed the human race with the ability to communicate through words. God has given us some words that are crucial for understanding what is involved in our salvation. As David writes, "The unfolding of your words gives light; it gives understanding to the simple" (Psalm 119:130 NIV). Here are some words to know:

Conviction. The first step in the process of salvation is performed by the Holy Spirit, who makes us conscious of sin and the need for a Savior (John 16:8).

Confession. This is the act of telling God that you know you have sinned. Your willingness to own up to your sin is evidence that you are truly repentant (1 John 1:9).

Repentance. A person who is truly sorry for sins will be willing to turn away from them. True repentance means to turn away from sin and turn toward God in your heart and mind. It means you're ready to make a new start (2 Corinthians 7:10).

Atonement. Once we own up to our sin, we go free. But who paid the price for our sins? *Atonement* refers to the fact that Christ died in our place. Our sins require the penalty of death, so Christ died so we could live. Christ's death atoned for—made full payment for—our sins (Romans 5:17).

Redemption. When you redeem something from a pawnshop, you buy it back. Christians were redeemed by God when He purchased us back from death with Christ's blood (Romans 3:25).

Justification. This is the process by which unjust sinners are made right (or just) in the sight of a just and holy God. Faith is the cause of justification in that faith is the means by which the righteousness of Christ is credited to us. When we are justified "in Christ," God looks at us and sees the perfection of Christ rather than our imperfections (Romans 5:18).

Regeneration. At the point of salvation, our old sinful nature is replaced by a new, righteous nature. We are regenerated by the power of God's

Spirit living in us. We don't suddenly become perfect, but we have a new power available in our lives to free us from being slaves to sin (2 Corinthians 5:17).

Is Jesus the Only Way?

Christianity is often accused of being an intolerant belief system because it says it offers the only way to God and the only way to salvation. But does that disqualify the Christian faith? Just because people think it's non-inclusive, does that mean it's not true? After all, nobody complains that there is only one way to be born. Why should it be so hard to believe there's only way to be born again? Besides, Christianity is completely inclusive. Anyone can come to Christ: Jew or Gentile, slave or free, male or female (Galatians 3:28).

A Reasonable Faith, a Reasonable Plan

If the Christian faith is a reasonable faith—if it's reasonable to believe that God is real, that He has spoken through His world and His word, that Jesus is God in human form—it is perfectly reasonable to believe that God's plan is valid.

Even then, just knowing about God's eternal plan and believing that it is true is not enough. We have to accept it personally. This is where so many people get stuck. They believe in God, and they even believe that the only way to salvation is through Jesus Christ, but they can't get past the fact that they can't do anything to earn their salvation. They want a ticket to heaven, but they want to be able to pay for it.

Here's what separates the Christian faith from all other belief systems in the world. In every other religion, you earn your way to heaven or the afterlife by the good deeds you do, like a Boy Scout collecting merit badges. With God's eternal plan, there is no earning. Salvation is a gift (Romans 6:23), and we can't do anything to earn it (Ephesians 2:8-9).

Understanding Why

Why did God set up His eternal plan this way? This is not easy to understand. In many ways God's eternal plan defies all logic. But on another, deeper level, it makes perfect sense because God based His plan on something much greater than logic. He based His plan on love. Faith is a requirement for salvation, and our faith gives us hope, but the love of God is greater than faith and hope.

> *Three things will last forever—faith, hope, and love—and the greatest of these is love* (1 Corinthians 13:13).

Accepting God's free gift of salvation through Jesus Christ is the only way to avoid God's eternal death penalty, but it is much more than fire insurance. You don't have to wait until the end of the world (or the end of your life) to enjoy the benefits of being a Christian. Your new life in Christ begins the moment you receive Him into your life.

The Divine Conspiracy

In his compelling book *The Divine Conspiracy,* Dallas Willard writes that entering into a life with Jesus Christ is not merely accepting what happened in the past (when Jesus came to earth to die on the cross) so that we can have a secure future (when Jesus comes back to earth again). "Jesus offers himself as God's doorway into the life that is truly life," Willard writes. "Confidence in him leads us today, as in other times, to become his apprentices in eternal living."[2]

Jesus satisfies our hunger for significance, which God has planted in every human being. All of us want to count for something. We want to find meaning somewhere outside ourselves. Willard says, "We are, all of us, never-ceasing spiritual beings with a unique eternal calling to count for good in God's great universe."[3] The only way for that to happen is to access and accept God's eternal salvation plan.

What's That Again?

1. We know that we matter immensely to God because He created us in His image. As human beings, we have His divine imprint.

2. Humans are the only beings personally and lovingly crafted by God. As a result we have several unique qualities.

3. In addition to having physical qualities, each person has a heart, soul, mind, and will. Of these, the soul is said to be the "real you."

4. The evidence of sin is everywhere: in our history, in our culture, and in our own lives. Yet many people have trouble admitting that they are sinners.

5. Sin is anything contrary to God's perfect nature. Both our nature and the actions that come from our nature are sinful. Sin matters to God because it brings consequences to His beloved children and because it separates us from Him.

6. As a consequence of Adam and Eve's act of rebellious disobedience, we are sinners in three critical ways: (1) We inherit a sin nature, (2) we carry a sin debt, and (3) we suffer sin's penalty.

7. Salvation describes how each of us can be saved *from* the penalty of sin *to* eternal life in God. Salvation restores the relationship between sinful humans and a holy God.

8. Salvation does not come from doing good works, being religious, keeping tradition, or even believing God exists. Salvation comes from God and is offered to us by God's grace as a gift. Our task is to understand the gift and accept it by faith.

Dig Deeper

This chapter is dealing with two of the most basic elements of the Christian faith, so the kind of books we recommend to help you dig deeper into the topics of sin and salvation are very elemental:

Essential Truths of the Christian Faith by R.C. Sproul covers 100 key doctrines in plain language. An entire section is called "Human Beings and the Fall," and another section is simply called "Salvation."

Know What You Believe by Paul Little is a book every Christian should read because it covers the basics of the Christian faith.

Another essential book is our own *Knowing God 101*. Each chapter covers a basic fundamental truth related to your Christian life.

■ ■ ■

Questions for Reflection and Discussion

1. Have you ever felt as if you didn't matter to God? What were you going through? What helped you to realize that you do matter to God?

2. When you look at the qualities that make us unique among all God's created beings, what kind of responsibility do you feel? Where has the human race blown it in living up to these unique qualities that God has given us?

3. Both Moses (in Deuteronomy 6:5) and Jesus (in Matthew 22:37) tell us to love God with all our heart, soul, and mind. How do you love the Lord with all your heart? With all your soul? With all your mind?

4. According to the Westminster Confession of Faith, what is our "chief end"? How do you glorify God? (Hint: A practical definition of *glorify* is to make someone look good.) How do you enjoy God forever, which is to say, how do you enjoy Him now, and how will you enjoy God in heaven?

5. Why are people so reluctant to admit they are sinners or even that they have sinned? Do we fool anybody by trying to deflect attention from our sins? Do we fool God? (We know, that last one is a dumb question, but we need to be

reminded that even if we think we're fooling other people, we aren't putting anything past God.)

6. What is the nature of the human race after the fall? What are the practical implications of the condition we are in? Does this mean we can never do good? Why or why not?

7. As best you can, describe how salvation is arranged for by God, how it is accomplished by Christ, and how it is applied by the Holy Spirit.

8. Why do you think it is reasonable to believe that God's salvation plan is valid and true?

Moving On...

Salvation is all about a restored relationship with God through Jesus Christ. Your new life in Christ begins here on earth, but it doesn't end here. Death is not the final curtain. Something unimaginable beyond this life awaits every Christian. And something equally unimaginable—but in a different way—beyond this life awaits those who have not put their faith in Jesus.

It's easy to believe that a loving and all-powerful God would create heaven. But why would He create hell? Is God that vengeful and that cruel? We'll consider questions like those in the next chapter.

Chapter 9

> For since the world began, no ear has heard,
> and no eye has seen a God like you,
> who works for those who ait for him!
>
> —*Isaiah*

Everybody thinks about heaven and hell and wonders, *Do they really exist, or are they made-up places?* Not surprisingly, more people are likely to believe in heaven than hell, which doesn't really prove anything. And speaking of proof, we don't have a whole lot of evidence for either place except for this lingering idea in all of us that something or perhaps even some place must exist beyond this mortal life.

But what is it that's beyond death? And do two distinct places exist—one for saints and one for sinners? These universal questions have no easy answers, but we can sensibly approach them and deal with some of the doubts people have about heaven and hell and the way they reflect God's character.

So let's spend some time in eternity. Our journey will require some faith, but we're also going to find some evidence along the way.

Heaven and Hell

*G*reat writers and poets put into words one of the greatest of all human desires—the longing for immortality. In his play *Antony and Cleopatra*, Shakespeare has Antony say:

> Give me my robe, put on my crown; I have
> Immortal longings in me.

In a letter to his beloved Fanny Brawne, the poet John Keats expresses a deep desire that all lovers have:

> I long to believe in immortality...If I am destined to
> be happy with you here—how short is the longest
> life. I wish to believe in immortality—I wish to live
> with you forever.

Is immortality—unending life—the stuff of wishes and fairy tales, or is it real? As with so many other issues we've covered so far, it all depends on your worldview. Let's take a look at immortality in the framework of the three major belief systems:

- The naturalist believes there is no such thing as immortality because it can't be demonstrated or experienced with the five senses. Immortality falls in the same category as the supernatural. Since there's no hard evidence for either one, neither one exists.

- The relativist probably doesn't have a strong opinion one way or the other. If believing in immortality floats your boat, go ahead and believe. If you prefer to believe that only your mortal body and only this natural world are real, that's fine too.

- The theist believes immortality is not only possible but also probable. If God exists as an immortal, immaterial, supernatural being, then immortality is what you would expect.

Evidence for Immortality

Can we find evidence for immortality? How can we possibly prove something that is immaterial and beyond our ability to measure? Well, we've already gone over the cumulative case arguments for God's existence, and He is an immaterial being beyond our ability to measure, so we should be able to find some evidence that would make it reasonable to believe that there is such a thing as immortality.

Evidence Based on God's Existence

Miracles are what you would expect from a supernatural God, and immortality is what you would expect as well. If you have good reasons to believe that an immortal, invisible God exists, then you also have good reasons to believe that immortality exists.

In their book *Beyond Death,* J.P. Moreland and Gary Habermas list four arguments based on God's existence that help make the case for immortality.

Divine imprint. The Bible tells us that God created humans in His image (*imago dei*). Obviously, this doesn't mean we look like God (which would be impossible because God is spirit), but we do share some of His qualities. One of these qualities has to do with God's dwelling place. "Heaven is a suitable place for a being like

God," write Moreland and Habermas. "Perhaps we are like God in this respect. We were meant to live a type of life suited for a heavenly mode of existence."[1] Maybe this is what the apostle Paul had in mind:

> *But we are citizens of heaven, where the Lord Jesus Christ lives* (Philippians 3:20).

Divine justice. Another quality we share with God is justice. All humans have a sense of justice. We want justice to be done when someone has wronged someone else (especially when that someone else is us). Yet on this earth, we see a great deal of injustice and inequity. Justice isn't always done. If God is completely and infinitely just, He must deal with injustice. We know He isn't dealing with all injustice in this mortal life, so we can reasonably believe He will take care of injustice in the life to come.

Divine love. As beings created in God's image, we know what it's like to love and be loved. This argument says that an infinitely loving God wants the best for His created beings. For humans, the best is a relationship with their Creator that goes on forever. Besides, God has placed in each person a desire for eternity and immortality:

> *God has made everything beautiful for its own time. He has planted eternity in the human heart* (Ecclesiastes 3:11).

Divine revelation. This argument simply says that if God exists, and the Bible is His trustworthy message to humanity, and if the Bible contains God's revelation that all people will live forever, then we can take God at His word.

Evidence Based on Human Desire

Okay, the arguments from God's existence are great if you already believe in God. But what if you don't buy into Christian theism? Is there any evidence for immortality apart from that worldview? Moreland and Habermas talk about several, including documented cases of near death experiences (or NDEs), such as the vivid description offered by Don Piper. In our view, one piece of evidence stands out above the others. It's called the argument from desire, and one of its greatest advocates is C.S. Lewis.

> If I find in myself a desire which no experience in this world can satisfy, the most probable explanation is that I was made for another world.
>
> —C.S. Lewis

According to Lewis, every person desires heaven, although that desire can be hidden. Moreland and Habermas write, "Sometimes we desire lesser, finite goods (such as beauty), but these are symbols of and pointers to the transtemporal, transfinite good that is our real destiny. The desire for heaven is a desire that no natural happiness will satisfy."[2]

The Resurrection of Jesus

So far all of the evidence we've presented for a life beyond this life is philosophical. It's compelling enough, but what if we had empirical evidence as well? Moreland and Habermas pose the question like this:

> What if we had evidence based on historical and scientific research that verified what philosophy showed was rational? What if we could find events that have occurred in our world that show that life beyond the grave is true? In fact, what if we could find at least one person who survived death and returned to tell us and show us what immortality is really like?[3]

If you haven't guessed it by now (and if the title of this section isn't a big enough clue), the answer to these "what if" questions is wrapped in the most significant event in history: the resurrection of Jesus Christ. We have already talked about Christ's resurrection in chapter 6, so you can go back and review the evidence presented there. What we want to do now is look at the apostle Paul's case for the resurrection in 1 Corinthians 15. Here Paul makes a case that the resurrection of Jesus is a historical event that proves that we too will experience life after death.

Jesus Died and Was Raised from the Dead

Paul is very meticulous as he tells his readers that the resurrection of Jesus Christ is a literal event with far-reaching implications.

And this isn't something that originated with Paul. He tells the Corinthians, "I passed on to you what was most important and what had also been passed on to me" (1 Corinthians 15:3). And he recites an early Christian confession that contains the very essence of the gospel (the good news) of Christ:

> *Christ died for our sins, just as the Scriptures said. He was buried, and he was raised from the dead on the third day, just as the Scriptures said. He was seen by Peter and then by the Twelve. After that, he was seen by more than 500 of his followers at one time, most of whom are still alive, though some have died. Then he was seen by James and later by all the apostles. Last of all, as though I had been born at the wrong time, I also saw him* (1 Corinthians 15:3-8).

Notice two certainties that form the bedrock of the Christian faith: Jesus died for our sins (the proof is that He was buried), and Jesus was raised from the dead (the proof is that more than 500 people, including all of the apostles, saw Him).

Jesus Was Raised from the Dead, so We Will Be Too

The certainty of the resurrection of Jesus assures us that we will be raised from the dead as well. If the resurrection didn't happen, then there's no afterlife, no immortality. Or to look at it another way, if you don't believe in immortality, then you don't believe that Christ was resurrected. The two are inextricably linked (1 Corinthians 15:12-13).

If Jesus Has Not Been Raised, the Christian Faith Is Worthless

Paul pushes his argument even further and says something truly astounding:

> *And if Christ has not been raised, then your faith is useless and you are still guilty of your sins. In that case, all who have died believing in Christ are lost! And if our hope in Christ is only for this life, we are more to be pitied than anyone in the world* (1 Corinthians 15:17-19).

Paul is so sure of the resurrection that he is willing to bet the house: If the resurrection didn't happen, then our faith is worthless and anyone who believes this stuff is a fool. But the resurrection of Jesus did happen, which gives us tremendous assurance of our own immortality.

So we know that we are going to live on after we die. But do we know what is going to happen? What is the afterlife like? Are heaven and hell real places? That's what we want to talk about next.

*W*hat Happens Between Death and Eternity?

When Christians die, they immediately go into the presence of the Lord. When the thief on the cross said, "Jesus, remember me when you come into your Kingdom," Jesus told him he would be in "paradise" that very day (Luke 23:42-43). And Paul writes that he longs "to go and be with Christ" (Philippians 1:23). However, departed Christians will not receive resurrected, glorified bodies until the future resurrection, when Jesus returns to earth. Paradise, then, is not a final destination but, as N.T. Wright explains, "the blissful garden, the parkland of rest and tranquility, where the dead are refreshed as they await the dawn of the new day."[4] Non-Christians will experience no garden, no rest, and no tranquility. Upon their death, it's off to *hades* (the Greek word) or *sheol* (the Hebrew word), where they wait for judgment.

Heaven: Our Greatest Hope

Not long ago a prominent Christian leader died suddenly after a long life of serving the Lord he loved. The memorial service was packed with people—family, friends, colleagues, and those who simply admired his life of integrity and selflessness. As the service was coming to an end, something very unusual happened. The familiar voice of the departed man of God could be heard throughout the auditorium. No, it wasn't some macabre parlor trick, but a recording the dear saint had made—as if he knew his time on earth was drawing to a close—to describe the world he had always longed for.

"I want to thank you all for coming, but you don't worry about me," the recording began. "I am having the time of my life. You should see this place!" He went on to paint a visual picture of heaven, using descriptions such as "walls of jasper" and "streets of gold" as found in Revelation 21. He talked about conversations with the apostle Paul and other heroes of the faith, and he said he would be waiting for those he loved, especially his wife of more than 50 years.

It was a tender and uplifting moment that brought tears and smiles to everyone in attendance. And even though this faithful servant of the Lord wasn't quite following the sequence of N.T. Wright's "life after life after death," his point was clear: Heaven will be a place of indescribable beauty and wonder. As much as he tried to describe its features, and as much as we may try to envision what heaven will be like, we can capture only a shadow of this glorious place where God Himself will dwell with His people.

> No eye has seen, no ear has heard, and no mind has imagined what God has prepared for those who love him.
>
> —the apostle Paul

A Brief Description of Heaven

Heaven is a real place, created by God, that will exist forever. Heaven is where Jesus lives now (Acts 3:21) and where those who have trusted Jesus by faith will live in the future (John 14:2). Gary Habermas writes, "the life of heaven is eternal life." And it isn't merely a continuation of our life now. There will be no sorrow, crying, or pain in heaven, and the inhabitants of heaven will never again experience death (Revelation 21:4).

Sometimes people think that heaven will be a boring place, with nothing to do but sit on a cloud strumming your harp. Hardly. Heaven will be a busy place filled with activity. We will be reunited with our believing loved ones who died before us (Matthew 8:11). Even more, we will see Jesus face-to-face in heaven and will be able to interact with Him (1 John 3:2). In fact, believers will be *glorified*—that is, raised with Jesus, seated and exalted with Him in heaven (Ephesians 2:6). While we're there, we will serve God

(Revelation 5:10) and give praise to Jesus, the Lamb who is worthy (Revelation 5:12).

Heaven Is a Place

In certain circles—including some religious ones—people deny that a real heaven exists in a real place. Instead, they say heaven is a state of mind—it if exists at all. Other people criticize thoughts about heaven as wishful thinking. To believe in heaven is to believe in fairy tales.

Don't be fooled. Heaven is not an alternative to reality. Heaven *is* reality. C.S. Lewis puts it this way:

> If Heaven is not real, every honest person will disbelieve it simply for that reason, however desirable it is, and if it is real, every honest man, woman, child, scientist, theologian, saint, and sinner will want to believe in it simply because it is real, not just because it is desirable.

If heaven is real, then it is a real place. Jesus confirms this:

> *There is more than enough room in my Father's home. If this were not so, would I have told you that I am going to prepare a place for you? When everything is ready, I will come and get you, so that you will always be with me where I am. And you know the way to where I am going* (John 14:2-4).

Just like Disney World

You've seen the television ads. Moments after some team wins the Super Bowl, the star player looks in the camera in a moment of celebration and says, "I'm going to Disney World!" as if that is the ultimate destination after winning the ultimate game.

We can actually draw a parallel between the Magic Kingdom and God's kingdom. What's fun about Disney World is that when you get there, you've got lots to do. You aren't stuck with just one ride or just one area to explore. You've got a choice of different lands or theme areas. Well, we would like to propose that heaven is a place with different lands, just like Disney World (only without the long lines). Let's take a tour of what heaven will include.

A New Heaven and a New Earth

Several times the Bible asserts that after the end of the world as we know it, God will create "a new heaven and a new earth" (Revelation 21:1). The old earth and heaven won't be completely destroyed but will be regenerated. According to one scenario, the process will begin during the millennium (the thousand-year reign of Christ and His saints) and will be completed after the great white throne judgment, when Satan and death have been conquered (Revelation 20). At this point, Jesus will turn the kingdom over to God the Father.

> *After that the end will come, when he will turn the Kingdom over to God the Father, having destroyed every ruler and authority and power. For Christ must reign until he humbles all his enemies beneath his feet. And the last enemy to be destroyed is death...Then, when all things are under his authority, the Son will put himself under God's authority, so that God, who gave his Son authority over all things, will be utterly supreme over everything everywhere* (1 Corinthians 15:24-28).

Because of what Christ has done on the cross to make all this possible, God will in turn elevate His Son to the highest place in heaven and earth. In fact, God has already done it.

> *Therefore, God elevated him to the place of highest honor and gave him the name above all other names, that at the name of Jesus every knee should bow, in heaven and on earth and under the earth, and every tongue confess that Jesus Christ is Lord, to the glory of God the Father* (Philippians 2:9-11).

*W*ill We Have Bodies in Heaven?

Peter Kreeft, who has written two wonderful books about heaven, says Christianity is the only belief system in which we "become more than we were before death." In every other belief system you are either gone forever (naturalism), you become a spirit or ghost (pantheism), your consciousness becomes one with the cosmos (Buddhism), or you are reincarnated (Hinduism).

In Christianity, if you have received God's plan for salvation, you are guaranteed a resurrected, glorified body. Paul draws a remarkable contrast between our present bodies, which die and decay, and our resurrected bodies, which will be full of glory and power and will never die. "For our dying bodies must be transformed into bodies that will never die; our mortal bodies must be transformed into immortal bodies" (1 Corinthians 15:53). All of this is made possible by the resurrection of Jesus, who became "the first of a great harvest of all who have died" (1 Corinthians 15:20).

Will our resurrected bodies bear the same imperfections and scars of our earthly bodies? That's hard to say. After His resurrection, Jesus asked doubting Thomas to place his hands into His scars. On the other hand, Kreeft writes that God is the author of healing. "Heaven will be the answer to every prayer, every desire for healing, physical, emotional, mental, and spiritual. All healings on earth are previews of coming attractions."

A New City

A lot of people love the country, but not everyone. Some prefer cities. They love the excitement, the lights, the streets, the glamour. Did you know that heaven will include a city? It's called the New Jerusalem, and it's described in detail in Revelation 21:

> *And I saw the holy city, the new Jerusalem, coming down from God out of heaven like a bride beautifully dressed for her husband. I heard a loud shout from the throne, saying, "Look, God's home is now among his people! He will live with them, and they will be his people. God himself will be with them* (Revelation 21:2-3).

You really need to read all of Revelation 21 because this is where we get the idea that the streets of heaven will be made of gold, and the gates of heaven will be made of pearls. The New Jerusalem is undoubtedly a literal city, probably the city that Abraham hoped for:

> *Abraham was confidently looking forward to a city with eternal foundations, a city designed and built by God* (Hebrews 11:10).

It's also the city that we long for:

> *For this world is not our permanent home; we are looking forward to a home yet to come* (Hebrews 13:14).

> Your place in heaven will seem to be made for you and you alone, because you were made for it.
>
> —C.S. *Lewis*

This city is heaven, but it's not all of heaven. Think of the New Jerusalem as the celestial capital city of heaven, visible from all parts of the new heaven and the new earth.

Heaven Is a State

When we say heaven is a state, we don't mean that heaven is a place like Missouri. By *state* we mean that heaven will offer opportunities far beyond anything we can imagine. Habermas writes that speaking of heaven as a state "encompasses all of the rich blessings not true of earth, including intimate knowledge of God and fellowship with him." This is where your thoughts about heaven can really begin to expand.

One of the incredible things about heaven is that we will continue to grow in knowledge and truth. Peter Kreeft writes that when we get to heaven, we will begin "the endless and endlessly fascinating task of exploring, learning, and loving the facets of infinity, the inexhaustible nature of God."[5] We will not be omniscient in that we know everything, but throughout eternity we will continue to learn things about heaven, about each other, and about God.

Heaven will also provide several conditions we can only dream about. Take note of the fact that though we experience each of these in some measure now, we always fall short of being able to enjoy them completely. Habermas presents five images from the

Bible that help us to see what our experience in heaven might be like:

Complete peace (Psalm 23:1-3). Even though we cannot experience complete peace in a world characterized by conflict, we know enough of what peace feels like to long for it. We long for peace in our world, we long for peace in our relationships, and we long for peace of mind. In heaven we will experience total, wonderful, blissful peace because God will care for our every need. For a beautiful picture of what this will feel like, read Psalm 23.

Complete rest (Psalm 91:1). Everybody's tired. Sometimes the greatest longing we have is for a good night's sleep. Even more than rest from physical weariness, we desire rest from our daily stress and pressures. In heaven we will have complete rest because God will have removed all of our burdens. Our bodies will be continually fresh, our minds always sharp, and our hearts forever light.

*W*ill There Be Sin in Heaven?

The easy answer is, of course not. But how do we know? And even if there is no sin, will it be like the Garden of Eden, where sin is absent but temptation is present? Will we have a free will in heaven, just like we do on Earth? Remember our little Latin lesson in chapter 8? Adam and Eve were *able to sin* and *able not to sin.* After the fall, they were *not able not to sin.* Habermas notes that in heaven, as in the Garden of Eden before the fall, we will not have sin natures. However, the great tempter, Satan, will be in "the fiery lake of burning sulfur" (Revelation 20:10). Consequently, we will be *able not to sin* (this is still different from God, who is *not able to sin*). "In this case," writes Habermas, "we would still be free to sin, but we would always choose not to because the glories and virtues of heaven would be so marvelous that no one in heaven would ever choose to act against those benefits."

Complete security and protection (Psalm 91:2). We worry so much about security. As a result, we take great measures to protect ourselves and our possessions. But even then, we have no guarantee that we will be completely safe. How would you feel if you were totally protected from harm of any kind, whether inflicted by people, diseases, or disasters? That's how we'll feel in heaven.

Complete beauty (Psalm 19:1). One of the unique qualities about being human is that you can appreciate beautiful things. You find joy in the beauty of nature. You recognize the beauty of great design and quality construction. But this is nothing compared to heaven. Heaven will provide a feast for the senses as we find ourselves surrounded by the natural beauty of the "paradise of God" (Revelation 2:7). As if that weren't enough, the wonders of the city "designed and built by God" will be yours to explore and enjoy for as long as you like.

*W*ill We Recognize Each Other in Heaven?

The resurrected body of Christ provides us with some clues about our own resurrection bodies. Although His body was glorified, His disciples recognized Him. Therefore, we may logically conclude that we will also recognize one another in heaven. Jesus said as much to His disciples (Matthew 8:11). Besides, our fellowship with each other will be much more meaningful if we know each other.

A related question is this: What age will we be in heaven? Will our resurrected bodies be the same age as when we die or are caught up in the clouds to meet Jesus in the air (1 Thessalonians 4:16-17), or will we all be the same age? The Bible gives us no answer, so we can only speculate. We do know that our heavenly bodies will not decay or die, so they will not age. Perhaps we won't even see age. Kreeft refers to Thomas Aquinas' belief that the perfect age is 33, the age of Christ when He was crucified and resurrected. He thought everyone in heaven will have 33-year-old bodies. Interesting thought.

Complete fellowship (Matthew 26:29). Nothing is sweeter than enjoying a delicious meal with family and friends (especially if you don't have to cook). More than once, Jesus described heaven by using the image of sitting down together for a meal. He told His disciples that He was looking forward to having fellowship with them in His Father's kingdom. And Jesus has promised you that He will share a meal as a friend with anyone who opens the door of his or her heart and invites Him in (Revelation 3:20).

Can you imagine? The King of kings wants to sit down with you for a meal in heaven! The thought should take your breath away. Not only that, but when you are in heaven, you will have the luxury of spending time with people you love and care about, not to mention the incredible people in history whom you can only wonder about. It's true! Jesus said that we would be able to "sit down with Abraham, Isaac, and Jacob at the feast in the Kingdom of Heaven" (Matthew 8:11).

$\mathcal{W}$ill There Be Animals in Heaven?

This is a very important question for many people. Often, to comfort children, we tell them that Fido, who has just been hit by a car, has gone to heaven, and someday we will see our beloved pet. Does the childlike belief that we will see our pets in heaven have any merit? Habermas doesn't think so because the animals weren't created in God's image and therefore don't have an eternal soul.

Peter Kreeft answers the question of animals in heaven (but not specific pets) by saying, "Why not?" He says that other nonhuman things will be in heaven (such as green fields and flowers), so why not animals? "Animals belong in the 'new earth' as much as trees," he writes. He also makes the point that from the beginning, human beings were meant to have stewardship over the animals (Genesis 1:28). We haven't done a very good job of fulfilling that divine directive on earth now, so "it seems likely that the right relationship with animals will be part of heaven."

Hell: The Terrible Choice

Heaven is a wonderful place to think about. Hell, not so much. Few people take hell seriously. But hell is real. In His parables, Jesus uses various terms to describe what seems to be hell:

> a place of outer darkness (Matthew 8:12)
>
> a fiery furnace where there is weeping and gnashing of teeth (Matthew 13:42)
>
> eternal fire (Matthew 25:41)
>
> eternal punishment (Matthew 25:46)

Paul refers to "terrible punishment" in store for those who refuse to turn from their sin (Romans 2:5) and to the judgment of those "who don't know God."

They will be punished with eternal destruction, forever separated from the Lord and from his glorious power (2 Thessalonians 1:9).

And then you have these graphic descriptions by John in Revelation:

the bottomless pit (Revelation 9:1)

a huge furnace (Revelation 9:2)

fire and burning sulfur (Revelation 14:10)

no relief day or night (Revelation 14:11)

the fiery lake of burning sulfur (Revelation 21:8)

the second death (Revelation 21:8)

There's no question we should take these descriptions of hell seriously even though they can be troubling. If people are bothered with the idea that a loving God allows evil and suffering in this life, you can only imagine how they feel about the idea that this same God is going to torture people in hell—forever! Maybe you're bothered by this. Honestly, we struggle with it. In fact, we think everyone should be at the very least uncomfortable with the reality of hell.

What Hell Is Not

Before we consider what hell really is, let's look at what hell is not. Our good friend J.P. Moreland was interviewed by Lee Strobel in his book *The Case for Faith.*[6] Strobel hammers Moreland with questions about hell so he can answer an important objection people have to the Christian faith: A loving God would never torture people in hell. Moreland has thought long and hard about this subject. Here are two of his most important conclusions about what hell is *not:*

A torture chamber. Moreland maintains that hell is a punish*ment,* not a place of punish*ing.* It's not torture. The punishment of hell is separation from God, bringing shame, anguish, and terrible regret. Because we will have both body and soul in the resurrected state, the misery people will experience in hell will be both mental and physical. "But the pain that's suffered will be due to the sorrow from the final, ultimate, unending banishment from God, his kingdom, and the good life for which we were created in the first place. People in hell will deeply grieve for all they've lost."[7]

A place of fire. No doubt this is a controversial statement, and while no one can say they know for sure, Moreland does make a pretty good case. Clearly, Jesus and John used *fire* to describe hell. But how could hell be a place of both "outer darkness" and "eternal fire"? Fire would light things up! Okay, you might be asking, if the fire isn't literal, then what does it symbolize? In Scripture, fire and flames are an image for God's judgment. In Revelation, John writes of the "Word of God," who will come with eyes like "flames of fire" and a sharp sword coming out of his mouth (Revelation 19:11-15). The flames stand for Christ coming in judgment, and the sword represents the word of God in judgment. In Hebrews 12:29, God is called a "devouring fire," but that doesn't mean He is literally made of fire. The fire is an image for God's judgment.

What Hell Is

Even if you take away these descriptions that people have used through the ages to describe hell—a place of torture and fire—you still have a terrible place.

Yes, hell is a place. Hell may not be a place like a dungeon or a lake of fire, but it is a place in the sense that it will be a part of the universe where people will be cut off from that glorious place where God and His people will be in blissful harmony. Moreland believes that the reason Jesus used the image of people gnashing their teeth in hell is that people will be in a state of anger and anguish, realizing what a great loss they are suffering.

Hell is also a choice. Most people don't deliberately reject heaven and choose hell. They reject Christ and thereby end up in hell. For all the sins that people can commit, says Moreland, "they pale in light of the worst thing a person can do, which is to mock and dishonor and refuse to love the person that we owe absolutely everything to, which is our Creator, God Himself."[8]

Before we get angry at God for creating hell, we need to keep in mind that hell was not part of God's original creation. Hell was something God had to create because people chose to rebel against Him, and it saddens Him. We know this for two reasons. One, in a dramatic moment before His triumphal entry into Jerusalem, Jesus weeps over Jerusalem even as He is pronouncing judgment because the city did not accept its opportunity for salvation (Luke 19:44). Peter tells us that God is being patient with us because He doesn't want anyone to perish (2 Peter 3:9). But someday God's patience will run out, and the "day of the Lord will come as unexpectedly as a thief" (2 Peter 3:10).

Two Extremes to Avoid

As you might expect, there are two extreme views on how God will deal with those who have chosen to reject Him:

Universal salvation: God will let everyone off the hook. People who hold this view believe that God will save every person in the end due to His love and compassion. True, God is loving and compassionate, but He is also completely just and holy. As a just God, He must deal with injustice. As a holy God, He must deal with sin.

Annihilation: God will destroy those who have not chosen Him. People who hold this view believe that God won't send people to hell; He will destroy them. The problem with this view is that it doesn't account for God's perfect morality. The truth is that everlasting separation from God is morally superior to annihilation. God created humans with His divine imprint, which gives each person intrinsic value. God loves intrinsic value, so He has to be a sustainer rather than a destroyer of persons. Another way to say it is this: God refuses to snuff out a creature that was made in His own image.

Eternity Begins Now

The evidence seems to show that immortality is real and that we will continue to live eternally in heaven or hell, depending on the choice we make now. For the person who is choosing hell, the life he or she has on earth is as good as it gets. For the person who is choosing heaven, this life on earth will pale when compared to what lies ahead in heaven.

For those who respond by faith to God's plan of salvation, eternity with Him begins now. Eternal life is not just life in heaven. "With Jesus," says N.T. Wright, "the future hope has come forward into the present."

What's That Again?

1. Your view of immortality depends on your world-view. The naturalist denies that immortality exists, the relativist can take it or leave it, and the theist believes immortality is possible.

2. Immortality is what you would expect from a supernatural God. If you have good reason to believe God exists, it's reasonable to believe that immortality exists.

3. Four arguments for immortality are based on God's divine imprint, His divine justice, His divine love, and His divine revelation.

4. The resurrection of Jesus—a factual, historic event—provides empirical evidence for immortality. The apostle Paul asserts that if Christ has not been raised, the Christian faith is worthless.

5. Heaven is a real place, created by God, that will exist forever. Heaven is where Jesus lives now and where all believers will live in the future.

6. Heaven includes a new heaven, a new earth, and a new Jerusalem. When we get to heaven, we will be able to explore and learn things about heaven, each other, and God.

7. Jesus, Paul, and John used graphic images like fire and burning sulfur to describe hell. Many people take the description literally. J.P. Moreland believes they are symbolic images of God's judgment.

8. Hell is a place where people will be in a state of anger and anguish, realizing the horror of their eternal separation from God and the glorious place where He is dwelling with His people.

Dig Deeper

Here are three different books on the afterlife and heaven that will help you think about your own immortality:

Beyond Death by J.P. Moreland and Gary Habermas is our personal favorite, but it's a bit technical. You may use it more as a reference book than something you would read for enjoyment.

On the other hand, Peter Kreeft's *Everything You Always Wanted to Know About Heaven* is a book you can read just for pleasure. It's a delight.

N.T. Wright is one of today's most imaginative and thought-provoking Christian writers. His book *Surprised by Hope: Rethinking Heaven, the Resurrection, and the Mission of the Church* will challenge you and stimulate your thinking.

■ ■ ■

*Q*uestions for *R*eflection and *D*iscussion

1. How much time do you spend thinking about immortality and eternity? Did you ever think there was actual evidence for eternal life?

2. What does it mean to you to be a citizen of heaven? If you took this seriously, how should that change the way you view your citizenship on earth?

3. Why would Paul hinge the Christian faith on the resurrection of Christ? Would you be a Christian if you had no hope of eternal life in heaven? Why or why not?

4. What kind of images of heaven have you had throughout your life? How has this chapter changed your thinking about heaven? What are the first three things you will do when you get to heaven?

5. What does it mean to you to know that you will have complete peace, rest, security and protection, beauty, and

fellowship in heaven? In what ways are these things distorted here on earth?

6. What's the difference between hell being a place of punish*ment* and a place of punish*ing*? Do you agree with J.P. Moreland's opinion that hell, while a terrible place of eternal separation, is not God's personal torture chamber?

7. Why was it necessary for God to create hell? In what ways would God's character be diminished if He didn't deal with sin and injustice?

8. Summarize the two extreme views on the afterlife: universalism and annihilation.

Moving On...

As we move to the last chapter in this section on faith, we're going to take a look at the institution that has done more good for people and also more damage to people than any other institution on earth. We're talking, of course, about the church, a place that has helped many people to believe and caused many others to doubt.

At its worst—when people corrupt it—the church can be like hell on earth. But at its best—the way God intended it—the church can be more like heaven.

Chapter 10

Before Christ sent the church into the
world he sent the Spirit into the church.
The same order must be observed today.

—*John Stott*

The church means different things to different people. For some it's a place of sacred community where they can worship God and learn about Him with others who share their beliefs. For others it's like a social club where they can go to meet people with shared values. But for a certain segment of the population, the church represents power, oppression, and corruption. For those who view the church positively, it serves to reinforce their beliefs, or at least it doesn't detract from them. For those who have negative feelings, however, the church can be a barrier to true faith.

In this chapter we're going to take a brief look at the church, from its 2000-year history to its current state. For those who are already big fans of the church, what you're about to read should be an encouragement. And for those who think the church is an idea that has run its course, what you're about to read will cause you to think again. That's because the church is God's idea, and His ideas never go out of style.

Church and Culture

*T*he church is getting hammered from all sides these days. The easy targets are the people who call themselves Christians but don't live up to the family name—the prominent minister who fails morally, the television evangelist who comes under scrutiny for questionable financial practices, the pastor who makes homophobic or racial comments, the priest accused of sexual abuse. The media love to showcase these people.

And it isn't just the people themselves who are getting shot at. Whenever people claiming allegiance to a particular religion commit an atrocity, social critics point out that religion itself is the cause of much of the violence in history. Christianity is not immune to these allegations, especially when you consider the Crusades, the Inquisition, and other violent acts inspired by the church. And then there is the shameful thread of anti-Semitism that is woven through the church's history. Not a pretty picture.

The Church Under Fire

Without a doubt, the church is under fire. When you combine the history of violence with the negative publicity currently plaguing the church, you can understand why many people are skeptical that the church is a place where you can go to experience authentic spirituality. For a growing number of spiritual people, including many committed Christians, the church is no longer a place where they go to develop their faith relationship with God.

In fact, new studies on religious life in America show that up to one-fourth of all church attenders have either switched churches or left the church altogether. Protestant and Catholic churches alike have lost members. Today just half of all Americans consider themselves Protestant, compared with two-thirds of the population in the 1970s. Catholic churches have experienced similar declines.

People Are Still Spiritual

People are leaving the church in record numbers, but that doesn't mean they aren't spiritual. To the contrary, people are more spiritual than ever. They just aren't interested in the kind of spirituality offered by the institutional church. For many people, their relationship with God has become a private matter. Others don't want their faith confined to a church building or program. They want to live out their relationship with God in the culture rather than to separate from the culture.

In his groundbreaking book *Revolution,* George Barna identifies upward of 20 million spiritual people who have left the church because "they are seeking a faith experience that is more robust and awe inspiring."[1] These "Revolutionaries" believe the church has failed to meet their need for intimate worship and intentional spiritual growth. Furthermore, they don't think the church encourages the very things they value: faith-based conversations, servanthood, and resource investment.

*W*hat Emerging Generations Think About the Church

In his book *They Like Jesus but Not the Church,* Dan Kimball identifies six perceptions that the emerging generation—and this includes Christians as well as non-Christians—have of the church:[2]

The church is an organized religion with a political agenda.

The church is judgmental and negative.

The church is dominated by males and oppresses females.

The church is homophobic.

The church arrogantly claims all other religions are wrong.

The church is full of fundamentalists who take the whole Bible literally.

What's Going to Happen to the Church?

With all that's going on in the church and with all the people leaving the church, what's going to happen to the church? Barna is convinced that the Revolutionaries are already finding alternate places—homes, cafes, schools, parks, the Internet—where they can gather together to experience authentic spirituality. For them, the world—not a building—is the church. For this reason, this twenty-first-century "spiritual awakening" (as Barna calls it) is different from past spiritual movements.

> In the great awakenings of America's history, the pattern was always the same: draw people into the local church for teaching and other experiences. In this new movement of God, the approach is the opposite: it entails drawing people away from reliance upon a local church into a deeper connection with and reliance upon God.[3]

Does this mean the church as we know it is dead, or at least dying? Hardly. It may be going through a dynamic transformation, but the rumors of the church's demise are greatly exaggerated. How do we know? Because there's a difference between the church—the

building on the corner with the First Baptist Church sign in front—
and the church—the body of believers who have committed themselves to Jesus Christ by faith. Before we suggest some remedies for
the local church (and we'll do that at the end of this chapter), we
need to see what the universal church is all about.

What Is the Church?

In reality, the church includes all Christians—those who believe
in the God of the Bible and have received Jesus Christ as their
personal Savior—for all time. In other words, all Christians living
today are part of the church, but so are all believers who have
died.

*T*he Church Belongs to God

The word *church* means "belongs to the Lord." In the New Testament,
the Greek word *ekklesia* was used by the writers to describe a group of
people who were "called out" by God. In the Old Testament, the nation
of Israel was referred to as a group of people "called out" by God, so in a
sense there was a church before Jesus came to earth. But the church we
know today came into existence with the coming of Christ. Jesus loved
and died for the church (Ephesians 5:25), and He has promised to build
the church (Matthew 16:18) by calling people to Himself through salvation
(Acts 2:47). Jesus began calling out people to Himself when He chose the
original 12 disciples. Think of these 13 men as a little church that eventually experienced explosive growth on the Day of Pentecost, when the Holy
Spirit first came in power to all believers (Acts 2:1-42).

The Church Is Invisible and Visible

Because the church includes all genuine believers for all time,
and because it is more than a collection of buildings and groups of
people, there is a sense in which the church is invisible. From our
human perspective, we don't know for sure who the true believers
are. That's because we can't see people the way God sees them.
Only God knows the true condition of the heart (2 Timothy 2:19).
As theologian Wayne Grudem states, "The invisible church is the
church as God sees it."

At the same time, the church is definitely visible. When we claim to be Christians and there is evidence of our faith in our lives, we can rightly say we are members of God's church. Professing Christians are the visible representative of the church. Here's the way Grudem puts it: "The visible church is the church as Christians on earth see it."

The Church Is Local and Universal

The word *church* can apply to local groups, whether they meet in special buildings, schools, homes, cafes, or even outdoors. And it can also apply to the universal church, which is the church throughout the world and throughout time. The bottom line is that those who have been called out by God at any level are part of the church.

Metaphors for the Church

To help us understand the true nature of the church, the Bible gives us several helpful metaphors and images. Here are three that relate to the three persons of the Trinity:

The people of God. We talked about this image when we said the church is made up of those who are "called out" by God. In the history of salvation, God has always called out people for Himself, for His purpose, and for His glory. In the Old Testament, God called out the Hebrew nation, and since Christ came to Earth, God's church has been grafted like branches into the plan God has for the people who belong to Him (Romans 11:17-18). The church can also be called the family of God. As believers, God is our heavenly Father (Ephesians 3:14), and we are His sons and daughters (2 Corinthians 6:18).

The body of Christ. This is the apostle Paul's favorite metaphor for the church, and he uses it in two ways. First, *the body of Christ* refers to the church as a body where the various parts or members (such as the foot, hand, ear, or eye) function together for service. This part of the metaphor emphasizes the diversity and mutuality of the church. We all have different gifts, and we all need each other (1 Corinthians 12:12-17). The other way Paul uses the metaphor emphasizes the unity of the church. We are all one body, and Christ is the head (Ephesians 1:22-23; 4:15-16).

The temple of the Holy Spirit. A temple is a physical place where God dwells. Similarly, the church is where God dwells with His people through the Holy Spirit. This happens to each of us individually (1 Corinthians 6:19) and to the church corporately (1 Corinthians 3:16).

A Brief History of the Church

You might be tempted to skip over this section (after all, it is about history), but we would urge you to take this whirlwind tour of the two-thousand-year history of the church. Knowing where the church came from will give you a greater appreciation for where the church is today. We're going to divide this section into three periods in church history: the ancient church (5 BC to AD 590), the church in the Middle Ages (590 to 1517), and the modern church (1517 to the present).

The Ancient Church (5 BC to AD 590)

The church as we know it began with Jesus Christ. Christianity and the church cannot exist apart from the life, death, and resurrection of Christ.

The Apostles and the Early Church

After His resurrection and before His ascension, Jesus gave His followers a set of instructions known as the Great Commission:

> *But you will receive power when the Holy Spirit comes upon you. And you will be my witnesses, telling people about me everywhere—in Jerusalem, throughout Judea, in Samaria, and to the ends of the earth* (Acts 1:8).

The early church followed these marching orders to the letter. The first 12 chapters of Acts tell us how the good news message of Jesus was first proclaimed in Jerusalem, where Peter preached on the day of Pentecost. Initially the early church was primarily Jewish as the message spread from Jerusalem to the rest of Judea and to Samaria. Then, beginning in Acts 13, the apostle Paul followed these instructions from the Lord: "Take my message to the Gentiles and to kings, as well as to the people of Israel" (Acts 9:15). Through the tireless efforts of Paul and the other apostles (the word *apostle* means sent one), the gospel went to every corner of the known world.

The Apostolic Fathers

With the martyrdom of Peter and Paul in AD 64 and 68, the destruction of Jerusalem in AD 70, and the death of John at the end of the first century, the apostolic age came to an end. With all of the original apostles dead, the leadership of the church passed to the next generation, known as the Apostolic Fathers. Despite the persecution inflicted by Roman authorities during the second century, Christianity spread west from Antioch and across the Mediterranean to Northern Africa. Two of the most prominent Apostolic Fathers, Ignatius and Polycarp, were executed for their belief in Jesus Christ.

Peace at Last

At the beginning of the fourth century, the persecution of the church was still pretty bad, but there was some hope. The Roman Empire was ruled by two imperial leaders—Galerius in the east and Constantius Chlorus in the west. Galerius was determined to wipe out Christianity, but Constantius stopped the persecution of Christians in his realm. His son, Constantine, assembled an army to capture Rome from the eastern powers. When he encountered his opponent at the Milvian Bridge just outside the walls of Rome, Constantine turned to the Christian God for help. In a vision he saw a cross with the words, "In this sign conquer." He took this as a sign to advance, and he subsequently defeated the enemy and took control of the Roman Empire. In 313 Constantine issued the Edict of Milan, officially ending all persecution against Christians.

Orthodox Theology

Finally, after more than 200 years of persecution, Christians were able to take a breath and address a very important issue: what they believed. When you live in a culture where it's illegal and downright dangerous to practice your faith, thinking about the details of your belief is difficult. You either believe in Jesus or you don't. But when the pressure of persecution is lifted, you tend to look deeper into your beliefs. This is what Christians in the fourth and fifth centuries did. They defined what it meant to have orthodox theology.

*T*heology and Orthodoxy

Theology comes from two Greek words: *theos* (God) and *logos* (word or rational thought). In essence, theology is rational thought about God. *Orthodox* theology is theology that conforms to what church leaders through the ages have agreed is correct.

From 313 to 481, several theological controversies erupted and resulted in four major church councils (like our modern-day conventions). The purpose of these councils was to resolve the conflicts by forming creeds, or statements of belief. Although there were several issues, the core of the debates centered on the person, the nature, and the essence of Jesus Christ. Four major church councils met over a period of 150 years in order to correctly understand the true person of Christ.

- *The Council of Nicea (325).* As the Roman emperor, Constantine called the first council to deal with the controversy concerning the divine nature of Christ. The central statement of the Nicene creed is that Jesus is "true God from true God" and "begotten, not created."

- *The Council of Constantinople (381).* Another debate centered on the humanity of Christ. Just as Nicea declared Jesus to be fully God, Constantinople declared Jesus to be fully human. The position of Constantinople was this: "The word of God has become flesh."

- *The Council of Ephesus (431).* Once the two natures of Christ were fully defined, another conflict arose: How do the two natures of Christ interact? Some people at this council thought the two natures had to be completely distinct and could never mix. Yet Scripture clearly teaches that Jesus' two natures were in a perfect relationship. Therefore, this council insisted on the unity of Christ's person. In other words, Christ was one person with two natures.

- *The Council of Chalcedon (451).* This council also confronted an issue concerning the natures of Christ. Chalcedon came up with this orthodox position: The two natures of Jesus are joined in one person without confusion, change, diversion, or separation. The reason this is so important is that salvation depends on it. Jesus died and was resurrected as both God and man. As God He saved us, and as man He identified with us.

We need to be thankful for the hard work done at these councils by people who cared deeply about correctly stating the truth of their faith. Whether they were dealing with the nature of Christ or the reality of the Trinity, their focus always remained on the deity and the redemptive work of the Lord Jesus Christ. They showed us that the church has always been and forever will be about Jesus.

The Church in the Middle Ages (590 to 1517)

Many people think of the Middle Ages—also known as the medieval era—as the Dark Ages. Nothing could be further from the truth. Historians agree that the medieval period provided the very foundation of Western thought both in philosophy and theology. Consider some of this period's significant contributions:

- Augustine and Aquinas produced their writings;
- the university was born;
- the great cathedrals of Europe—some of history's greatest architectural wonders—were designed and constructed; and
- the printing press, which led to a flowering of literacy and knowledge, was developed.

Culturally, the church had a huge influence on how people lived. As we will see, abuses arose as the church gained more and more power, but the overall benefit to society was profound. There was no such thing as a secular culture. If you lived in the Middle Ages, you lived your life fully aware of the one true God.

The First Medieval Pope

The reason the year 590 is usually considered the beginning of the Middle Ages is that this was the year Gregory I (also called the Great) became the bishop of Rome (he refused the title of pope). The Roman Empire had collapsed, leaving a vacuum that was filled by the Roman Catholic Church and its new leader. Gregory the Great was a strong advocate of Scripture as the measure for life, and he encouraged missionary activity throughout the world.

The Rise of Islam and the Crusades

During the seventh century and later, Christianity was confronted with a new monotheistic faith—Islam. Founded by Muhammad (570–632), Islam was based on a series of revelations Muhammad claimed to receive from the angel Gabriel. The revelations were eventually collected in a new scripture called the Qur'an (Koran).

Islam spread quickly as Muhammad preached faith in Allah. In 622 Muhammad and his followers were forced to flee to Yathrib (later renamed Medina, "the city of the prophet"). This flight to Medina, known as the Hegira, marks the beginning of the Islamic calendar and is considered the most important event in Islamic history. By 630 Muhammad had gained control over most of the Arabian peninsula. Within a hundred years, his successors had conquered Palestine, northern Africa, and Spain.

Arabs dominated Islam until the eleventh century, when the Seljuk Turks took over. Much more fanatical than the Arabs, the Turks harassed Christians making pilgrimages to Jerusalem, and they threatened the security of the Eastern church. In 1095, Pope Urban II issued a call to deliver the holy places of Palestine from Muslim control, officially kicking off the Crusades. As church historian Earle Cairns writes, "The whole movement may be characterized as a holy war against the enemies of the cross by the spiritual forces of Western Christendom." There were seven major crusades, but the First Crusade was the only successful one. The liberation of Jerusalem in 1099 and the creation of feudal states were the main results.

Christianity as a Reasonable Faith

Is the Christian faith a blind leap in the dark, or is it reasonable? That's what we've been wrestling with in this book, and we can thank a group of medieval theologians known as the Scholastics for answering this question in the affirmative. Two of the most important Scholastics were Anselm of Canterbury (1033–1109) and Thomas Aquinas (1225–1274).

Crisis and Corruption

During the fourteenth and fifteenth centuries, the Roman Catholic Church experienced two things that paved the way for the Reformation: a crisis of leadership and increased corruption and fraud. Immorality and greed among many church leaders undermined their authority. It was common for clergy to buy and sell church offices (a practice known as *simony*). Even worse, the church raised money by selling holy relics (called *indulgences*) in exchange for forgiveness of sin and a reduced time in purgatory.

Beginning in the fourteenth century, several prominent people were openly disagreeing with the Roman Church and calling for reform. John Wycliffe (1330–1384), an English reformer, boldly questioned papal authority, church hierarchies, and other Catholic practices. He believed that the only way to overcome abusive authority was to make the Bible available to everyday people in their own language. (Until then the Bible was available only in Latin, and only church leaders could read it.) Wycliffe was convinced that if people could read Scripture for themselves, they would understand how they could have a personal relationship with Jesus Christ without going through the church. He was the first to translate the Latin Bible into English. By the sixteenth century, church reform seemed inevitable. All that was needed was a strong leader.

The Modern Church (1517 to the Present)

The strong leader was Martin Luther (1483–1546), generally considered the father of the Protestant Reformation. Luther was educated in the finest Roman Catholic schools and became both a monk and a priest. As he studied the Scriptures, however, he became increasingly disillusioned with Roman Catholic practices, particularly the sale of indulgences for forgiveness of sin. Luther was convinced that pardon for sin came through faith alone (*sola fide*). Works had nothing to do with it. And he believed that the Bible alone (*sola scriptura*) is the source of final authority and truth. By 1516 Luther was teaching that our inward righteousness was the gift of God and was the source—rather than the result—of good works.

The Reformation

On October 31, 1517, Luther went public with his arguments against the sale of indulgences by posting the 95 Theses on the door of the Castle Church in Wittenberg, Germany. Luther wasn't thinking that by doing this, he was going to create a whole new movement. He simply wanted to reform certain abuses that had negative consequences for morality and faith.

Essentially the 95 Theses were an invitation to debate the issues publicly (that was the protocol back then). But no one wanted to debate Luther, mainly because most of the professors and students at Wittenberg agreed with him. Instead, someone translated the theses from Latin into German and circulated them. As Luther's beliefs spread throughout Europe, the Reformation caught on like wildfire. Other leaders, such as the Swiss reformers Ulrich Zwingli and John Calvin, gained followers with their own theological interpretations. In fact, Calvin's influence was so strong that he inspired the Dutch Reformation and the English Reformation, as well as the Puritans who sailed to the New World in search of religious freedom a hundred years later.

The Impact of the Reformation on Culture

Church historian Earle Cairns explains how the Reformation impacted culture in positive ways:[4]

- It helped to create a demand for universal elementary education, because if people were able to interpret the Bible for themselves, they must be able to read;

- its insistence on spiritual equality motivated people to seek political equality;

- it promoted the rise of democracy in both the church and the state;

- it stimulated capitalism.

The Catholic Counter-Reformation

The energy and the commitment of the Protestant Reformers (they were called that because the reformers were seen as protesting the teaching and practices of the Catholic Church) put Catholicism on the defensive. Under the leadership of Pope Paul III, a Counter-Reformation began. For 18 years—from 1545 to 1563—a group of bishops met 25 different times at the Council of Trent to craft a response. The council acknowledged some of the abuses and established new guidelines for clergy. However, Trent rejected justification by faith alone and emphasized the need for works in order to be saved. Furthermore, the council declared that church tradition had equal authority with Scripture. These declarations did nothing to bring about a reconciliation between Catholics and Protestants.

Protestantism Gets Cold

Protestantism flourished in the sixteenth century, but by the seventeenth century it had become cold and impersonal. Christianity was little more than a set of beliefs, and churches weren't instructing people on how to live those beliefs in everyday life. As you would expect, the chilly condition of Protestantism produced two main reactions. One was *rationalism,* a philosophy that says the only way to know truth is through reason. In religious terms, this led to *deism,* which is basically a religion of reason.

Deism and Its Consequences

The deist believes that God created the universe, but He isn't involved with it. In fact, God left His creation to operate by natural laws. The world as we know it doesn't include the supernatural (such as miracles), the Bible is not God's revealed word, and there's no such thing as the deity of Christ. He was simply a moral teacher who insisted that God alone was worthy of worship. Because deism ignored human sin, it was very optimistic about man's goodness and potential to achieve greatness—even perfectibility. Deism became the belief of choice of many of America's founding fathers, such as Benjamin Franklin and Thomas Jefferson.

Revivalism Takes Hold

The other reaction to cold Protestantism was *revivalism,* which emphasized the importance of the Bible and living out your beliefs in everyday life. Quakerism, founded by George Fox (1624–1691) in England, stressed personal experience and taught that the true freedom of Christianity was found in the Spirit—or "inner light"—something each person must follow in order to find God.

Methodism, founded by John Wesley (1703–1791), also in England, taught that the gospel should impact culture. To do this he trained lay preachers (including women) to spread the salvation message across the British Isles to the American frontier, where it flourished. Wesley personally traveled more than 200,000 miles on horseback and preached 42,000 sermons. His brother, Charles, wrote more than 7000 hymns.

The Great Awakenings in America

The Methodist Church laid the groundwork for revivals and growth in America in the eighteenth century. Two Great Awakenings impacted the emerging American culture in significant ways. The first Great Awakening began in the 1720s and was led by George Whitfield and Jonathan Edwards, a brilliant and powerful preacher who had a unique ability to combine the logic of the gospel message with the emotion of the human heart. Out of the first Great Awakening came new denominations, such as the Baptists.

The second Great Awakening came after the American Revolution and affected the new nation even more than the first. Most significantly, it brought about a shift from a theology that stressed God's sovereignty and man's inability to save himself, to a theology that emphasized man's free will and ability in salvation.

Evangelism and the Modern Mission Movement

It was only natural that the revivals and Great Awakenings of the seventeenth and eighteenth centuries would motivate Christians to take the good news message of Jesus around the world. William Carey (1761–1834), considered the father of modern missions, moved his family to Calcutta, India in order to fulfill the Great Commission. His efforts there became a model for modern missions. J. Hudson Taylor (1832–1905) was a pioneer missionary in China, and others took the gospel to previously unreached places, such as Africa. In America, evangelists such as D.L. Moody (1837–1899), Billy Sunday (1869–1935), and Billy Graham have preached the gospel to untold millions of people in this country and throughout the world.

What Is a True Church?

With such a rich and varied history, you might be wondering if all churches today are true to God's original intention. Have some strayed from the values and practices that characterized the early church (the one the Revolutionaries often look to for inspiration)? You might even be in the process of looking for a church to attend. How do you know which church is the best?

First of all, if you're looking for the best or the perfect church, you're going to be disappointed. The only perfect church is the church God sees from His perspective—the invisible church. This is the church that's been called out by God Himself and made possible by the saving life of Christ. But the visible church—the one we can see—is far from perfect, mainly because it contains imperfect people. At the same time, a church can live up to God's intention for His people by displaying at least two characteristics first suggested by Martin Luther and John Calvin: preaching the word of God and practicing baptism and the Lord's supper.

Beyond that, we want to give you three "purposes of the church" suggested by theologian Wayne Grudem:

> Worship—a church's ministry to God.
>
> Nurture—a church's ministry to believers.
>
> Evangelism—a church's ministry to the world.

When a church keeps those purposes in balance, it will be in line with God's purposes for His people who are called by His name.

Confronting the Church Crisis

At the beginning of this chapter, we listed a number of problems facing the church—problems that have caused many people not only to question the church but also to have doubts about

God. We've explained that the church as a building or an institution is distinct from the church as the family of God or the body of Christ. One is an organization, and the other is a living organism. The problems that have existed in the church from the first century to the twenty-first century are produced by human beings, not by God. Still, because the church represents God and claims to speak for Him, we need to sort through some of the more nagging issues and do our best to come up with some responses. These will help you deal with your own doubts about the church and answer questions from those who criticize the church.

When Church Leaders Go Bad

How do you respond when a church leader does something that brings dishonor to the church and the name of Christ? First, remember the difference between the visible church and the invisible church. People can say they are Christians, but that doesn't mean they are. If their actions or words clearly and consistently contradict Christlike behaviors and attitudes, they may not have a personal relationship with Jesus Christ.

In addition, we need to be aware that some people call themselves Christians, but in fact they are teaching a different gospel. This is nothing new. The apostle Paul warns Timothy, a young pastor, about these false teachers:

> *These people always cause trouble. Their minds are corrupt, and they have turned their backs on the truth. To them, a show of godliness is just a way to become wealthy* (1 Timothy 6:5).

Knowing that some people like that are claiming to speak for God doesn't mean that you can excuse every wrongdoing by saying, "Well, that guy isn't really a Christian," or "That crackpot is a false teacher." Authentic Christians and true teachers also do and say the wrong things. We aren't capable of judging who is and who isn't an authentic Christian, so we have to take professions of faith at face value and be ready to give an answer for some of the negative stuff that happens. Here are some suggestions:

- *Acknowledge the problem when it happens.* The worst thing we can do is make excuses for someone's behavior or try to cover it up.

- *Hold the wayward church leader accountable.* As the body of Christ, we need to hold one another accountable for our actions, whether we are on a national stage or in a local church. This doesn't mean that we condemn the sinner (if we did that, none of us would be able to stand!). Instead, as Paul instructs, we need to restore our fallen or wayward brothers and sisters in Christ:

  > *Dear brothers and sisters, if another believer*
  > *is overcome by some sin, you who are godly*
  > *should gently and humbly help that person*
  > *back onto the right path* (Galatians 6:1).

- *Realize that the Bible doesn't gloss over flawed characters.* The Bible is an honest book. As far as human nature goes, it gives us the good with the bad. And it doesn't gloss over the fact that some of the people who loved God the deepest had the most serious character flaws. Moses (called a friend of God) murdered a man. David (called a man after God's heart) committed adultery and then tried to cover up his sin by having the husband killed. Paul (the greatest Christian missionary in history) struggled with his own sins.

When the Church Engages in Violence and Abuse

How do you respond to the history of violence in the church? Remember the difference between cultural and authentic Christianity. Sadly, at various times throughout history, the institutional church has merged with culture as it has gained political and economic power. From this power has come violence, oppression, and abuse. In fact, some of the most intense persecution against Christians has been carried out by the institutional church. Although these actions do not discredit the true church, we need to acknowledge that the church has been guilty of them.

Additionally, people have often done things in the name of Christ that they should not have done. Consequently, we can't blame Christianity for everything done in Christ's name.

Finally, we have to keep this in mind: Although violence in the name of Christianity is inexcusable, even the harshest critic of Christianity has to admit that much (if not most) of the violence in the world is done by people and regimes that don't claim any connection to Jesus Christ or Christianity. "We can only conclude," writes Tim Keller, "that there is some violent impulse so deeply rooted in the human heart that it expresses itself regardless of what the beliefs of a particular society might be."[5]

When the Church Isn't Meeting Your Needs

We're not going to spend a whole lot of time with this response because the answer is pretty straightforward. If you aren't happy with a particular church or the church in general because it's not meeting your needs, perhaps it's time to realize that church exists for a higher purpose than to meet your needs and make you happy.

---

*W*hat to Do If You're Unhappy with Your Church

Your church may meet in a beautiful building with stained-glass windows, a rented school cafeteria, or a corner café. If you're unhappy with the way things are going, there are three productive things and three unproductive things you can do.

Three productive things you can do:

> Stay where you are and help make improvements.

> Find another church where you can exercise your spiritual gifts.

> Help start a new church.

Three unproductive things you can do:

> Do nothing.

> Complain.

> Stop going to church altogether.

Yes, the church can help you deal with your problems. After all, as the old saying goes: "The church is a hospital for sinners, not a museum for saints."[6] Needy people shouldn't be turned away (if that were the case, none of us would qualify to join). At the same time, we need to realize that the reason God wants us to go to church and participate in the living organism called the body of Christ is that we are needed! God has given each one of us spiritual gifts so that we can build up the body, not tear it down. Here's the way Paul puts it:

> *In his grace, God has given us different gifts for doing certain things well...If your gift is serving others, serve them well. If you are a teacher, teach well. If your gift is to encourage others, be encouraging. If it is giving, give generously. If God has given you leadership ability, take the responsibility seriously. And if you have a gift for showing kindness to others, do it gladly* (Romans 12:6-8).

Before you bail on your church because it's not meeting your needs, evaluate your own spiritual condition to make sure you are doing your part to meet the needs of others by putting your spiritual gifts into practice.

What's That Again?

1. The church is under fire because of past troubles, current negative publicity, and the perception that it is not meeting the spiritual needs of people.

2. People today are just as spiritual as they ever were. Many just aren't interested in the kind of spirituality offered by the institutional church.

3. The word *church* means "belongs to the Lord." The true church includes all Christians for all time.

4. The church relates to all three persons of the Trinity. Those who belong to the true church are part of the family of God, the body of Christ, and the temple of the Holy Spirit.

5. The ancient church era (5 BC to AD 590) included the apostles, the apostolic fathers, and the church councils of the fourth and fifth centuries, when the orthodox theology of the church was defined.

6. The church in the Middle Ages (590–1517) encouraged the birth of the university, the construction of great cathedrals, and the development of the printing press. During this era, Christianity was established as a reasonable faith.

7. The modern church (1517 to the present) included the Protestant Reformation, revivalism, the American Great Awakenings, and the modern missionary movement.

8. A true church is one where the Bible is preached and the sacraments of baptism and the Lord's Supper are practiced. The three purposes of the church are worship, nurture, and evangelism.

9. When church leaders go bad and the institutional church engages in violence and abuse, we need to acknowledge the problems and deal with them. At the same time, we need to remember that Christianity can't be blamed for everything done in Christ's name.

Dig Deeper

Here are the three books we found most helpful as we researched this chapter:

The Case for Faith by Lee Strobel. Lee interviewed an expert in church history who had some valuable insights into ways we can respond today to things that happened a long time ago.

The Reason for God by Tim Keller contains a terrific chapter on ways to respond to the perception that the church is responsible for so much violence.

We would recommend that you read a book on church history once in your life. One of the best is called *Christianity Through the Centuries* by Earle Cairns.

■ ■ ■

Questions for Reflection and Discussion

1. What is your current church experience? Are you active in a local church? Why or why not? If you are, do you believe your church is meeting your spiritual needs?

2. Take a look at the emerging generation's six perceptions of the church. Why do you think these perceptions exist? Which ones do you agree with? Which ones do you disagree with?

3. Explain the difference between the invisible and visible church. What is the difference between the local and universal church? To which of these do you belong?

4. Which of the three metaphors for the church do you most closely identify with? Explain why.

5. Why was it important for the church councils to recognize that Jesus is both fully human and also fully God? Why is this important for you personally?

6. John Wycliffe believed that the way to overcome abusive church authority was to make the Bible available to everyday people in their own language. Why was this so important? Why is it still important?

7. When you look at the characteristics of a true church, including the three purposes we listed, how well do you think your church is measuring up?

8. Several years ago Pope John Paul II began calling for the church to acknowledge its role in "the dark side of history." Do you think church leaders are responsible to do this?

What can you do as an individual to help people deal with the hurt the church has caused them?

9. Why are we prone to want the church to meet our needs? What can you do to help meet the needs of others in your church?

Moving On...

We hope we've helped you answer some of the questions you've had about the church. Even more, as we have come to the end of this section on questioning faith, we hope you are ready to move on to a couple of chapters that are going to show how the Christian faith stands apart from other belief systems and how the experience of faith is a powerful component of a reasonable faith.

Part IV
A Faith You Can
Live With

Introduction to Part IV

What's Ahead

*I*f you feel a little overwhelmed at this point, we don't blame you. Over the span of ten chapters, you've taken in a lot of information. It's time to take a deep breath and think about what you're going to do with all of this knowledge. That's what the final two chapters in the book are about.

In chapter 11, we will consider how Christianity—essentially, the Christian faith—stacks up in the marketplace of ideas. It's one thing for you to believe this stuff, but how do you engage the culture—that would be your friends, family, coworkers, fellow students, even complete strangers—in conversations about faith? Let's face it, if you're a Christian, and you're breathing, and you leave the house each day, you're going to run into all kinds of people with all kinds of beliefs. How do you live out your faith in a pluralistic culture?

An Example You Can Follow

When it comes to talking to people about faith, it helps to have people we can look to as examples. You may know people who are "in the world" sharing their faith in creative ways. Great! Follow them around and learn from them. If you don't have a model you can follow, we have one, and he's probably the second-best example you could ever find.

Aside from Jesus, the apostle Paul is considered the most influential person in the history of Christianity. He was a brilliant man, but he never came across as a know-it-all. He had two qualities that made him an extremely effective witness for his faith: He was humble, and he had a great love for people. One particular episode in Paul's life provides a glimpse into the way he related to people on a spiritual level. The story is told in Acts 17:16-34.

Paul and the Philosophers

The year is AD 50, and Paul is in the middle of his second missionary journey. He makes a stop in Athens—a major cultural, intellectual, and religious center—to wait for the rest of his missionary team, who are supposed to meet him there. Paul is probably relaxing, taking in the sights, eating some Greek food. He isn't looking for a debate, but he is ready to let God use him.

As he is walking around the city, he notices dozens and dozens of idols, many representing classic Greek gods, and this troubles him (Acts 17:16). But instead of going back to his motel to get away from the spiritual darkness, Paul goes into the public square, where he talks to everyone. The Bible says he has a debate with some Epicureans and Stoic philosophers (17:18). The Epicureans didn't care a whole lot about religion, but instead pursued pleasure by trying to live a tranquil life free from pain. The Stoics believed that God lived in all things and that the happy life was lived as one with nature.

There may not be any Epicureans and Stoics around today, but their philosophy lives on. These belief systems are still around today. In Paul's day, neither of these groups could relate to Paul's faith. When Paul told them about Jesus, they thought he was strange. "He seems to be preaching about some foreign gods," they said (17:18).

So Paul, who has done his homework and knows what these philosophers believe, changes his tactic. He isn't ashamed of Jesus. He is just being wise in his approach. When the philosophers ask him to further explain his beliefs, Paul doesn't condemn them for their religiosity—he commends them. And he comments specifically on the inscription he sees on one particular idol: "To an Unknown God."

Paul compliments them for their desire to know God, and then he offers to tell them about the one true God. It's a brilliant move on Paul's part, and he pulls it off because he knows what the philosophers believe.

Gerald McDermott, author of *Can Evangelicals Learn from World Religions?*, is critical of Christians who approach people of other faiths "with the assumption that their religions are totally false or wholly demonic, and that if they accept Christ they must discard everything they have ever known about the divine."[1] When we assume that people who hold other beliefs are completely in the dark, we risk alienating them from wanting to know more about our faith. Paul doesn't do this.

In a very reasonable yet loving way, Paul tells them about the Unknown God who is closer to them than they realize. Here's what he says about the God they can know (Acts 17:24-31):

> He is the God who made the world and everything in it.
>
> He doesn't live in man-made temples.
>
> He doesn't need anything from us, but we need everything from Him.
>
> He created everything and is involved with all He created.
>
> He wants us to seek Him and find Him, and He's not far away.
>
> He has given us evidence of His existence.
>
> He wants everyone to turn to Him.
>
> He is being patient, but someday there will be judgment.

Not Everyone Will Respond—But Some Will

You would think that after Paul's eloquent, loving, and persuasive explanation of his Christian faith, the people would line up to receive Christ. But that doesn't happen.

> *When they heard Paul speak about the resurrection of the dead, some laughed in contempt, but others said, "We want to hear more about this later." That ended Paul's discussion with them, but some joined him and became believers* (Acts 17:32-34).

This is what's great about the Bible. It's realistic about life and the way things are. The writer of Acts doesn't have to reveal that some people laughed at Paul, but he leaves it in as an encouragement to the rest of us. Not everyone is going to respond to our explanations of Christianity. Some will even laugh, but others will want to hear more about our faith. Notice that Paul is content to stop talking. He doesn't feel the need to continue explaining or pleading with these people. He trusts God that he will be able to continue the discussion at another time and another place.

That's the way we need to be when we witness for Christ. The timing isn't up to us. Only God knows when and where someone will respond to His love and His plan. If people do become believers, it's because the Holy Spirit is moving in their lives, not because we are so persuasive.

Your Faith Is More Than You Know

As important as it is to know what you believe, you need to remember that your faith is more than you know. What do we mean by that? Simply this. Your own experience of faith—the personal way you can sense God's presence in your life—is another way that you can know God is real. That's what we're going to talk about in chapter 12 as we conclude our journey together.

Chapter 11

I believe in Christianity as I believe that the
sun has risen, not only because I see it,
but because by it I see everything else.

—*C.S. Lewis*

Many people believe that the various religions express the same truth in different ways. In their view, God sits at the top of a great mountain, and all of the belief systems out there are like trails leading upward to God. What you believe doesn't matter as long as you sincerely believe in God and are doing your best to reach Him.

That may sound wonderful, but it's not reasonable. By definition, all religions are different and even mutually exclusive at different points. It would be more reasonable to say that all religions are false than to say they are all true. Let's assume for a moment that there is at least one religion that's true. If that's the case, the next question is this: Which one is it? What a great question! In fact, it's *the* question because the answer will point you to the ultimate source of truth, which is the main business of religion. As Paul Tillich writes, "Religion is all that is connected to one's ultimate concern."

How do you go about finding which religion is true? A good way would be to investigate the truth claims made by each of the major religions and belief systems. That's what any reasonable and open-minded religious seeker would do. But before you or any honest seeker does that, we would like to suggest that you do something first: Investigate the claims of Christianity. We're going to tell you why in this chapter.

A Case for Christianity

*L*ike the church, Christianity has taken it on the chin lately. *But wait a minute,* you might be thinking. *Aren't the church and Christianity the same thing?* Not exactly. Whether you think of the church as a visible and local organization or an invisible and universal organism, the church involves people called out by God.

By comparison, Christianity is more closely related to the Christian faith (in fact, we've used those two terms interchangeably throughout the book). It's more about the beliefs of people than it is about the people who believe. So when critics complain about Christianity, they are generally focusing on the Christian belief system that claims to point people to the ultimate source of truth.

So what do people complain about when the subject turns to Christianity? Nine times out of ten, it's the reputation that Christianity has for being a narrow, intolerant, and judgmental belief system. Nobody likes to be told they're wrong in what they believe (especially if they are told they are going to hell as a result), yet that's exactly the perception many people have of Christians and Christianity. Mike Erre puts it this way:

> From behind our fortress of objective, absolute truth, Christianity has traditionally been defended with a "we're right, you're wrong," "us versus them" mindset that alienates, divides, and threatens. Such a paradigm is unbiblical and wrongheaded.[1]

Taking a Different Approach

Some people may have taken the wrong approach in defending Christianity, but that doesn't mean it shouldn't be defended. After all, Christianity is a belief system, and we are told in Scripture to offer an *apologia*—a defense—for our hope (which is based on what we believe), so we should be ready, willing, and able to defend Christianity. But we shouldn't get defensive. Like the apostle Paul in the ancient city of Athens, we need to show respect for the beliefs of others by actually knowing what they believe. Only then do we earn the right to share what we believe.

Now, you could spend a lifetime studying other religions. There are dozens—make that hundreds—of religions and belief systems out there, and you wouldn't have to go very far to get a firsthand look. If you live in America, you live in the most religiously diverse nation in the world. Chances are good that your neighborhood has its share of people who believe much differently from the way you do—with just as much sincerity and devotion.

Whether you are a Christian or not, it makes sense to study other religions. If you are a Christian, studying what others believe will help you relate to your neighbors as you engage them in conversations about faith. Paul was able to find common ground with the philosophers of Athens because he knew their beliefs. He could even quote their poets! Studying other religions has another benefit: It gives you a greater appreciation for what you believe.

If you are not a Christian and you are honestly searching for truth, you would be wise to investigate the truth claims of all the major religions and belief systems. How else are you going to find the ultimate source of truth, which is the main business of religion?

$\mathcal{A}$ll Truth Is God's Truth

Sometimes Christians believe they have a corner on truth and that somehow God has confined everything that's true into one single system (namely, Christianity). But how can that be? If something is true and God is true, why wouldn't that truth be God's truth? Just because the person or religion making the truthful statement isn't Christian doesn't invalidate the statement. Mike Erre makes the point that Christians don't need to feel threatened by truth outside of the Bible, "for all truth is a reflection of the Holy Creator God."

Start with Christianity

As we said, a lot of religions are out there. If you were to study them one by one, where would you start? Would you make an alphabetical list, starting with Buddhism and moving through the alphabet until you got to Zoroastrianism? Or would you go from the oldest religion to the newest?

You could certainly conduct your study that way, but it would take a while. You could easily get discouraged (or grow old) before you finish. So we'd like to make another suggestion that comes from our good friend, Dr. Craig Hazen. He advises that anyone who wants to study world religions and make a comparison between them should start with Christianity. "It's the only religion that's testable," he says. "So you start with Christianity and measure all of the other religions against it rather than the other way around."

Dr. Hazen explains that this feature of Christianity is unnerving because many people generally conclude that religion is subjective. They think it's merely a personal experience that takes place inside you. What you believe doesn't matter as long as you're sincere. Well, that's fine if you're talking about personal preferences. But if you're talking about truth—that which corresponds to reality—then belief does matter, especially as it relates to immortality and the afterlife. And if belief matters, then knowing with reasonable certainty that your belief is true matters even more.

If Christianity Is True, Are All Other Religions False?

At this point you may be wondering, *Doesn't every religion contain at least some truth?* Absolutely. But that doesn't mean the entire religion is true, or that it points to the ultimate source of truth. That's why we like to say that truth is in everything, but not everything is true.

Five Reasons Why Christianity Is Unique

When it comes to God and your eternal destiny, it just makes sense to make sure your beliefs are as true as they can be. After all, your life is at stake. That's why we want to take a little time to make some comparisons between Christianity and some other belief systems and show you why it is unique.

Christianity Is Testable

Many religious traditions are defined by the subjective inner feelings of their followers. Certainly Christianity includes an emotional element, as does any belief system or any community where people share things in common. People get fired up about their favorite sports team (have you ever met a loyal, passionate Green Bay Packers fan?), the company they work for, or even the city where they live. So nothing is wrong with having subjective inner feelings about something.

But if people can't back up their subjective feelings with objective truth or knowledge, they start to question their own experience. The great thing about Christianity is that the feelings and experiences people have in their faith are rooted in objective truth. You could even say Christianity has a knowledge component that is unique among world religions. In fact, the Bible writers emphasize knowledge. Here are just a few examples:

> *Intelligent people are always ready to learn. Their ears are open for knowledge* (Proverbs 18:15).

> *To those who listen to my teaching, more understanding will be given, and they will have an abundance of knowledge.*

*But for those who are not listening, even what little under-
standing they have will be taken away from them* (Matthew 13:12).

*May God give you more and more grace and peace as you
grow in your knowledge of God and Jesus our Lord* (2 Peter
1:2).

*I have written this to you who believe in the name of the
Son of God, so that you may know you have eternal life*
(1 John 5:13).

The reason these writers can say this is that the Christian faith
is based on the person of Christ. Christianity makes astounding
claims about His life, His words, His death, and His resurrection—
all of which, according to Dr. Hazen, are testable.

What I mean by this is that these claims are such that
any thinking person can examine the evidence and
reasonably determine whether the claims are historically accurate or justified. I think this is one of the primary reasons a thoughtful person sorting through the
various religious traditions would obviously start with
Christianity. Christianity is unique in that it actually
invites people to investigate carefully its claims about
God, humankind, the universe, and the meaning of
life.[2]

In chapter 9, we talked about the Christian faith hinging on
the fact of the resurrection. Dr. Hazen, who is an expert on world
religions, says he has not been able to find any other religious tradition or belief system "that so tightly links the truth of an entire
system of belief to a single, testable historic event."[3]

For thoughtful people who want to make sure their beliefs are
linked to historic, verifiable facts, Christianity stands apart.

Christianity Is Consistent with What We Already Know About God

In chapter 3 we outlined a cumulative case for believing in
the existence of God. One of the components of this argument is

that the universe had a beginning that was caused by a necessary being that is self-existent, eternal, and uncaused. By definition, this necessary being must be...

> independent of the universe
>
> all-powerful
>
> supremely intelligent
>
> infinite
>
> supernatural
>
> purposeful

Christianity is unique in that it describes God in just these terms in a book written centuries before scientists developed a profile for the necessary being. Other religions and belief systems may describe God by using one or more of these descriptions, but some of their accepted beliefs about the nature of God will contradict other descriptions. For example, pantheistic religions, such as Hinduism, view God as being one with the universe, not independent of it. Deism doesn't allow for a purposeful God.

Another part of this idea is that Christianity is consistent with what we know about God through the natural world. In chapter 4 we talked about the evidence from the world as a compelling proof for God's existence. Christianity is unique among world religions and belief systems in that it portrays God in ways that are consistent with natural revelation. For example, the evidence for an intelligent designer points to the kind of all-knowing, all-powerful, purposeful Creator portrayed by the Christian belief system.

> *The heavens proclaim the glory of God. The skies display his craftsmanship. Day after day they continue to speak; night after night they make him known* (Psalm 19:1-2).

When you bring the Bible into the picture, you have a holy book that offers an elegant framework for the creation story, even though the Bible is not a scientific book and makes no attempt to explain origins in scientific terms. But the way it outlines the order of the creation events is completely consistent with scientific understanding.

Christianity's Picture of the World Matches the Way the World Really Is

Remember our discussion of worldviews in chapter 2? In the theistic worldview, an infinite, personal God created the universe and everything in it. He created human beings in His image, giving them meaning and value as they invest in His eternal values. Christianity further defines theism by emphasizing that each of us has an eternal destiny and can, by God's grace and an exercise of faith in Jesus Christ, choose to spend eternity in heaven.

Perhaps you once thought that these features of the Christian worldview were more like fantasy than reality. Even if you believed them, you may have thought they weren't reasonable. This may have been your opinion before reading this book.

Now, we don't want to presume that we are persuasive enough to change your mind in just ten chapters, but it may be that after getting some new information and a few compelling arguments, you now view these components of the Christian worldview differently. Together these constitute the Christian story:

- God exists and is the Creator of the universe;
- God has revealed Himself through His world and His word;
- God has most fully revealed Himself through Jesus Christ, who is God in human form;
- Jesus lived a perfect life, died a painful death, and came back to real life so that we could have life by believing in Him; and
- human beings are immortal.

Far from being a fairy tale or a story believed by dummies, this is reality. This isn't the product of wishful thinking, but a description of the way the world really is. It doesn't take a blind leap in the dark to believe it. All it takes is a reasonable step of faith.

Okay, we know some people still don't buy it, and we can understand. So let's approach this particular uniqueness of Christianity from another angle. Craig Hazen uses the existence of evil, pain, and suffering as a litmus test for whether or not a particular belief system or worldview paints a picture of the real world. "It seems obvious that any religion that doesn't do justice to these common human experiences," he writes, "should probably not be at the top of the list for a thoughtful religious seeker."[4]

So how do the other religions and worldviews tackle the question of evil and suffering? According to Hazen, they all struggle to find a satisfactory answer. The Eastern religions (Hinduism, Buddhism, and the like) simply say that evil and suffering are illusions and will fade away as the practitioners of these belief systems gain enlightenment. Atheism and relativism make little or no attempt to provide an answer. People with these worldviews prefer to direct their frustration over evil and suffering toward Christianity.

As we said, that's okay. Christianity can handle the question because God has answered it. Christianity doesn't try to deny or minimize evil and suffering. In fact, just the opposite is true.

> The Scriptures of Christianity confront the issue of evil head-on starting with the first pages of Genesis. A whole section of the Bible, the book of Job, is dedicated to the unanswerable questions involved in personal suffering. Although the Bible never provides an answer to the *why* question in the case of individual instances of suffering (such as, why did the drunk driver crash into *me*?), it does provide the most satisfactory context for coming to terms with the existence of evil.[5]

The most important answer, of course, is found in the person and work of Christ, because He knows what it's like to suffer, and by His death and resurrection He gave us a promise that a new world is coming, where there won't be any more death or suffering or crying or pain.

Christian Salvation Is Free and Open to All

Of the five unique characteristics of Christianity, this one offers the clearest distinction. Among all of the world religions and belief systems, Christianity is the only one that says salvation is a gift. In every other religion you have to work for salvation. Here are examples from three popular belief systems:

- In Islam, salvation is awarded on the basis of a divine judgment scale. If your good deeds outweigh your bad ones, you have a shot at heaven. Furthermore, the only deeds that qualify for the judgment scale are those that are compatible with the teachings of the Qur'an and the Hadith. Chief among those are the Five Pillars of Faith that each Muslim must perform if the scale is going to tip in his or her favor.

- In Mormonism, you are saved by doing good works and by obeying "the laws of the Gospel," meaning people are saved by following the beliefs of the LDS Church.

- In Hinduism, salvation is based on karma, or good works. If your good works outweigh your bad works, you have a better chance of experiencing salvation. There's no such thing as sin against a holy God. Life is lived on the scales of good and bad, and in the cycle of reincarnation.

The Golden Rule Isn't Enough

If there's one principle that almost every religion has in common, it's the Golden Rule: "Do unto others as you would have them do unto you." This ethical principle actually goes back to the time of Confucius. Buddha had a variation, Socrates taught the Golden Rule, and Jesus said it in His Sermon on the Mount (Matthew 7:12). But this isn't the essence of what Jesus taught. He knows that our problem isn't *knowing* what we should do, but actually *doing* it. Jesus goes beyond the Golden Rule by forgiving us and covering us in His perfect life, thereby giving us the power to live as we should.

As we discussed in chapter 8, Christianity teaches a different way. Salvation does not come from doing good works, being religious, or keeping traditions. Pure and simple, salvation is a gift from God, made possible by the person and work of Christ. All we have to do is understand the gift and accept it by faith. We like what Paul Little says:

Christianity is what God has done for human beings in seeking them and reaching down to help them. Other religions are a matter of human beings seeking and struggling toward God.[6]

And here's another thing to consider. In every works-based religion, you really don't know if you've done enough to earn your salvation. "Fear persists because there's no assurance of salvation," Little writes. Christianity offers assurance because it's based on God's grace rather than our works.

---

*B*reaking Down Barriers

In works-based religions, there are barriers to entry. If you don't have the right background or pedigree, if you don't have the right education or training, if you question certain beliefs, if you aren't the right sex, you may be denied access. Christianity has no barriers. As Paul writes, "There is no longer Jew or Gentile, slave or free, male and female. For you are all one in Christ Jesus" (Galatians 3:28).

Christianity Has Jesus At the Center

We made the point in chapter 6 that everybody wants a piece of Jesus. He is unquestionably the most popular person who ever lived. Religions want Jesus too. Muslims respect Him as a prophet. Jews acknowledge His status as a rabbi. It is not unheard of for Hindus and Buddhists to view Jesus as a prominent spiritual man. In fact, as Dr. Hazen remarks, "Jesus is without a doubt the closest thing the world has to a universal religious figure."

Yet only one religion—Christianity—is built around the person and work of Jesus. In reality, Christianity is more than a religion about Jesus. More accurately, it's a relationship with Jesus, whom God sent to earth to save humanity from spiritual death. That is the heart and soul of Christianity. This is where Christianity stands apart from every other religion and spiritual belief in the world. A Christian is one who accepts the claims of Jesus:

- *He is God in human form.* Jesus didn't say He was *like* a god. He said that He *was* God (John 10:30). The apostle Paul writes, "For in Christ lives all the fullness of God in a human body" (Colossians 2:9). This "Jesus is God" premise is the foundation of Christianity.

- *He rose from the dead and is alive today.* Anybody can claim to be God, and many have. But a claim like that is ridiculous unless you can back it up. The same goes for Jesus. His claim to be God wouldn't mean a thing unless He had proved it to the world, which He did. Jesus offered several proofs for His divine nature: He performed miracles, forgave sins, and most of all, came back from the dead.

- *All who follow Him can have an exceptional life.* In addition to offering an eternal relationship with God in heaven, Jesus makes it possible for His followers to enjoy a moment-by-moment personal relationship with Him on earth. No other religion proposes this sort of amazing familiarity with the founder. Everyone who accepts God's offer of salvation through Jesus can be in intimate contact with God.

These claims are amazing, but they aren't any good if those who profess to follow Him don't take them to heart. Mike Erre reminds us that Christianity should always be about truly knowing Jesus.

> There is a difference between being religious and following Jesus. We can allow our religiousness to get in the way of truly knowing Jesus (as opposed to just knowing *about* him). The cure for this, I think, is to get a glimpse of Jesus. He often goes unrecognized and unknown, even in the church. But those who get a glimpse of the real thing will never settle for a substitute. Those who catch a glimpse of Jesus will never settle again for simply being religious.[7]

Christianity Is Probably True

Just because Christianity is unique among world religions doesn't mean it's true. But when you look at why Christianity is unique, the case for Christianity as a compelling belief system that points to ultimate truth becomes much stronger.

Still, for those who are looking for a smoking gun to validate Christianity may be disappointed that no such final proof exists. About the best anyone can do in making an apologetic case for Christianity is to say that it is *probably* true rather than positively true. But is that so bad? Not really.

As William Lane Craig says, "the fact that Christianity can only be shown to be probably true need not be troubling," as long as we keep two things in mind:[8]

- Just about everything we know, we know with probable, not positive, certainty. For example, we may believe it is safe to fly, even though we know that a passenger airplane will probably crash at some point in the future. Knowing that a plane might crash doesn't diminish our conviction that it is safe to fly.

- Even though we can at best show Christianity to be probably true, we can know that it's true based on the inner witness of the Holy Spirit. Craig uses the example of someone on trial for a crime he knows he didn't commit, even though the evidence is against him. He may not be able to show his innocence, but he knows that he's innocent.

It is not necessary—nor is it reasonable—to have logically demonstrative proofs as a pre-condition for making a commitment to Christ and Christianity. If the evidence is reasonable, and the distinctives make sense, and you have an inner conviction that what you believe is true, then you can trust it to be true.

What's That Again?

1. Whereas the church involves people called out by God, Christianity is a belief system that claims to point people to the ultimate source of truth.

2. We should be ready, willing, and able to defend Christianity, but we shouldn't get defensive. We should show respect for the beliefs of others by actually knowing what they believe.

3. Studying other religions has two benefits: It helps you relate to your neighbors, and it gives you a greater appreciation for your own faith.

4. Anyone who wants to study world religions and make a comparison between them should start with Christianity because it's the only religion that's testable.

5. Christianity has a strong knowledge tradition based on the truth about God and Jesus Christ. In fact, Christianity is unique in that it actually invites people to investigate its claims.

6. Christianity is consistent with what we already know about God, including what we know through the natural world.

7. Christianity paints a picture of the world that matches reality. The Christian story isn't the product of wishful thinking, but a description of the way the world really is.

8. In Christianity, salvation is free and open to all, and Jesus is at the center. However, Christianity is more than a religion about Jesus. It is a relationship with Jesus.

9. About the best anyone can do in making an apologetic case for Christianity is to say that it is probably true. This should not be troubling.

Dig Deeper

We've recommended two of these books in previous chapters, but they are worth repeating:

Passionate Conviction contains several wonderful essays about God and the Christian faith, and the chapter by Craig Hazen on Christianity in a world of religions outlines the distinctives in an easy-to-follow way.

The Jesus of Suburbia by Mike Erre is our favorite book about Jesus. It will challenge and inspire you to follow Jesus more fully.

Our own *World Religions & Cults 101* is a good place to start if you're interested in studying other religions.

We also want to highly recommend a novel called *Five Sacred Crossings* by Dr. Craig Hazen. This page-turner presents the five unique characteristics of Christianity in a well-told fictional story.

■ ■ ■

Questions for Reflection and Discussion

1. What kind of complaints and criticisms have you heard about Christianity? Do you have any complaints and criticisms of your own? What are they?

2. What are some of the religions and belief systems you are familiar with? Make a list and give a brief description or impression of each one.

3. Mike Erre says, "All truth is a reflection of the Holy Creator God." Give at least one example of a truth that exists outside of Christianity.

4. Have you ever had an inner subjective feeling about something or someone, only to be disappointed? What happened? Why is it important to have objective truth behind your experience?

5. Give an example of how Christianity portrays God in a way that is consistent with natural revelation.

6. Have you ever been at a place in your life where you thought the Christian story didn't correspond with the way the world really is? Have you changed your mind? Why?

7. In what ways does Christianity adequately address the problem of evil and suffering?

8. Explain why you can have assurance of salvation in Christianity but not in other religions.

9. How sure are you that Christianity is true? Do your beliefs outweigh your doubts? Can you live with that? Why or why not?

Moving On...

We are quickly coming to the end of our book, and we want to thank you for hanging in there with us. In case you didn't notice, this chapter was kind of a summary of many of the concepts and arguments presented in the previous chapters. But that doesn't mean we're done. Before we say goodbye, we want to move from the objective to the subjective, and talk about the dynamic dimension of your inner spiritual life and how that helps to validate your Christian faith.

*C*hapter 12

> Thou hast formed us for Thyself,
> and our hearts are restless
> till they find rest in Thee.
>
> —*Augustine*

Earlier in the book we quoted Jesus responding to the question, "What is the most important commandment?" Today we might ask, "What does God wants from us?" Either way you phrase the question, the answer Jesus gives is the same: "You must love the LORD your God with all your heart, all your soul, and all your mind" (Matthew 22:37).

This book has emphasized the mind, which is what we intended to do. As you learn to know God better and better—who He is, what He's like, how He created the universe, what He's done about humanity's rebellion against Him, why He sent Jesus—your faith is strengthened. But loving God and a life of faith include more than the mind. The heart and soul dimension is just as important. We've already defined the soul as the eternal you. The heart is the real you, the place of emotion and will. The heart is where your experiences are stored.

As we conclude this book, we want to focus on the ways your heart for God—your feelings for God and your experiences with God—are as important as your knowledge of God in shaping your faith.

The Experience of Faith

Feelings are a gift from God. Our emotions are part of our DNA. Our ability to laugh, cry, love, fear, hope, and wonder makes our lives interesting and livable. We aren't robots programmed to do what our Maker wants us to do. We are free beings endowed by our Creator with the capacity to be, well, *human*.

God must be very fond of the human species because even though we snubbed Him, He sent his only Son to become one of us. Jesus didn't become an angel or a superhero. He became human. How much God must love us for that to happen!

Experiencing God

God sent Jesus so that we could get a picture of Him. "If you had really known me, you would know who my Father is. From now on, you do know him and have seen him," Jesus tells His disciples on the night before He is crucified (John 14:7). Imagine the emotions that welled up in those early followers when they fully realized the meaning of that statement: The all-powerful, all-knowing, infinitely vast Creator God was present among them.

The astonishing thing for us, 2000 years later, is that God is present with us today, and not just in the same room. He is literally inside of us, part of us, intimately involved with each person who has entered into an eternal relationship with Christ by faith. And this is no ordinary human relationship. This is God establishing His presence in us through the indwelling power of the third person of the Trinity, the Holy Spirit.

We can know how this process works, but knowing it and experiencing it are two completely different things. The mind can grasp the truth of the gospel, but the heart embraces it. To love God with our mind is to understand what He has done to save us and to realize what His will is for us. But to love Him with our heart is to experience God Himself—with no barrier, no wall, and no veil between us. When Jesus cried out from the cross, "It is finished," the curtain between the people and the Holy of Holies was ripped from top to bottom. At last, because of the saving life and death of Christ, humanity was free to experience the power of God in a profoundly personal way.

The Presence of God

How our world and even our churches long for this experiential presence of God. "I speak to thirsty hearts whose longings have been welcomed by the touch of God within them," writes A.W. Tozer. "They need no reasoned proof. Their restless hearts furnish all the proof they need."[1] The eternal soul of every person is on an "interior journey," Tozer continues. Every soul starts in "the wilds of sin," but all who believe by faith in the reality of God and His eternal plan to save them move into "the enjoyed presence of God."[2]

> The presence of God is the central fact of Christianity. At the heart of the Christian message is God Himself waiting for His redeemed children to push in to conscious awareness of His presence.
>
> —A.W. Tozer

A great many Christians know the presence of God in theory. Fewer have experienced the presence in reality. No wonder the church has little attraction for restless hearts. The world may be dying because it doesn't know God, but God's church is starving because it isn't experiencing God.

The instant cure for most of our religious ills would be to enter the Presence in spiritual experience, to become suddenly aware that we are in God and God is in us. This would lift us out of our pitiful narrowness and cause our hearts to be enlarged. This would burn away the impurities from our lives as the bugs and fungi were burned away by the fire that dwelt in the bush. What a broad world to roam in, what a sea to swim in is this God and Father of our Lord Jesus Christ.[3]

Practicing the Presence of God

Living in the presence of God is a two-way street. God is present in us, but we must respond daily by giving ourselves—our hearts and wills, our passions and desires, our goals and ambitions—to Him. This isn't something that comes automatically. We need to have a plan, and we need to practice, practice, practice.

In his book *Kingdom Triangle*, J.P. Moreland outlines a three-part strategy that will help you experience God in ever increasing ways.[4]

1. Develop your mind. Yes, loving God with your mind is important. But as we have talked about several times, it's more than just knowing *about* God. It's knowing God and all that He has revealed to us, and then deliberately living your life with confidence that it's true. Don't just know *what* you believe. Know *why* you believe as well. Read, study, memorize, and meditate on God's word. Ingest the Scriptures as routinely as you take in food. Read books, listen to audio recordings, and watch videos about God and the Bible. Access the wisdom of others who are further along the interior journey than you are. Get involved in a Bible study, preferably one where you are accountable to others for your progress and personal habits. Lead others who learn from you.

2. Discipline your soul. In addition to reading and studying God's word, practice the presence of God by getting involved in a program of spiritual formation. This simply means that you discipline yourself to imitate the life of Jesus. It's one thing to *know* what you should do, and quite another to actually do it. In his classic book *The Spirit of the Disciplines,* Dallas Willard tells us what this means:

> What we need is a deeper insight into our practical relationship with God in redemption. We need an understanding that can guide us into constant interaction with the Kingdom of God as a real part of our daily lives, an *ongoing spiritual presence* that is at the same time a *psychological reality.* In other words, we must develop a psychologically sound theology of the spiritual life and of its disciplines to guide us.[5]

Space does not allow us to go into these disciplines in detail, but we can at least list the ones Willard explains in his book. He puts them in two categories:[6]

Disciplines of Abstinence	Disciplines of Engagement
solitude	study
silence	worship
fasting	celebration
frugality	service
chastity	prayer
secrecy	fellowship
sacrifice	confession
	submission

3. Draw upon the Holy Spirit. Moreland calls upon Christians to open themselves to experience the power of the kingdom of God and the Holy Spirit by "becoming naturally supernatural." The Christian life is a supernatural life, yet most of us are content to live in the natural world with very little sense of God's miraculous power. For Paul the good news of Christ in all its fullness includes three elements: the presentation of the message, the personal example of His work, and the power of God's Holy Spirit:

> *Yet I dare not boast about anything except what Christ has done through me, bringing the Gentiles to God by my message and by the way I worked among them. They were convinced by the power of miraculous signs and wonders and by the power of God's Spirit. In this way, I have fully*

presented the Good News of Christ from Jerusalem all the way to Illyricum (Romans 15:18-19).

We'll be the first to admit that this third part of the strategy is the most foreign to many Christians. Most of us aren't very good at living a "naturally supernatural" life.

> The gospel is animated by God's powerful Spirit, and its result is Spirit-empowerment for new living.
>
> —*Scot McKnight*

Moreland offers three words of advice so we can begin moving forward in this important area of faith:[7]

- *Never try to make something happen.* If you force it and act like God is doing something when He isn't, you're going to come across as "inauthentic and contrary to the nature of God's Kingdom."

- *Be gentle, humble, and patient with yourself and others.* As you "grow in the miraculous," realize that not everyone understands the concept of signs and wonders. "At the end of the day," writes Moreland, "this is not about us. It's about becoming more effective colaborers with God in the Great Commission enterprise."

- *You can't create faith by simply trying to believe something more strongly.* "By study, meditation, risk, learning from successes and failures, and in related ways, one can grow in faith."

The result of living in this Kingdom Triangle will help you "enter more and more deeply into progress in the way of Jesus," writes Moreland.[8] As you develop your mind, you will grow in truth. As you discipline your soul, you will gain passion for your inner journey. And as you draw upon the Holy Spirit's power, you will gain faith and confidence to risk more and more for God.

For Seekers Only

Before we close the book, so to speak, on evidence for faith, we want to turn our attention to those who are still seeking God but have not yet made a decision to trust Him. If you've hung in there until now, we commend you! And if you're still not sure about committing yourself to this life of faith in the one true God, we want to offer three words of encouragement.

Keep seeking. Don't give up your search for the ultimate truth. You're on the right path, and it's just a matter of time before God grabs your heart and you make a decision to believe. God doesn't mind your taking time, as long you keep three things in mind. The writer of Hebrews reminds us what they are:

> *And it is impossible to please God without faith. Anyone who wants to come to him must believe that God exists and that he rewards those who sincerely seek him* (Hebrews 11:6).

At the very least, you must believe God exists. That's a given. Then you must be willing to exercise faith, which adds trust and commitment to belief. Then you must believe God will reward you as you follow Him in faith.

Doubt your doubts. We devoted four chapters to faith and doubt, and even though we hit the major topics that cause many people to doubt God, we didn't cover them all. You may have other doubts, which is fine. Just don't let them stand in your way unnecessarily. You don't have to have every one of your questions answered before you come to faith. You just have to say, as William Lane Craig observes, "The weight of the evidence seems to show this is true, so even though I don't have answers to all my questions, I'm going to believe—and then hope for answers in the long run."

Even after you believe, some doubt will always be there. Remember, absolute certainty isn't necessary. In fact, it isn't even possible. But reasonable certainty is not only possible, but also very inviting.

Taste and see. David, the king of Israel, tells us to "taste and see that the Lord is good" (Psalm 34:8). What great advice! It means to give God a try. If you have reason to believe God exists, and your unbelief doesn't outweigh your belief, why not spend some time in God's neighborhood, so to speak? Read the Bible, hang around some Christians, pray and ask God to give you a sense of His presence. Your goal should be to trust God in the biblical sense, not just believe in the philosophical sense.

If you stay at it, something incredible will happen. You will move from believing God exists to trusting in the plan God has made through Jesus.

Why Jesus Matters

We've considered a lot of evidence for faith in this book, but as we conclude we want to come back to the greatest evidence of all—the person of Jesus Christ. The way to know God by faith is to know Him through Jesus, yet that can be a problem for some people. Even though Jesus is widely considered to be the most influential person who ever lived, no individual has caused more debate. For such a central figure in history, there is little consensus about Him. It seems that either Jesus is respected and revered, or He is despised and denigrated.

So what's all the fuss about? It's not about His morality. Jesus is universally recognized as the greatest moral teacher of all time. It's not about His miracles. Whether they were supernaturally caused is not what impassions the debate. It's not even about His resurrection. As important as that fact of history is, people don't seem to stay away from God because they do or don't believe that Jesus came back from the dead.

The controversy about Christ centers on His theology. Not only did Jesus claim to know God, but He also claimed to be God. And most controversial of all, He claimed that His death on the cross is the only way a sinful humanity can be forgiven by God and experience eternal life.

Every person must take a side in the controversy. You must decide if Jesus was just a good man, or if He was the God-man. Your faith in God must ultimately be directed to belief in Jesus—not just an intellectual agreement that He existed, but a belief that He is the sole solution for humanity's spiritual void. Your decision will take you far beyond knowing why Jesus matters to the human race. On a more personal level, you will know why Jesus matters *to you*.

What's That Again?

1. God is present with us, and He is intimately involved within us through the Holy Spirit.

2. Loving God with our heart is to experience God with no barrier or wall between us.

3. The world may be dying because it doesn't know God, but God's church is starving because it isn't experiencing God.

4. Living in the presence of God is a two-way street. God is present in us, but we must respond daily by giving ourselves to Him.

5. J.P. Moreland outlines a three-part strategy that will help you experience God in ever-increasing ways. This involves developing your mind, disciplining your soul, and drawing upon the Holy Spirit.

6. Spiritual formation is the process of disciplining yourself to imitate the life of Jesus. Dallas Willard calls it a "psychologically sound theology of the spiritual life and of its disciplines to guide us."

7. The Christian life is a supernatural life, yet most of us are content to live in the natural world with very little sense of God's miraculous power.

8. Those who have not yet made the decision to commit themselves to a life of faith in the one true God should keep seeking God, doubt their doubts, and give God a try.

9. Jesus is the greatest evidence for faith.

Dig Deeper

We recommend the three books we have referred to in this chapter:

Kingdom Triangle by J.P. Moreland is a refreshing and somewhat unconventional guide to living the kind of life God has in mind for us.

The Spirit of the Disciplines by Dallas Willard is a true classic. Every Christian who desires to live a life characterized by spiritual formation should read this book.

A.W. Tozer is one of the finest spiritual writers of the past 50 years. You can't go wrong with any of his books, but we would recommend you start with *The Pursuit of God.*

■ ■ ■

Questions for Reflection and Discussion

1. What has been your experience with God to this point in your life? Have you loved Him with your mind, your heart, or both?

2. Explain how your heart can furnish proof for the reality of God. In what ways is the presence of God real to you?

3. How systematic have you been in giving yourself to God? Do you have a plan? If so, what is it?

4. Summarize the components necessary to develop your mind for God. Why does this take such discipline?

5. Look at the two lists of disciplines. Write a one-sentence description of each of the disciplines of abstinence. Now do the same thing for the disciplines of engagement.

6. What is your reaction to the third part of the Kingdom Triangle strategy? How good are you at living a "naturally supernatural" life? What can you do to get better at it?

7. Why is it important for seekers to keep seeking? What

happens when they stop? Why is it impossible to achieve absolute certainty in the Christian life?

8. What is it about Jesus that is so controversial? What are the two sides of the controversy?

Moving On...

Congratulations! You've made it through a book that probably challenged you at some points. We don't expect that you agreed with everything, but we hope that it made you think about the Christian faith in new ways. As we said at the beginning of the book, if you're a Christian, we hope you have a greater appreciation for your faith. If you haven't yet made the decision to put your faith in Jesus, we pray that you will continue to seek the one who loves you more than you could ever know.

Notes

Introduction to Part 1

1. Peter Kreeft, *Handbook of Christian Apologetics* (Downers Grove, IL: InterVarsity Press, 1994), 22.

Chapter 1—A Case for Faith

1. Mike Erre, *The Jesus of Suburbia* (Nashville, TN: W Publishing Group, 2006), 171-72.
2. Peter Kreeft, *Handbook of Christian Apologetics* (Downers Grove, IL: InterVarsity Press, 1994), 30.
3. Wayne Grudem, *Systematic Theology* (Grand Rapids, MI: Zondervan, 1994), 710.
4. Grudem, 730.

Chapter 2—A Place for Evidence

1. J.P. Moreland, *Loving God with All Your Mind* (Colorado Springs, CO: NavPress, 1997), 25-26.
2. Moreland, 24.
3. Peter Kreeft, *Handbook of Christian Apologetics* (Downers Grove, IL: InterVarsity Press, 1994), 37.
4. C.S. Lewis, "Man or Rabbit?" in *God in the Dock: Essays on Theology and Ethics,* ed. by Walter Hooper (Grand Rapids, MI: Eerdmans, 1970), 108-9.
5. Norman L. Geisler, *Baker Encyclopedia of Christian Apologetics* (Grand Rapids, MI: Baker Books, 1999), 785.
6. William Lane Craig, *Reasonable Faith* (Wheaton, IL: Crossway Books, 1994), 31.

Introduction to Part 2

1. "U.S. Religious Landscape Survey," The Pew Forum on Religion & Public Life, www.religions. pewforum.org.

Chapter 3—Evidence for God

1. R. Douglas Geivett, "Two Versions of the Cosmological Argument," in *Passionate Conviction,* ed. Paul Copan and William Lane Craig (Nashville, TN: Baker Academic, 2007), 56.
2. Peter Kreeft, *Handbook of Christian Apologetics* (Downers Grove, IL: InterVarsity Press, 1994), 58.
3. Robert Jastrow, *God and the Astronomers* (New York, NY: Norton, 1992), 13.
4. Geivett, 66.
5. Kreeft, 74.
6. Kreeft, 75.
7. Paul Copan, "A Moral Argument," in *Passionate Conviction,* 92.

Chapter 4—Evidence from the Natural World

1. William Dembski, *The Design Revolution* (Downers Grove, IL: InterVarsity Press, 2004), 63.
2. Jay Richards, "The Contemporary Argument for Design: An Overview" in *Passionate Conviction,* ed. by Paul Copan and William Lane Craig (Nashville, TN: Baker Academic, 2007), 72.
3. Charles Darwin, *On the Origin of Species* (Cambridge, MA: Harvard University Press, 1964), 280.
4. Hugh Ross, *The Creator and the Cosmos* (Colorado Springs, CO: NavPress 2001), 194.
5. Darwin, 189.
6. Dembski, 33.

7. Dembski, 33.

Chapter 5—Evidence for the Bible

1. Tim Keller, *The Reason for God* (New York, NY: Dutton, 2008), 99.
2. Henrietta Mears, *What the Bible is All About* (Ventura, CA: Regal Books, 1983), 20.
3. Norman Geisler, *A General Introduction to the Bible* (Chicago, IL: Moody Press, 1968).
4. Keller, 100-109.
5. Elaine Pagels, *Beyond Belief* (New York, NY: Random House, 2003), 40.
6. Bruce M. Metzger, *The Canon of the New Testament* (Oxford: Clarendon Press, 1987), 173.
7. Gordon Fee and Douglas Stuart, *How to Read the Bible for All It's Worth* (Grand Rapids, MI: Zondervan, 2003).
8. R.C. Sproul, *Knowing Scripture* (Downers Grove, IL: InterVarsity Press, 1977).

Chapter 6—Evidence for Jesus

1. PAX-TV's *Faith Under Fire*, "Faith Under Scrutiny," episode 12, April 23, 2005.
2. Elaine Pagels, *Beyond Belief* (New York, NY: Random House, 2003), 32.
3. Ben Witherington III, "Why the 'Lost Gospels' Lost Out," *Christianity Today*, June 2004, 32.
4. William Lane Craig, "Rediscovering the Historical Jesus: Presuppositions and Pretensions of the Jesus Seminar," www.leaderu.com.
5. R. Douglas Geivett, "The Evidential Value of Miracles," in *In Defense of Miracles*, ed. by R. Douglas Geivett and Gary Habermas (Downers Grove, IL: InterVarsity Press, 1997), 179.

Chapter 7—Evil and Suffering

1. John Marks, *Reasons to Believe* (New York, NY: HarperCollins, 2008), 381.
2. Peter Kreeft, *Handbook of Christian Apologetics* (Downers Grove, IL: InterVarsity Press, 1994), 139.
3. Wayne Grudem, *Systematic Theology* (Grand Rapids, MI: Zondervan, 1994), 197.
4. Peter Kreeft quoted in Lee Strobel, *The Case for Faith* (Grand Rapids, MI: Zondervan, 2000), 37.
5. Norman Geisler and Ron Brooks, *When Skeptics Ask* (Grand Rapids, MI: Baker Books, 1990), 64-65.
6. Geisler and Brooks, 65.
7. Gary DeWeese, lecture at Biola University, October 13, 2005.
8. C.S. Lewis, *The Problem of Pain* (New York, NY: Macmillan, 1970), 89.
9. Kreeft, 123.

Chapter 8—Sin and Salvation

1. R.C. Sproul, *Essential Truths of the Christian Faith* (Wheaton, IL: Tyndale House, 1992), 147-48.
2. Dallas Willard, *The Divine Conspiracy* (San Francisco, CA: HarperSanFrancisco, 1998), 12.
3. Willard, 21.

Chapter 9—Heaven and Hell

1. J.P. Moreland and Gary Habermas, *Beyond Death* (Wheaton IL: Crossway Books, 1998), 20.
2. Moreland and Habermas, 32.
3. Moreland and Habermas, 111.
4. N.T. Wright, "Heaven Is Not Our Home," *Christianity Today*, April 2008.
5. Peter Kreeft, *Everything You Ever Wanted to Know About Heaven* (San Francisco, CA: Ignatius Press, 1990), 52-53.

6. Quoted in Lee Strobel, *The Case for Faith* (Grand Rapids, MI: Zondervan, 2000), 169-94.

7. Quoted in Strobel, 174-75.

8. Strobel, 181.

Chapter 10—Church and Culture

1. George Barna, *Revolution* (Carol Stream, IL: Tyndale House, 2005), 14.

2. Dan Kimball, *They Like Jesus but Not the Church* (Grand Rapids, MI: Zondervan, 2007).

3. Barna, 127.

4. Earle E. Cairns, *Christianity Through the Centuries* (Grand Rapids, MI: Zondervan, 1996).

5. Tim Keller, *The Reason for God* (New York, NY: Dutton, 2008), 56.

6. Keller, 54.

Introduction to part 4

1. Gerald McDermott, *Can Evangelicals Learn from World Religions?* (Downers Grove, IL: InterVarsity Press, 2000), 216-17.

Chapter 11—A Case for Christianity

1. Mike Erre, *The Jesus of Suburbia* (Nashville, TN: W Publishing Group, 2006), 163.

2. Craig Hazen, "Christianity in a World of Religions," in *Passionate Conviction*, ed. by Paul Copan and William Lane Craig (Nashville, TN: Baker Academic, 2007), 143.

3. Hazen, 144.

4. Hazen, 147.

5. Hazen, 149.

6. Paul Little, *Know Why You Believe* (Downers Grove, IL: InterVarsity Press, 1988), 147.

7. Erre, 54.

8. Craig, 40.

Chapter 12—The Experience of Faith

1. A.W. Tozer, *The Pursuit of God* (Camp Hill, PA: Christian Publications, 1993), 31-32.

2. Tozer, 33.

3. Tozer, 36.

4. J.P. Moreland, *Kingdom Triangle* (Grand Rapids, MI: Zondervan, 2007).

5. Dallas Willard, *The Spirit of the Disciplines* (New York, NY: HarperSanFrancisco, 1988), xi.

6. Willard, 158.

7. Moreland, 182-83.

8. Moreland, 199.

Index